Test Automation
WebDrive ... with C#

MW00356503

Vaibhav Mittal
Navneesh Garg

- Microsoft Visual Studio 2017
- Learn Automation on a Web Based Application
- Real Life Experiences
- Step by Step Instructions
- BDD and Continuous Integration

Selenium with C# - Step By Step Guide

Test Automation Using Selenium with C#

Vaibhav Mittal & Navneesh Garg

ISBN - 978-0-9922935-6-7

Publisher: Adactin Group Pty Ltd.

Contents

About the Author

Vaibhav Mittal

Vaibhav Mittal is a seasoned Consultant with experience in the complete life cycle of software development and testing. He has worked across geographies for multiple clients helping them solve their problems in the most efficient manner. He has exposure to multiple technologies including Microsoft .NET, Java, Oracle, ETL, Business Intelligence and Analytics.

As a Chief Information Officer at Adactin Group Pty Ltd, Sydney, he is responsible for multiple projects and works in the capacity of Testing and Automation expert. He is helping his clients grow in the space of software testing while using agile methodologies. As a trainer he has trained multiple professionals on various technologies.

Before joining Adactin Group, he worked with November Research Group, Oracle and Adobe Systems. He has consulted for clients from USA, Europe, Japan and India. He has presented multiple papers in international conferences held by SQS and IQNITE.

Navneesh Garg

Navneesh Garg is a recognized test automation architect and corporate trainer, specializing in test automation, performance testing, security testing and test management. As a tool specialist, he has worked on a variety of functional automation tools including Selenium, HP QTP/UFT, TestComplete, TestPartner, SilkTest, Watir, RFT, and on varied technologies including Web, Java, Dot-net, SAP, Peoplesoft and Seibel.

His previous book "Test Automation using Unified Functional Testing" is among the bestselling books on HP QTP. This book has consistently ranked among the top 100 testing books on Amazon. It was the first book to be released globally on the latest version of HP QTP.

He is an entrepreneur and founder of several successful IT companies which encompass the AdactIn Group, CresTech Software, and Planios Technologies.

As an experienced corporate trainer, he has trained professionals in Selenium and other test tools across a wide range of global clients such as Macquarie Bank, Corporate Express, Max New York Life, Accenture, NSW Road and Maritime Services, Australian Dept of Education, HCL Technologies, Sapient, Fidelity Group, Adobe Systems, and many more. He has training experience in diverse geographies such as Australia, India, Hong Kong and USA.

As a technical test delivery head for his company, he has led and managed functional automation testing and performance testing teams across a wide range of domains, using commercial tools and open source tools. Certified in HP QTP, HP Quality Center, HP LoadRunner, IBM Rational Functional Tester and as a Certified Ethical Hacker, he has designed several high-end automation frameworks including using Selenium and its integrations with tools like TestNG, JUnit, Selenium Grid, Jenkins and ANT.

Preface

The motivation for writing this book stems from my hands-on experience in the IT and testing domains and the experience I have gained as automation consultant working in numerous complex automation projects.

Selenium, being an open source tool, is gaining huge popularity but still is not conceived as an easy to use tool especially by testers due to a variety of reasons, including tool setup, programming background and support issues. A key objective of this book is showcase in a simple guided way to use Selenium WebDriver so that we can attain maximum return on investment from using the tool. Not only will we learn how to use the tool but also how to effectively create maintainable frameworks using Selenium.

Scope of Topics

As part of the scope of this book we will cover **Selenium with C#** as the programming language with Visual Studio 2017 community edition.

We will be using **Visual Studio 2017** as the main IDE for creating selenium tests.

No prior knowledge of C# language is required for this book but having an understanding of object oriented programming language concepts will definitely help. As part of this book we will be covering **Basics of C#** which would be required to use **Selenium** for beginner users.

We will also learn how Selenium integrates with **continuous Integration** tools like **Team Foundation Server.**

Our intent in this book is to discuss the key features of Selenium and cover all crucial aspects of the tool in order to help you **create effective automation frameworks using Selenium with C#.**

Target Audience

The target audience for this book are manual, functional testers who want to **learn Selenium quickly** and who want to create effective automation frameworks that generate positive ROIs to stakeholders.

Salient Features of this Book

This book has been designed with the objective of **simplicity and ease of understanding**.

A major fear amongst functional testers who want to learn Selenium is the fear of the programming language and coding. We address these fears by covering just enough **basics on C# programming language** that will give you the confidence to use Selenium.

This book follows a **unique training based approach** instead of a regular text book approach. Using a step by step approach, we guide you through the exercises using pictorial snapshots.

We also provide step by step installation and configuration of Visual Studio before using Selenium.

Instead of using custom html pages with few form fields and links, this book utilizes a custom developed, Web based application containing many form fields and links.

Another differentiator is that we have tried to include **many practical examples and issues** which most automation testers encounter in their day-to-day activities. We share our real-life experience with you to give you an insight into what challenges you could face while implementing an automation solution on your project. Our practical examples cover how to use most of the features within Selenium.

We also cover aspects of **Continuous Integration tool; Team Foundation Server** so that Selenium scripts can be integrated with the development environment and run on nightly builds.

Finally, the book includes a special section devoted to answering the most **common interview questions** relating to test automation and Selenium.

Sample Application and Source Used in Book

The sample application used in the book can be accessed at the following URL:

www.adactin.com/HotelApp/

The source code used in the book can be found at the following link

www.adactin.com/store/

Feedback and Queries

For any feedback or queries you can contact the author at www.adactin.com/contact.html or email info@adactin.com

Order this book

For bulk orders, contact us at orders@adactin.com

You can also place your order online at adactin.com/store/

Acknowledgements

My family has always been compassionate in this journey. My wife and two little ones (Vedaang and Sia) have always encouraged and supported me despite it took a lot of my time being away from them. It would not have been possible without their support.

I don't want to miss an opportunity to express my gratitude to all others, who saw me through this book; to all those who provided support, talked things over, read, write, offered comments, allowed me to quote their remarks and assisted in editing, proofreading and overall designing of this book. Thank you all – my co-workers, friends, peers and my commercial team for extending your support.

Vaibhav Mittal

I would like to thank my family (my parents, my wife Sapna, my wonderful kids Shaurya and Adaa) for their continued support. Without them this book would not have been possible.

I would also like to thank my colleagues and clients for the inspiration, knowledge and learning opportunities provided.

Navneesh Garg

1. Introduction to Automation

Introduction

In this chapter, we will talk about automation fundamentals and understand what automation is and the need for automation. An important objective of this chapter is to understand the economics of automation and determine when we should carry out automation in our projects. We will also discuss some popular commercial and open source automation tools available in the market.

Key objectives:

- What is automation?
- Why automate? What are the benefits of automation?
- Economics of automation.
- Commercial and Open Source automation tools.

1.1. What is Functional Automation?

Automation testing is to automate the execution of manually designed test cases without any human intervention.

The purpose of automated testing is to execute manual functional tests quickly in a cost-effective manner. Frequently, we rerun tests that have been previously executed (also called regression testing) to validate the functional correctness of the application. Think of a scenario where you need to validate the username and password for an application which has more than 10,000 users. It can be a tedious and monotonous task for a manual tester and this is where the real benefits of automation can be harnessed. We want to free up the manual functional testers' time so that they can perform other key tasks while automation provides extensive coverage to the overall test effort.

When we use the term "automation", there is usually confusion about whether automation scope includes functional and performance testing. Automation covers both.

- Functional Automation: Used for automation of functional test cases in the regression test bed.
- Performance Automation: Used for automation of non-functional performance test cases. An example of this is measuring the response time of the application under considerable (e.g., 100 users) load.

Functional automation and performance automation are two distinct terms and their automation internals work using different driving concepts. Hence, there are separate tools for functional automation and performance automation.

For the scope of this book, we will be referring only to **Functional Automation**.

1.2. Why do we automate?

Listed below are the key benefits of Functional Automation:

1. Effective Smoke (or Build Verification) Testing

Whenever a new software build or release is received, a test (generally referred to as the "smoke test" or "shakedown test") is run to verify if the build is testable for a bigger testing effort and major application functionalities are working correctly. Many times we spend hours doing this only to discover that a faulty software build resulted in all the testing efforts going to waste. Testing has to now start all over again after release of a new build.

If the smoke test is automated, the smoke test scripts can be run by developers to verify the build quality before being released to the testing team.

2. Standalone - Lights Out Testing

Automated testing tools can be programmed to kick off a script at a specific time.

If needed, automated tests can be automatically kicked off overnight, and the testers can analyseanalyze the results of the automated test the next morning. This will save valuable test execution time for the testers.

3. Increased Repeatability

At times it becomes impossible to reproduce a defect which was found during manual testing. The key reason for this could be that the tester forgot which combinations of test steps led to the error message; hence, he is unable to reproduce the defect. Automated testing scripts take the guesswork out of test repeatability.

4. Testers can Focus on Advanced Issues

As tests are automated, automated scripts can be baselined and rerun for regression testing. Regression tests generally yield fewer new defects as opposed to testing newly developed features. So, functional testers can focus on analysinganalyzing and testing newer or more complex areas that have the potential for most of the defects while automated test scripts can be used for regression test execution.

5. Higher Functional Test Coverage

With automated testing, a large number of data combinations can be tested which might not be practically feasible with manual testing. We use the term "Data driven testing" which means validating numerous test data combinations using one automated script.

6. Other Benefits

- **Reliable**: Tests perform precisely the same operations each time they are run, thereby eliminating human error.
- **Repeatable**: You can test how the software reacts under repeated execution of the same operations.
- **Programmable**: You can program sophisticated tests that bring out hidden information from the application.
- **Comprehensive**: You can build a suite of tests that cover every feature in your application.

- **Reusable**: You can reuse tests on different versions of an application, even if the user interface changes.
- **Better Quality Software**: Because you can run more tests in less time with fewer resources.
- **Fast**: Automated tools run tests significantly faster than human users.

1.3. When Should we Automate? Economics of Automation

Let us take a scenario. If your Test Manager comes up to you and asks whether it is advisable for your company to automate an application, how would you respond?

In this scenario, the manager is interested in knowing if functional automation will deliver the organization a better Return On Investment (ROI) besides improving application quality and test coverage.

We can determine whether we should automate a given test if we can determine that the cost of automation would be less than the total cost of manually executing the test cases.

For example, if a test script is to run every week for the next two years, automate the test if the cost of automation is less than the cost of manually executing the test 104 times (Two years will have 104 weeks).

Calculating the **Cost of Test Automation**

Cost of Automation = Cost of tool + labor cost of script creation + labor cost of script maintenance

Automate if:

Cost of automation is lower than the manual execution of those scripts.

The key idea here is to plan for the cost of script maintenance. I have seen a lot of automation projects fail because project managers did not plan for the labor costs involved in script maintenance.

Example Let me give you an example from my personal experience.

I performed some automation work for one of our investment banking clients. We had a five-member team, which automated almost 3000 test cases in about six months, which included around total 30 man-months of effort. At the end of the project, we gave the client's testing team a handover of the entire automation suite created by our team. Our recommendation to them was that they would need at least a one or two member team to continuously maintain the scripts. This was because there were still functional changes happening to the application and scripts would need maintenance. But since the client project manager had no budget allocated for this activity, they skipped this advice and continued to execute automation scripts. After the first six months of the 3000 test cases, only 2000 test cases were passing, while the rest started failing. These scripts failures were because script fixes were needed due to application changes. The client team was okay with that and continued to execute those 2000 working test cases, and got rid of the remaining 1000 test cases, which were now executed manually. After another six months, only scripts corresponding to 1000 test cases were passing. So they got rid of another 1000 test cases and started executing them manually. After another six months (1.5 years in total), all the scripts were failing, and testing had to move back to manual functional testing.

In the above real-life scenario, the cost of automation and its benefits could have been reaped, if the client had allocated 1-2 automation testers (could have been part-time) to maintain the scripts and had properly planned and budgeted for it.

1.4. Commercial and Open Source Automation Tools

This section lists some of the popular Commercial and Open Source Automation Tools.

Vendor	Tool	Details
OpenSource (free)	Selenium	Open Source tools and market leader in Open Source segment. Primary for Web-based automation. Support C#, Java, Python, and Ruby as programming language.
OpenSource (free)	Watir	Watir stands for "Web application testing in Ruby". It is again primarily for Web application automation and uses Ruby as the programming language.
HP	Unified Functional Testing	HP UFT (the previous version was called QTP) is the market leader in Test Automation in the commercial tools segment. It uses VBScript as the programming language and its ease of use makes it a tool of choice against other competing tools.
IBM	Rational Functional Tester	IBM Rational Functional Tester is another popular Test Automation Tool. We can program in VB.net or Java using this tool. Is recommended for technical testers.
Microfocus	SilkTest	Microfocus bought SilkTest from Borland. It is still a very popular Automation tool which uses 4Test (propriety) language. Good for technical testers.
Microsoft	VSTP – Code UI tests	Code UI tests come with Microsoft Visual Studio Enterprise version. You can program using VB.net or C# as languages of choice. Fairly good for technical testers.
SmartBear	TestComplete	Low-cost alternative to other commercial tools with good features for automation. You have the option to program using VBScript, JScript, C++Script, C#Script or DelphiScript language.

2. Training Application Walkthrough

In this chapter, we will introduce our customized Web-based training application, which we will use as a part of our book.

Key Objectives:

- Training application walkthrough.
- Understand a sample scenario.

2.1. Training Application Walkthrough

As part of this book, we will be working through a custom Web-based training application. The reason for planning to use our custom-built Web-based application was that this book is focussed around Selenium which only supports Web-based applications. Also, 80-90% of applications tested and automated in real projects are Web-based applications. We will have a much closer and a better understanding of how we need to automate Web-based applications.

Our sample application is a simple hotel booking web application, which has the following key features:

- Search for a Hotel.
- Book a Hotel.
- View Booked Itinerary.
- Cancel Booking.

Let us browse through the application.

1. Launch IE and enter URL *www.adactin.com/HotelApp* to see the Login page.

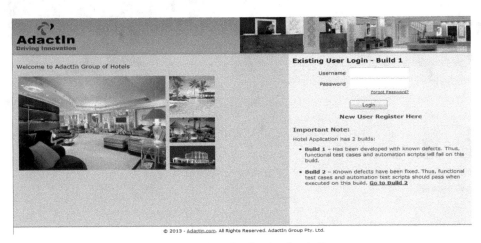

Figure 2.1 – Application Login Page

2. Click on "**New User Register Here**" to go to the Registration page.

Figure 2.2 – **Application Registration Page**

3. Register yourself by entering all the fields. Remember the username and password as you will be using this username/password to login to the application and the remaining part of automation.

4. After you register, an automatic email will be sent to your email-id for confirmation. In case you do not receive the email, reverify it in the junk folder as the email might have gone to your junk folder.

5. Click on the confirmation link in the email.

6. Go to Login page link.

7. On the Login page use the username/password with which you have registered earlier, and click on the **Login** button. You will come to Search Hotel Page.

8. Search for a Hotel.

   i. Select a location, e.g., Sydney.

   ii. Select Number of Rooms, e.g., 2.

   iii. Select Adults per Room, e.g., 2.

   iv. Click on **Search** button.

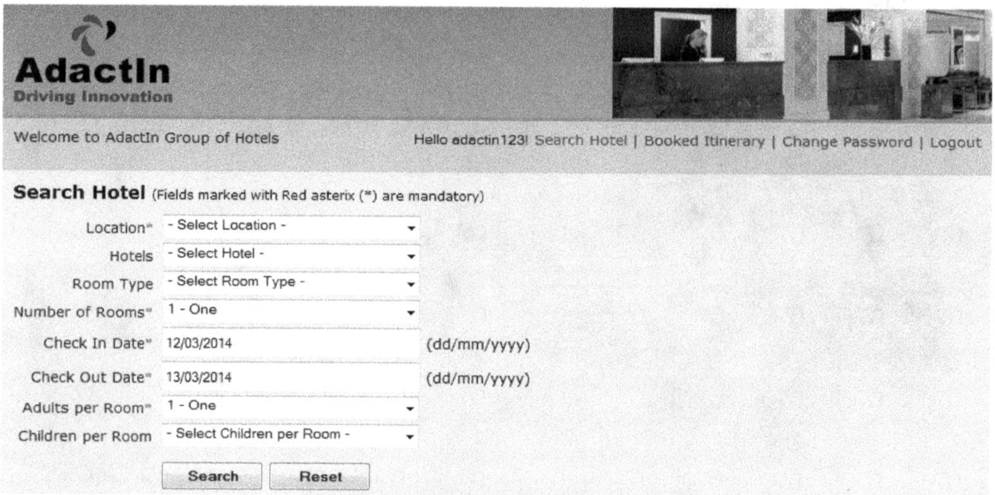

Figure 2.3 – **Application Search Hotel Page**

9. Select a Hotel.

    i. **Select** one of the Hotel Radio Buttons, e.g., select radio button next to Hotel Cornice.

Figure 2.4 – Application Select Hotel Page

10. Book a Hotel.

    i.   Enter First Name.
    ii.   Enter Last Name.
    iii. Enter Address.
    iv.   Enter 16-digit credit Card Number.
    v.   Enter Credit Card Type.
    vi.   Enter Expiry Month.
    vii. Enter Expiry Year.
    viii. Enter CVV Number.
    ix.   Click on **Book Now.**

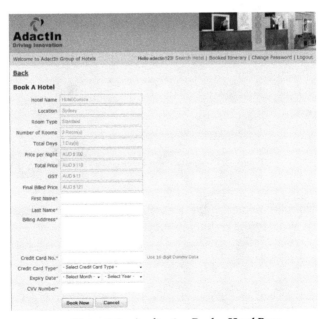

Figure 2.5 – Application Book a Hotel Page

11. After you see booking confirmation, you will notice that you get an Order number. generated.

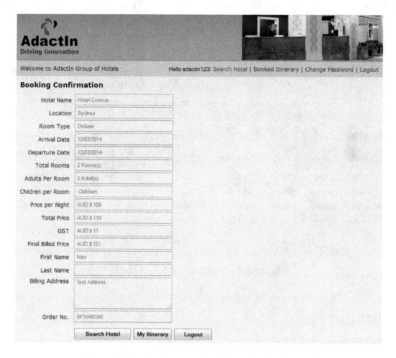

Figure 2.6 – Application Booking Confirmation Page

12. Copy the Order Number. to the clipboard. In our case it is 8K1I446G95.

13. Click on **My Itinerary** Button or click on the **Booking Itinerary** link at the top right corner of application. The user will go to the **Booked Itinerary** Page.

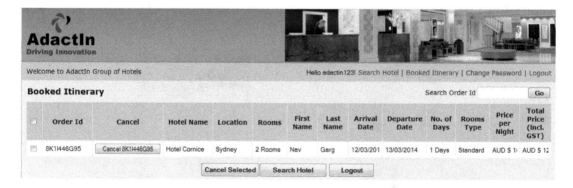

Figure 2.7 – Application Booked Itinerary Page

14. Enter the Order Number. copied in the previous step in search Order Id field, and click on the **Go** button. You will see the order you recently created.

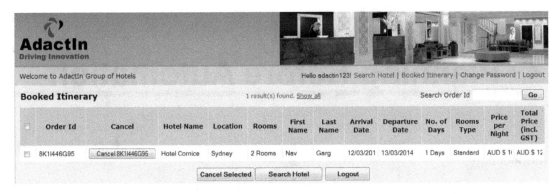

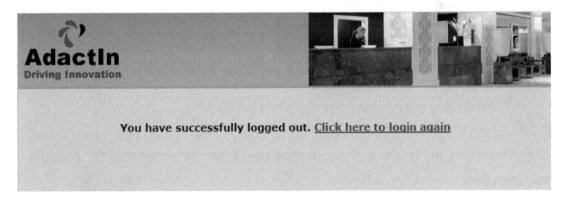

Figure 2.8 – Application Search Results Page

15. Click on **Logout** button or **Logout** link, on the top right corner to logout from the application. You will go to "**Click here to login again**" page.

Figure 2.9 – Application Click here to Login Again Page

16. Click on "**Click here to login again**" link to go to login page.

 Note: Hotel Application has two builds:

- Build 1: Has been developed with known defects. Thus, few functional test cases and automation scripts will fail on this build.

- Build 2: Known defects have been fixed. Thus, functional test cases and automation test scripts should pass when executed on this build.

The user can access either of the builds from the Login page of the Hotel Application.

3. Planning Before Automation

Introduction

Before you actually start recording your scripts and doing automation, it is important to plan the recording of your scripts. You need to plan:

- The test cases which need to be automated.
- Define priority of the test cases and automate key test cases first.
- The stability of your application.
- The data dependency of the tests.
- If there are tests which use the same data.
- If the automation tester knows the steps of the tests to be automated.
- Whether the automation testers have permission to access application components and systems.
- Who is going to automate which test within the team?
- When should the automation tasks be accomplished?

In this chapter, we will try to understand what we need to plan before we start our recording.

Key objectives:

- To understand the prerequisites before we record.
- To understand the Test Automation process.

3.1. Prerequisites Before you Start Recording

Let us try to understand some of the prerequisites before we start recording our scripts:

- **Prepare your Test Environment -- Check whether your environment and application are stable**

Determine that you have a test environment available in which you can record/replay and create your automation scripts.

Determine whether the application is stable from a development as well as functional point of view. Does the interface change very often?

As a recommendation, if the application interface is changing too often, or if the application is not stable from a functional point of view, or if the test environment is not stable, we should not start automation. It's important to understand the factual reason for that. Technically speaking, we can still perform automation, but it might increase maintenance and script modification effort later on when functional issues or UI issues are fixed. So a better approach is to wait until the environment is stabilized.

- **Ensure that the automation tester has permission to access application components and systems**

Ensure that the test suite and testers have permissions to access the database, host systems, and input/output data.

- **Execute the test case steps manually to determine the expected results**

Execute the test case steps manually on the application to verify that all the steps are listed and ensure that you are able to understand the business process. One of the most important factors to consider in automated testing is to ensure that the test duplicates the test steps in the most straightforward manner possible. It is important to **capture the actions** stated in the test case **exactly as an end user would perform** them in the business process.

Also, it helps you to understand if there is any **pre-data setup** required for the test. For example, if you need to automate login, you need to have a valid username and password. Rather than starting your recording first, you will realize that you need a valid login when you first manually execute your tests.

example Let me give you another example from my personal experience:

Once we were implementing functional automation for a client and we had a test case which required us to verify that the login expires after two months. We thought of changing the system date of our PC to two months in the past and then verifying that the login expires. But the question was: how do we change the system date using HP UFT? So we did some research, tried a couple of examples, and were able to figure out a way. But that took us about two days.

Now once we had implemented the solution, we found that whenever we ran the UFT script, the login did not actually expire and the user could still login. We ran the test case steps manually and found the login does not expire even when manually executed which got us perplexed. After some more investigations, we realized that we were changing the system date of our local PC and not the server. But as the expiry date was linked to the server date and not to the local machine, the login did not expire and the user could login. Also, we did not have access to the server, and due to authorization issues, it was not possible to change the date of the server machine.

The question is: Could we have foreseen this issue and saved our two days? If we would have manually tested this scenario, we would have realized our mistake and would not have spent two days trying to automate it.

- **Determine what data will be required to be used for test execution**

Ensure that you understand what input data you would need for test creation. You need to understand valid and invalid input data. Also, a lot of times there are scenarios where you would need data in a specific format or type.

example Let me take an example here:

I used to work for a mortgage domain client. One of their applications required the input date to be greater than or equal to the current date. How do we design an automation script to take a date that's greater than the current date without the test case depending on the already defined data? It needs better planning. As a solution, instead of using hard-coded data, we used some VBScript function to generate a date greater than today's date.

Apart from this, there might be scenarios where after the test verification has finished; you would need to roll back specific data that was earlier set up as part of test execution. So make sure to understand data dependencies before you start automation.

- **Determine the start and end point of the test and follow it for all your automation scripts**

Make sure that for all your automation scripts, you determine where your script will start from and where it will end.

Why is this important? This is important as you are going to run your scripts as a suite or a batch and not individually. So your current script should know where your previous script ended.

For instance, say you are working on a Web-based application and you open your browser at the start of every test but fail to close the browser at the end of each test. If you are running 50 tests you will have 50 browser windows open at the end of your script run which will cause script execution issues.

The correct way is to determine the Start and End point of your test and follow it for all your scripts. This will ensure that any automation tester in your team would know which form or page of application will be open when they start creating their automation script and where they should finish their script.

A better solution for Web-based applications will be to open the browser at the start of every test and close the browser at the end of every test.

- **Reset any master data if data is modified as part of the test**

Another important thing to do is to reset any master data to the default value after data is modified as part of your test. The reason is that future test scripts would be looking for default data and not the data which you have modified as part of your current test.

 Let me give an example here:

I was once working on a manufacturing based application which had units (centimeters, millimeters, and inches) defined as master data to measure the length of various manufacturing components. As a part of one test case we automated, we changed the master data of Unit field from centimeters to inches and verified that all the valid lengths are now in inches. Our automation script worked beautifully, and we integrated it with our automation suite and executed our overnight test run.

Next morning we found that all our scripts, following this script failed. We realized that though we had changed the master data of the Unit field from centimeters to inches, we never changed it back to default (which was centimeters). Hence, all the sequential scripts failed as they expected the unit to be centimeters, but found the unit in inches. So we had to fix the script to reset the Unit field back to default value at the end of the script.

So as a thumb rule, reset all the master data that you have modified at the end of your test to default values as it can impact other tests.

- **Standardize naming conventions**

Create standards and conventions on how you are going to name your automation scripts, setup naming conventions for your temporary variables, functions, and other components of your automation framework.

This will help to ensure that the whole team is following standardized naming conventions and the complete framework can be easily maintained in the future.

- **Plan and prioritize your test cases and identify your automation candidates**

Plan and prioritize which test cases you should automate first. We use the term *automation candidates* for regression test cases, which we select for automation.

A few key criteria for selection of automation candidates include:

- Test cases which are high priority or linked to high priority requirements. Usually, we automate Sanity or Build Acceptance test cases as a first step.
- Test cases which are data-oriented or which need to be executed multiple times for different sets of data.
- Test cases which take a long time to exe   automation will free up functional testers to perform more key task
- Existing or fixed defects in the systems w   to test cases.
- Frequency of execution of the test c   ecuted very frequently are better candidates for   estment (ROI).
- Test cases for operating syste   e automated, as the same scri   s or browsers.
- **Plan resources and sc**

Plan how many people will be au   edule will be.

3.2. Test Automati

This section describes automation p   tomate the regression test cases.

1. Defining the scope for automation: Define t   es that should be automated, check feasibility, and confirm return on investi

2. Selection of the Test Automation tool: Select right t omation tools, which will suit your application technology and fit into your budget. It can be an open source or a commercial tool.

3. Procurement of licenses: If a commercial tool is selected, procure the license for the commercial tool.

4. Training the testers to use the tool: If required, train the testing team on how to perform automation and how to use the automation tool.

5. Automation strategy and plan: Design the automation strategy and plan on how and when regression test cases will be automated. Also, define data dependencies, environmental needs, and risks.

6. Identification and development of Automation Framework and Test Automation Lab: Automation framework is required to make sure that automation scripts are maintainable. It involves setting up design and guidelines for automation components. This includes defining naming conventions, guideline documents, and structure of the automation scripts and setup of test machines in the test environment.

7. Creation of Automation Scripts: Actual recording or creation of automation scripts from regression test cases.

8. Peer Review and Testing: Review of Automation Scripts by peers to ensure that all conventions are followed and automation scripts are correctly mapped to functional test cases. Test case verification points are also verified as part of the review.

9. Integration of scripts: This involves the integration of automation scripts into a larger automation suite for overnight test execution, to be executed as a batch process.

10. Script maintenance: Regular script maintenance that is required when an application undergoes functional changes and needs fixes in automation scripts.

4. Introduction to Selenium

Introducing Selenium

Selenium is an Open Source tool for automating browser-based applications. Selenium is a set of different software tools, each with a different approach to supporting test automation. The tests can be written as HTML tables or coded in a number of popular programming languages and can be run directly in most modern Web browsers. Selenium can be deployed on Windows, Linux, and Macintosh and many OS for mobile applications like iOS, Windows Mobile, and Android.

Among all Open Source tools, Selenium functional testing tool is considered to be a highly portable software testing framework and one of the best tools available in the current market for automation of Web applications.

Key objectives:

- Understand Selenium Tool Suite.
- Choosing right Selenium Tool for use.
- Requirements for Selenium Setup.

4.1. Selenium's Tool Suite

Selenium is not just a single tool but a suite of software, each catering to different testing needs of an organization. **It has four components.**

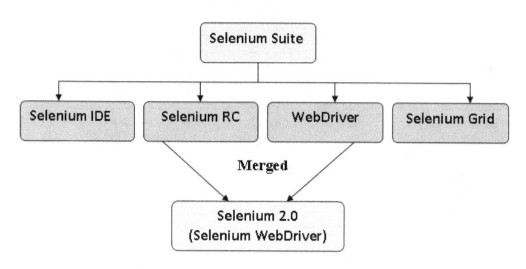

Figure 4.1 – Selenium Suite Structure

14

In the section below, we will understand more about each of these components.

1. Selenium IDE

Selenium IDE (Integrated Development Environment) is a prototyping tool for building test scripts. It comes as a Firefox plugin and provides an easy-to-use interface for developing automated tests. Selenium IDE has a recording feature, which records user actions as they are performed and then exports them as a reusable script in one of many programming languages for execution later.

Selenium IDE is simply intended to be a rapid prototyping tool. Selenium IDE has a "Save" feature that allows users to keep the tests in a table-based format for later import and execution. Selenium IDE doesn't provide iteration or conditional statements for test scripts. Use Selenium IDE for basic automation. Selenium developers usually recommend Selenium 2 or Selenium 1 to be used for serious, robust test automation.

2. Selenium 1 - Selenium RC or Remote Control

Selenium RC is the main Selenium project allowing user actions to be simulated in a browser like clicking a UI element, input data, etc. It executes the user commands in the browser by injecting Java script functions to the browser when the browser is loaded. As we know, Java Script has its own limitations and so does Selenium RC.

How Selenium RC Works

First, we will describe how the components of Selenium RC operate and the role each plays in running your test scripts.

RC Components: Selenium RC components are:

- The Selenium Server which launches and kills browsers, interprets, and runs the Selenese commands passed from the test program, and acts as an *HTTP proxy*, intercepting and verifying HTTP messages passed between the browser and the AUT.
- Client libraries which provide the interface between each programming language and the Selenium RC Server.

Here is a simplified architecture

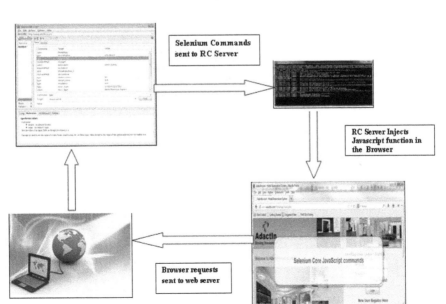

Figure 4.2 – Selenium RC Architecture

The diagram shows how the client libraries communicate with the Server passing each Selenium command for execution. Then the server passes the Selenium command to the browser using Selenium-Core JavaScript commands. The browser, using its JavaScript interpreter, executes the Selenium command. This runs the Selenese action or verification you specified in your test script.

3.   WebDriver

WebDriver was a new project developer due to the inherent limitation of the Selenium RC. WebDriver interacted directly with the browser using the "native" method for the browser and operating system, thus avoiding the restrictions of a sandboxed Javascript environment. The WebDriver project began with the aim to solve Selenium's pain points.

4.   Selenium 2 - Selenium WebDriver

Developers of both Selenium RC and WebDriver decided to merge both the tools and create Selenium 2.0 aka Selenium WebDriver. It was a new addition to the Selenium toolkit which provided all sorts of awesome features, including a more cohesive and object-oriented API as well as an answer to the limitations of the old implementation (Selenium RC). Both tools had their own advantages and merging the two provides a much more robust automation tool.

Selenium WebDriver supports the WebDriver API and underlying technology, along with the Selenium 1 technology underneath the WebDriver API for maximum flexibility in porting your tests. In addition, Selenium 2 still runs Selenium 1's Selenium RC interface for backward compatibility.

Selenium WebDriver's architecture is simpler than Selenium RC's.

WebDriver uses a different underlying framework from Selenium's Javascript Selenium-Core. It makes direct calls to the browser using each browser's native support for automation. How these direct calls are made and the features they support depend on the browser you are using.

- It controls the browser from the OS level.
- All you need are your programming language's IDE (which contains your Selenium commands) and a browser.

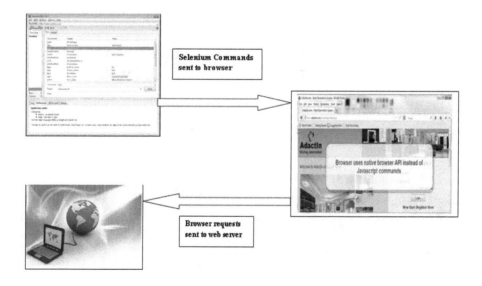

Figure 4.3 – Selenium WebDriver Architecture

It provides the following:

- A well-designed standard programming interface for Web application testing.
- Improved consistency between browsers.
- Additional functionality addressing testing problems not well-supported in Selenium 1.0 like handling multiple frames, pop-up, and alerts, better page navigation, drag-and-drop, and handling of AJAX-based UI elements.

5. Selenium Grid

Selenium Grid is a tool used together with Selenium RC and WebDriver to run parallel tests across different machines and different browsers all at the same time. Parallel execution means running multiple tests at once.

Features:

- Enables simultaneous running of tests in multiple browsers and environments.
- Utilizes the hub-and-nodes concept. The hub acts as a central source of Selenium commands to each node connected to it.

This has two advantages:

- First, if you have a large test suite or a slow-running test suite, you can boost its performance substantially by using Selenium Grid to divide your test suite to run different tests at the same time which will result in significant time savings.
- Also, if you must run your test suite on multiple environments you can have different remote machines supporting and running your tests in them at the same time.

In each case, the Selenium Grid greatly improves the time it takes to run your suite by making use of parallel processing.

4.2. How to Choose the Right Selenium Tool for your Need

Tool	Why Choose?
Selenium IDE	<ul><li>To learn about concepts on automated testing and Selenium, including:<ul><li>Selenese commands such as type, open, ClickAndWait, assert, verify, etc., are easy to understand.</li><li>Locators such as id, name, XPath, CSS selector, etc.</li><li>Exporting test cases in various programming languages.</li><li>To create tests with little or no prior knowledge of programming.</li><li>To create simple test cases and test suites that can be exported later to RC or WebDriver.</li></ul></li></ul>
Selenium RC	<ul><li>To design a test using a more expressive language than Selenese.</li><li>To run your test against different browsers (except HTML Unit) on different operating systems.</li><li>To deploy your tests across multiple environments using Selenium Grid.</li><li>To test your application against a new browser that supports JavaScript.</li><li>To test Web applications with complex AJAX-based scenarios.</li></ul>**Note**: Selenium RC has been superseded by Selenium WebDriver 2.0.

Tool	Why Choose?
Selenium WebDriver	• For all reasons above for Selenium RC. • To use a certain programming language in designing your test case. • To execute tests on the HTML Unit browser. • To create customized test results.
Selenium Grid	• To run your Selenium WebDriver/RC scripts in multiple browsers and operating systems simultaneously. • To run a huge test suite that needs to complete as soon as possible.

Advantages/Limitations of Selenium Tools

You'll find that Selenium is highly flexible. There are many ways you can add functionality to both Selenium test scripts and Selenium's framework and customize your test automation. This is perhaps Selenium's greatest strength when compared with other automation tools. In addition, since Selenium is Open Source, the source code can always be downloaded and modified.

Advantages of Selenium

1. Open Source tool.
2. Supports all browsers like Internet Explorer, Firefox, Safari, or Opera.
3. Runs on all operating systems – Windows, Mac OS, and Linux.
4. Supports various languages like Java, .NET, Ruby, Perl, PHP, etc.
5. Runs multiple tests at a time.
6. Provides the option of using a wide range of IDEs such as Eclipse, Netbeans, Visual Studio, etc., depending on the choice of development language.

Limitations of Selenium

1. Supports only browser-based applications, not desktop/windows applications.
2. Does not support file upload from a local machine.
3. Requires high technical skills to meet its full potential.
4. Being an open source, Selenium has no official technical support.

5. Installing Selenium Components

Introduction

Before we can start using Selenium, there are a few Selenium and non-Selenium components that we need to install. In this chapter, we will perform step by step installation and setup of the components which we will need to use cover the scope of this book.

 Note: You need access to the internet to download the required setup files.

Key objectives:

1. Setup Instructions for installing Katalon Automation Recorder.
2. Setup Instructions to install and setup Microsoft Visual Studio IDE.

5.1. Installing Katalon Automation Recorder

The Katalon Studio team has recently introduced **Katalon Automation Recorder** that has been developed for the users who are no longer able to continue the automation testing using obsolete Selenium IDE. It can be added as an extension in Firefox and Chrome and supported by the latest versions of these browsers (and will be supported by the upcoming versions as well). This tool is a perfect alternative for the Selenium IDE and other similar open source frameworks.

Pre-requisite – Firefox browser should be installed locally on the test machine.

1. Launch Firefox and navigate to the URL https://www.katalon.com/resources-center/blog/katalon-automation-recorder/ .

2. Click on Firefox and will navigate to URL https://addons.mozilla.org/en-US/firefox/addon/katalon-automation-record/

3. Firefox will protect you from installing add-ons, e.g., from unfamiliar locations, so you will need to click **"Allow"** to proceed with the installation

4. Click on "**Add To Firefox"**.

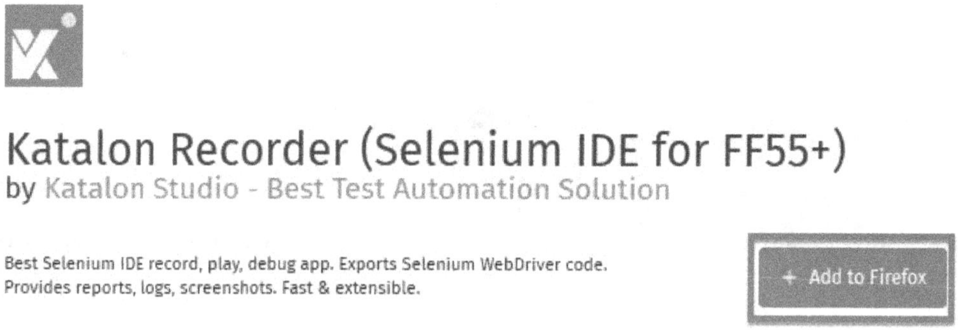

Katalon Recorder (Selenium IDE for FF55+)
by Katalon Studio - Best Test Automation Solution

Best Selenium IDE record, play, debug app. Exports Selenium WebDriver code.
Provides reports, logs, screenshots. Fast & extensible.

Figure 5.1 – Allow IDE Installation

5. Add-on will get downloaded and a pop-up appears. Click **Add.**

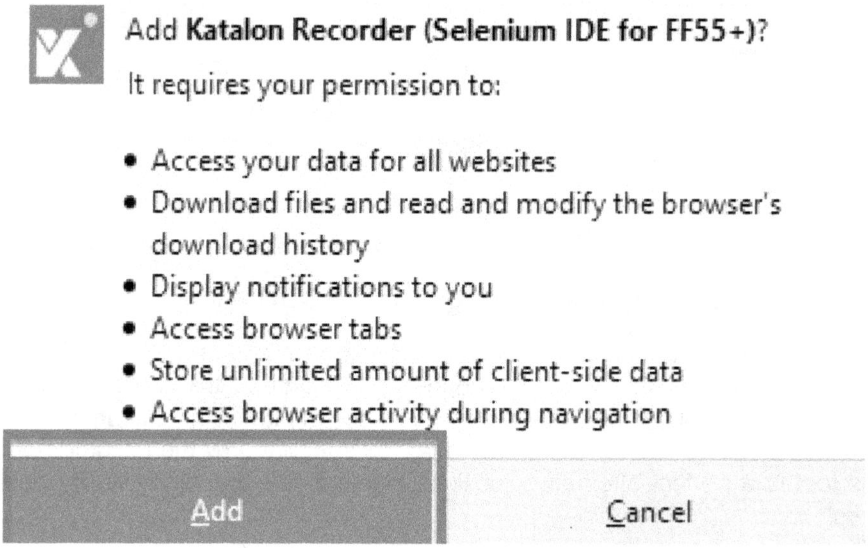

Add **Katalon Recorder (Selenium IDE for FF55+)?**

It requires your permission to:

- Access your data for all websites
- Download files and read and modify the browser's download history
- Display notifications to you
- Access browser tabs
- Store unlimited amount of client-side data
- Access browser activity during navigation

| Add | Cancel |

Figure 5.2 – Install Katalon Recorder from Firefox Add-on

6. Wait until the installation is completed. In the pop-up window, click **OK**

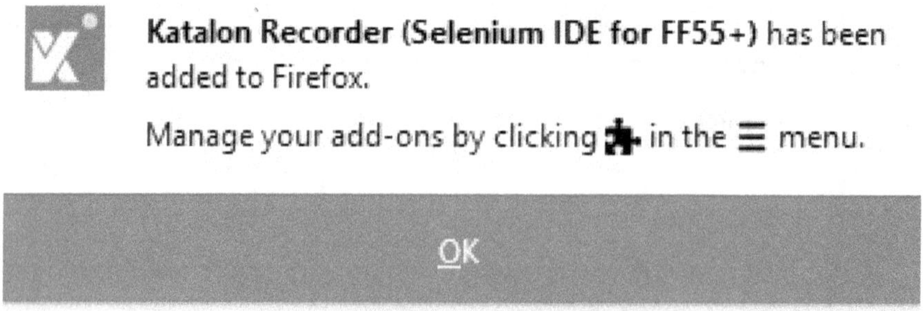

Katalon Recorder (Selenium IDE for FF55+) has been added to Firefox.

Manage your add-ons by clicking 🧩 in the ≡ menu.

OK

Figure 5.3 – Click "OK" Now

7. After Firefox reboots you will find the the Katalon Recorder on your Firefox toolbar in a jiffy (it will not take more than 10 seconds to get installed).

Figure 5.4 – Katalon Recorder

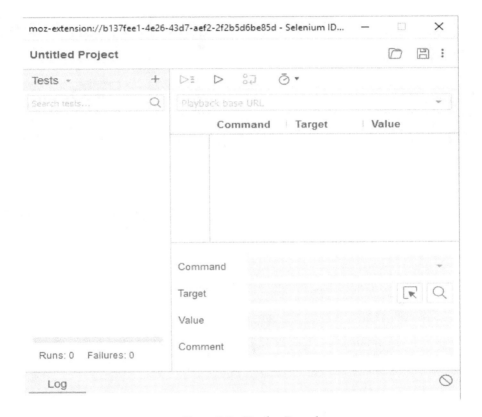

Figure 5.5 – Katalon Recorder

5.2. Installing and Configuring Microsoft Visual Studio

About Microsoft Visual Studio: Visual Studio is an integrated development environment (IDE) from Microsoft. It is used to develop computer programs for Microsoft Windows, as well as websites, web apps, web services, and mobile apps. Visual Studio supports different programming languages and allows the code editor and debugger to support (to varying degrees) nearly any programming language, provided a language-specific service exists. Built-in languages include C, C++ and C++/CLI (via Visual C++), VB.NET (via Visual Basic .NET), C# (via Visual C#), and F#.

We will be using Microsoft Visual Studio IDE for creating our NUnit based Selenium WebDriver tests.

Downloading and Installing Microsoft Visual Studio 2017 Community Free Edition

1. Go to https://www.visualstudio.com/downloads/. Click on Visual Studio Community.

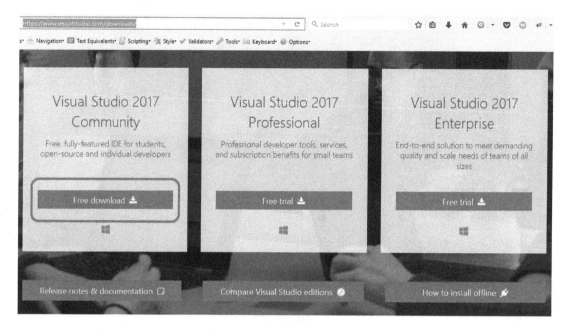

Figure 5.6 – Visual Studio Download

Note: You would see the latest version of Visual Studio at the time you initiate a download.

2. Click on **Save file** to download it on your machine.

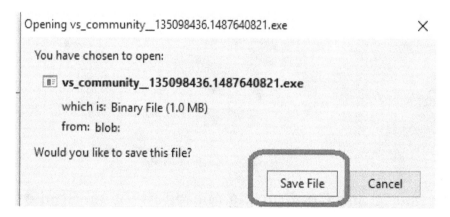

Figure 5.7 – Save File

3. Choose the location on your machine and click on **Save**.

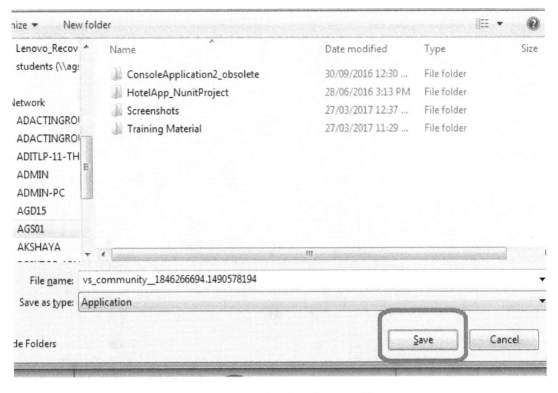

Figure 5.8 – Save the File in the Desired Location

4. Once the application is downloaded, click on the application to start.

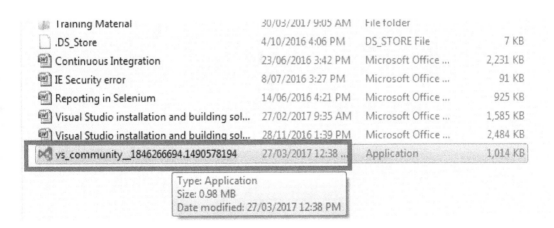

Figure 5.9 – Click on the Application

5. Double click on the .exe file. The Visual Studio Application will open prompting you to choose the components that you would like to install at the start.

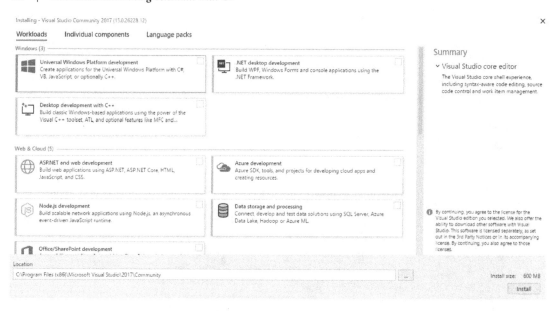

Figure 5.10 – **Installation Components**

💡 **Note:** There are a number of components that can be chosen from the list. However, for our application's sake, we're sticking to only those that are needed.

6. Click on the **Workloads** tab. Under the **Windows** section, choose the **Universal Windows Platform Development.** Under the **Web and Cloud** section, select **Office/SharePoint development.**

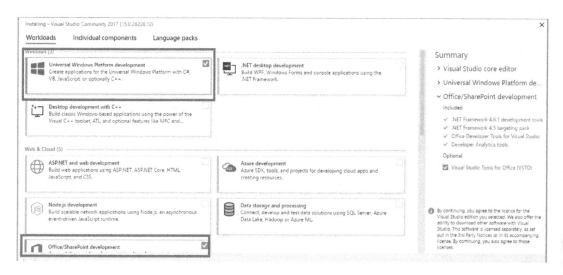

Figure 5.11 – **Choose Web and Cloud Components**

7. Scroll down and under **Other Toolsets**, select **Visual Studio Extension Develop, .Net Core cross-platform development**

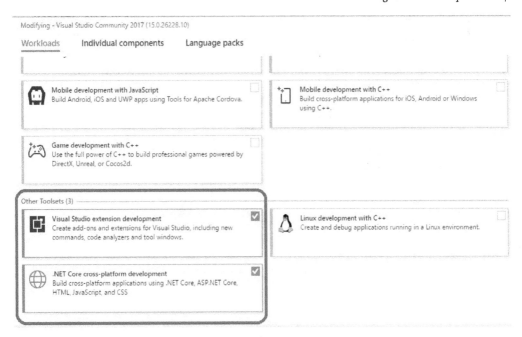

Figure 5.12 – Choosing Other Toolsets

8. Under **Individual Components,** the **.Net Components** will be selected automatically, as shown in the picture.

Figure 5.13 – Choose Individual Components .NET Framework

9. Scroll down. Under the **Development Activities**, select ASP .NET and web development tools, C# and Visual Basic and JavaScript and TypeScript language support.

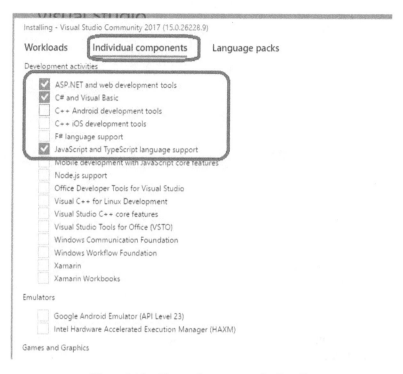

Figure 5.14 – Choose Components for Installation

10. Under the **Compilers, Build tools, and runtimes section**, C# and Visual Basic Roslyn compilers will be selected.

Figure 5.15 – Choose Cloud Components

11. Under the **Language packs,** English will be selected by default.

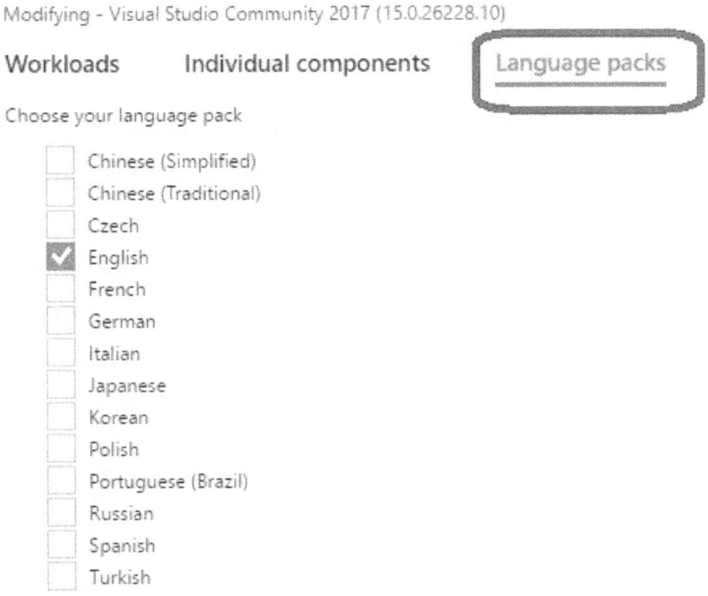

Figure 5.16 – Language Packs

Note: **We can choose any language of our choice. For the scope of this book, English has been chosen.**

12. Once all the required components are selected, click **Install.**

Figure 5.17– Install Components

13. The Installation may take a while to complete.

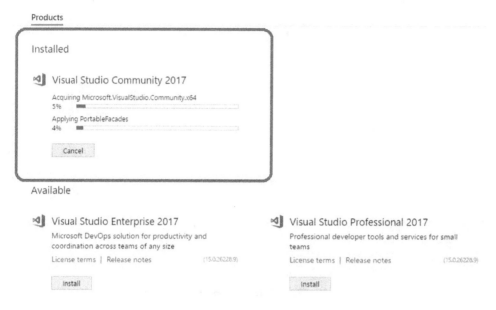

Figure 5.18 – Installation in Progress

14. Once the installation is complete, you will be able to see that all the components are installed. Click on **Launch.**

Figure 5.19 – Launch Visual Studio

15. Visual Studio will be launched. You will be prompted to sign in or sign up. At the moment, click on **Not now, maybe later.**

Figure 5.20 – Visual Studio User Sign Up

16. Choose the environment in which you want to work and click on **Start Visual Studio.**

Figure 5.21– Choose the Environment

17. The Visual Studio IDE will open up.

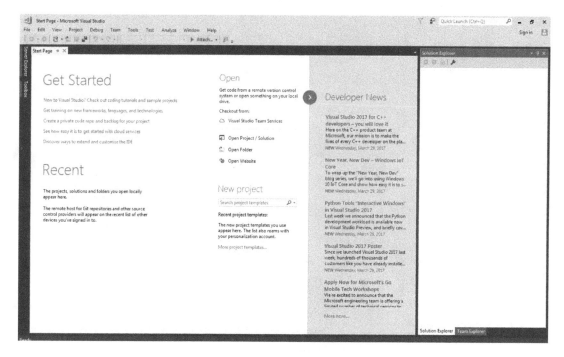

Figure 5.22 – Visual Studio Start Page

18. Click **File > New > Project** to create a new project.

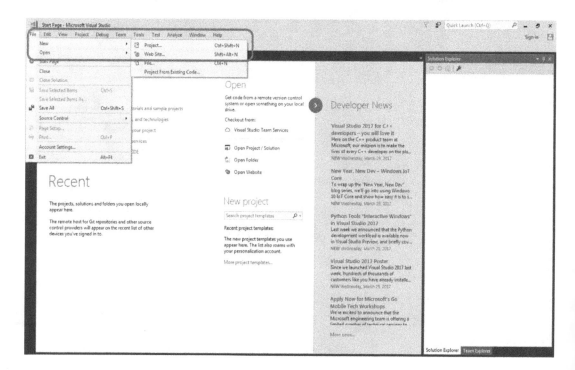

Figure 5.23 – Start New Project

19. Choose the template for **Visual C#** from the Installed tab in the New Project window. On the left hand pane, click on **Test**. On the right-hand pane, click on **Unit Test Project (.NET Framework)**.

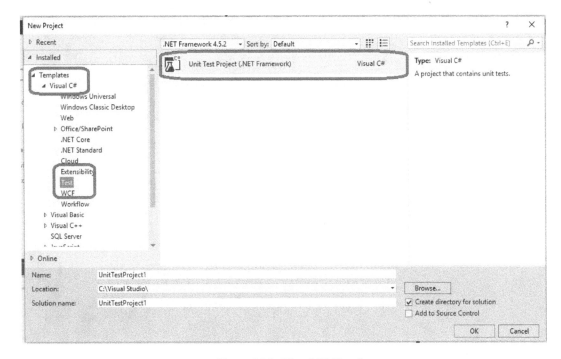

Figure 5.24 – Visual C# Template

20. Choose the Name as **HotelAppApplication** and the Location on your machine. Click **OK**.

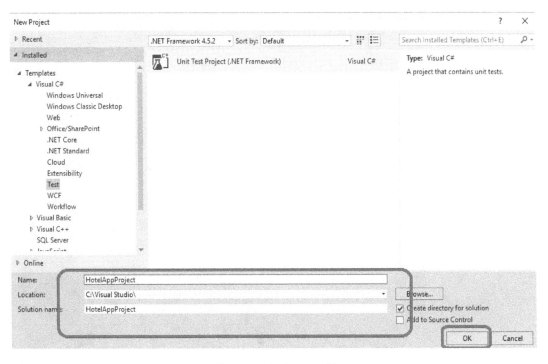

Figure 5.25 – Program Name

21. A new Visual C# Unit Test project will get opened.

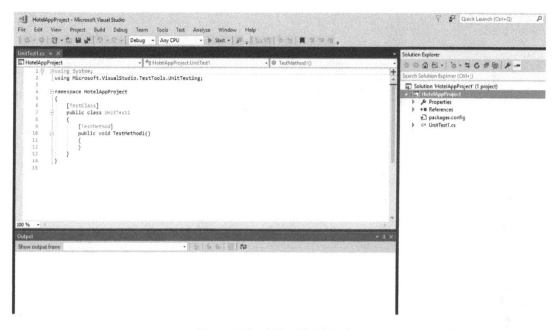

Figure 5.26 – A New Unit Test Project

6. Using Katalon Automation Recorder

Introduction

Many times, functional testers believe that they need to write programs to automate applications. This is not entirely true. Most of the automation tools come with record/replay features which allow you to record user actions and replay those actions without writing a single line of program. Yes, you might need to make some enhancements to your script, which again can be accomplished without any programming.

In Selenium, we can perform record/replay and automate test cases using Selenium IDE. Selenium IDE is an easy-to-use and Firefox plugin and is generally a quick and efficient way of developing test cases. As Selenium IDE has stopped working from Firefox 55 onwards, The **Katalon Studio team** has recently introduced **Katalon Automation Recorder** that has been developed for the users who are no longer able to continue the automation testing using obsolete Selenium IDE.

It can be added as an extension in Firefox and Chrome and supported by the latest versions of these browsers (and will be supported by the upcoming versions as well). This tool is a perfect alternative for the Selenium IDE and other similar open source frameworks. It is a very handy and powerful test steps recorder which is ported from Selenium IDE to Chrome and Firefox with major functions preserved.

It also contains a context menu that allows you to first select a UI element from the browser's currently displayed page and then select from a list of Selenium commands with parameters pre-defined according to the context of the selected UI element. This chapter is all about understanding the features of **Katalon Automation Recorder** and how to use it effectively.

example As consultants, we have to perform automation feasibility studies across various client applications. The simplest way to do the feasibility study using Selenium is by using **Katalon Automation Recorder**. By recording and replaying a basic script we can figure out if the application can be automated by Selenium. If yes, we can delve into the bigger effort of configuring Selenium WebDriver.

In this chapter, we will define how to record a basic script, replay the script, and save the script using **Katalon Automation Recorder**.

Key objectives:

- Understand Selenium interface.
- Record a basic script.
- Replay the script.
- Save the script.

6.1. Selenium Interface

1. To launch the Katalon Automation Recorder, Open Firefox browser

2. Go to Toolbar -→ Select  .

Figure 6.1 - Open Katalon Automation Recorder

3. It opens with an empty script-editing window and a menu for loading or creating new test cases

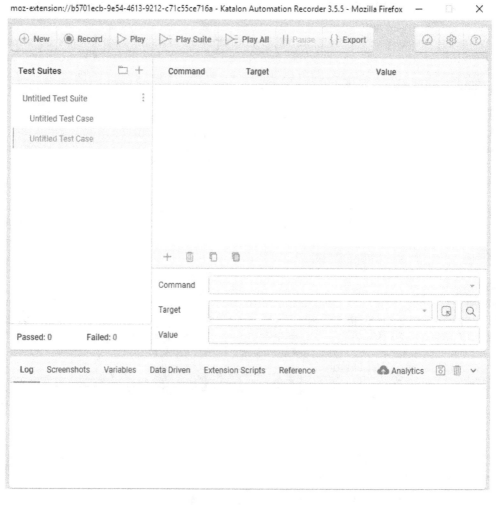

Figure 6.2 – Katalon Automation Recorder

4. Find below few of the IDE User Interface options.

6.2. Katalon Recorder User Guide

Katalon Automation Recorder main UI contains 4 sections as follow:

- Main Toolbar
- Test Case/ Suite Explorer
- Test Case Details View
- Log/Reference/Variable

Toolbar

Katalon Recorder main toolbar contains buttons to help you to manage web recording process.

Button	Description
New	Create new test case or test suite
Record	For recording automation test
Play	Execute selected single test case
Play Suite	Execute selected test suite
Play All	Execute all test suites
Pause/Resume	Pause and Resume current execution
Stop	Stop recording or the current execution
Export	Export current test suite/test case to various scripting languages and framework
Speed	Adjust execution speed
Setting	Port configuration for Katalon Studio Users. Allow users to change the default port used by Katalon Studio to communicate with the active browser
Help icon	Katalon Automation Recorder User Guide

The toolbar contains buttons for controlling the execution of your test cases, the extreme left button, the one with the red dot, is the record button.

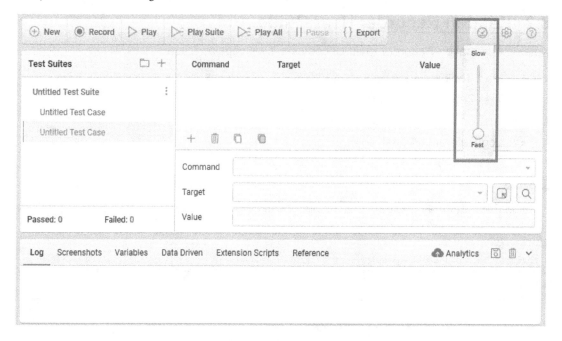

Figure 6.3 – Katalon Automation Toolbar

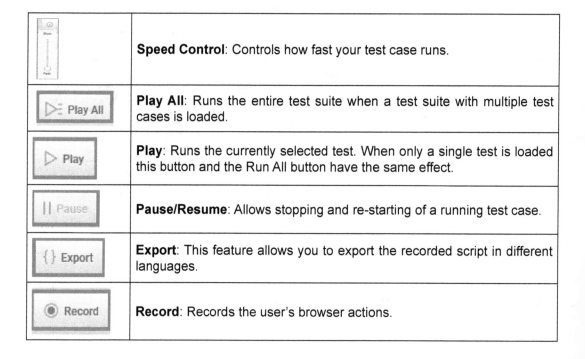

6.3. Recording Using Katalon Automation Recorder

Alright! Let us record our first script now.

Note: Many first-time users begin by recording a test case from their interactions with a website. When Katalon Automation Recorder is first opened, the record button is OFF by default

Recording your First Test Case

1. Open the **Firefox browser**.

2. Enter the URL of the site you want to test. Let's take our sample application:

   http://www.adactin.com/HotelApp/

3. Go to **Tools** → and open Katalon Automation Recorder.

4. Press the **red button** to start recording.

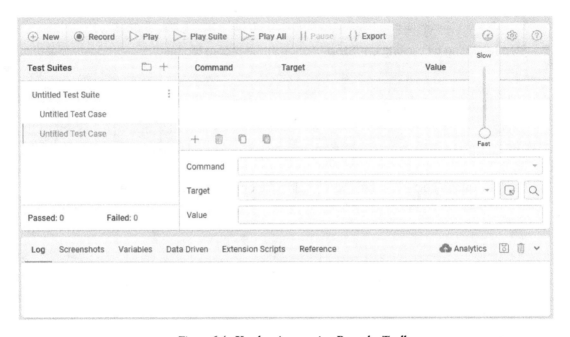

Figure 6.4 –Katalon Automation Recorder Toolbar

5. Assuming that the application is already open in the Firefox browser with the login page visible, perform the following steps:

   a. Login (use the username/password with which you have registered earlier).

   b. Search for the Hotel:

      i. Select a location, e.g., Sydney.

      ii. Select number of rooms, e.g., 2-Two.

      iii. Select adults per rooms, e.g., 2-Two.

      iv. Click on the Search button.

   c. Select a Hotel.

      i. Select one of the Hotel Radio buttons, e.g., select radio button next to Hotel Creek.

   d. Book a Hotel.

      i. Enter First Name.

      ii. Enter Last Name.

      iii. Enter Address.

iv.   Enter 16-digit Credit Card no.

v.   Enter Credit Card type.

vi.   Enter Expiry Month.

vii.   Enter Expiry Year.

viii.   Enter CVV number.

ix.   Click on Book Now.

e.   After you see the Booking confirmation page, click on the Logout link in the top-right corner.

f.   Click on "Click here to Login again" link to go back to the Home page.

6.   Stop recording by clicking on "**Stop**" button in the record toolbar.

Figure 6.5 – Stop Recording

7.   Verify the steps below that are recorded in Katalon Automation Recorder.

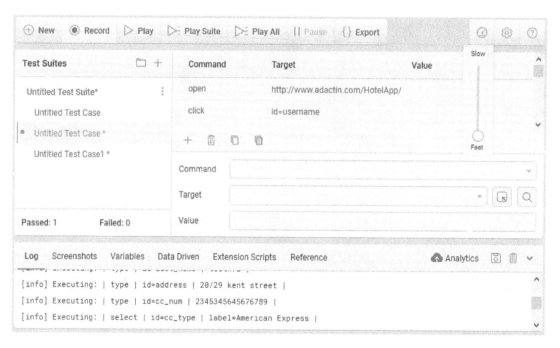

Figure 6.6 – Steps

If you look at the above steps, the first column "Command" represents the operation or method performed on user controls. For example, type method to enter value in the Username field.

The second column- "Target" represents the user controls of the application on which actions are done.

The third column "Value" represents all the input data that has been entered into the application for testing.

Note: Note that all the actions which we performed are captured as separate steps in the IDE script.

During recording, Katalon Automation Recorder will automatically insert commands into your test case based on your actions. Typically, this will include:

- Clicking a Web Element like a button or link - *click* or *clickAndWait* commands.
- Entering values - *type* command.
- Selecting options from a drop-down list box - *select* command.
- Clicking checkboxes or radio buttons - *click* command.

8. **Select** the step where location selection is Sydney.

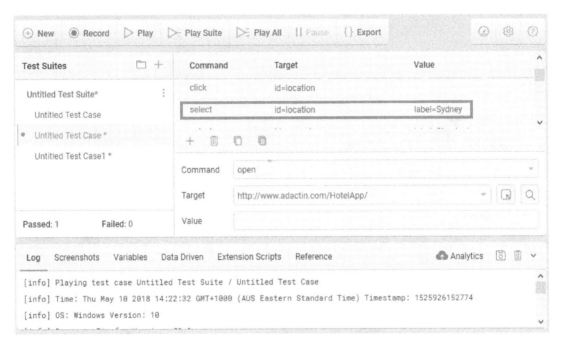

Figure 6.7 – Commands, Target, and Values

Note that in the bottom pane you can select values for Command and change Target and Data values.

6.4. Saving and Replaying the Script using IDE

Saving the Test case

Now you can save your script. Like most programs. However, Selenium distinguishes between test cases and test suites. To save your tests for later use, you can either save the individual test cases or save the test suite. If the test cases of your test suite have not been saved, you'll be prompted to save them before saving the test suite.

1. Select **Export** →Select the Format and **Save Test Case**.

Figure 6.8 – Option to Save Test Case

2. Save the Test Cases in your C:\Selenium Folder and name it as **MyIDEscript**.

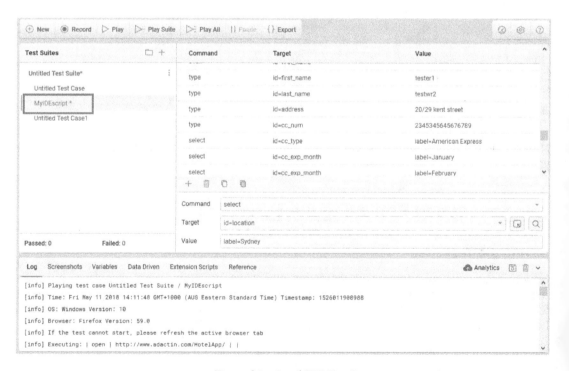

Figure 6.9 – Saved IDE Test Case

Running the Test Cases

The IDE allows many options for running your test case. You can run a single command you are currently developing, and you can do a batch run of an entire test suite. Execution of test cases is very flexible in the IDE.

Run a Test Case

Click the Play button to run the currently displayed test case.

Run a Test Suite

Click the Play All button to run all the test cases in the currently loaded test suite.

Stop and Start

The Stop button can be used to stop the test case while it is running. The icon of this button then changes to Record.

Run Any Single Command

Double-click any single command to run by itself. This is useful when writing a single command. It lets you immediately test a command you are constructing when you are not sure if it is correct. You can double-click it to see if it runs correctly. This is also available from the context menu.

3.   Click on Play Suite button and verify test suite run until completion.

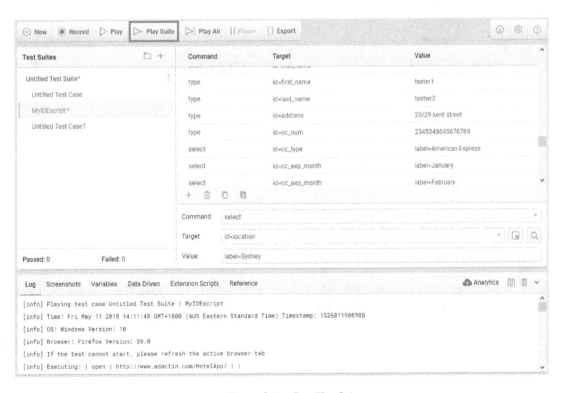

Figure 6.10 – Run Test Suite

Note: In case you have clicked on the Logout button (at the bottom of the Booking page) instead of the Logout link (on the top right corner of the Booking page) your script might fail due to a synchronization issue. Re-record your script and click on the Logout link on the top right corner of the application.

In the coming chapters, we will see how to deal with synchronization issues.

4. Verify the Results in the Log tab

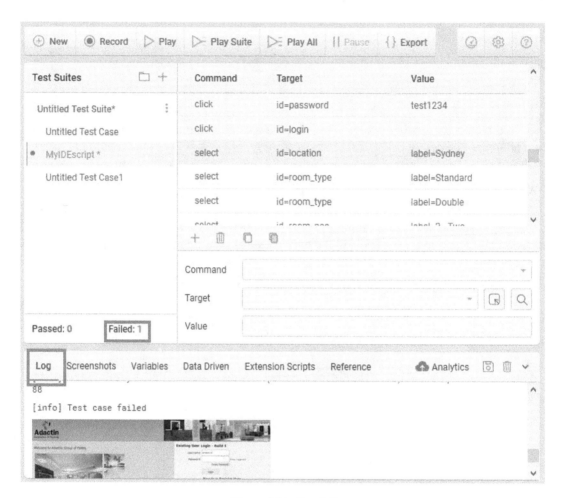

Figure 6.11 – Result Logs

Log/ Screenshots

When you run your test case, error messages and information messages showing the progress are displayed in this pane automatically, even if you do not first select the Log tab. These messages are often useful for test case debugging. Notice the Clear button for clearing the Log. Also, notice the Info button is a drop-down allowing selection of different levels of information to log.

Reference

The Reference tab displays the detail documentation of selected command. It helps users to ensure the correct types and the number of parameters for the command.

Variables

The Variables tab displays detailed information of the current selected command. Users can view command name, target, and values in this tab while the test is executing.

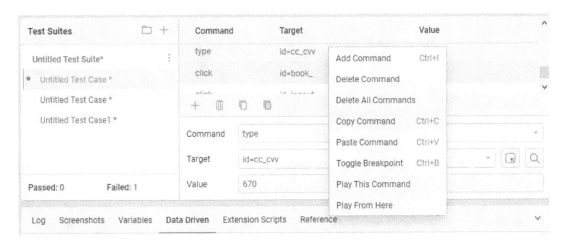

Figure 6.12 – Test Case Table Pane

Operations Pane: The **Command**, **Target**, and **Value** entry fields display the currently selected command along with its parameters. The user can modify Command, Target or Value in this pane.

If you select the step where we select location as Sydney you would see Command, Target, and Value as in the snapshot below.

Figure 6.13 – Operations Pane

6.5. Inserting/Editing Test Steps Manually

You can not only edit the steps inside the selenium IDE but can also add new steps or change the sequence of steps inside the IDE itself. To do that we need to understand the following:

Test Case Table Pane: Your script is displayed in the test case pane. It has two tabs, one for displaying the command and their parameters in a readable "**table**" format. The other tab is described below.

Command	Target	Value
select	id=room_type	label=Standard
select	id=room_type	label=Double
select	id=room_nos	label=2 - Two
select	id=adult_room	label=2 - Two
click	id=Submit	
click	id=radiobutton_2	
click	id=continue	
click	id=first_name	
type	id=first_name	tester1

+ 🗑 🗐 🗑

Operations Pane: The **Command**, **Target**, and **Value** entry fields display the currently selected command along with its parameters. The user can modify Command, Target or Value in this pane.

If you select the step where we select location as Sydney you would see Command, Target, and Value as in the snapshot below.

Command	select ▼
Target	id=location Find
Value	label=Sydney

Figure 6.14 – Operations Pane

If you start typing in the Command field, a drop-down list will be populated based on the first characters you type; you can then select your desired command from the drop-down.

6.6. Adding Verifications and Asserts with the Context Menu

One crucial part of any test case is the verification of your results against expected results. Your test cases will also need to check the properties of a Web page. To do the same in your script you can insert **assert** or **verify** commands In Katalon. Both the commands work to compare results, with different outcomes to the failure of a test condition.

Assert	"**assert**" will fail the test and **abort the current test case**
Verify	"**verify**" will fail the test and **continue to run the test case**

Choosing between "assert" and "verify" comes down to convenience and management of failures. There's little point in checking if the first paragraph of the page is correct if your test has already failed when checking if the browser is displaying the expected page. If you're not on the correct page, you'll probably want to abort your test case so that you can investigate the cause and fix the issue(s) promptly. So it is better to use the "assert" command.

On the other hand, you may want to check many attributes of a page without aborting the test case on the first failure as this will allow you to review all the failures on the page and take appropriate action. You can use the "verify" command in this case.

Problem: As an example, let us say we want to verify that our login is successful. We can verify this by checking that the Logout link exists once a user logs in.

To add a verification point:

1. Open your IDE test case MyIDEScript.

2. Select step where the user selects location Sydney.

Figure 6.15 – Select Location Step

3. Select **Step** and right click → **Toggle Breakpoint** to insert a Breakpoint at location step.

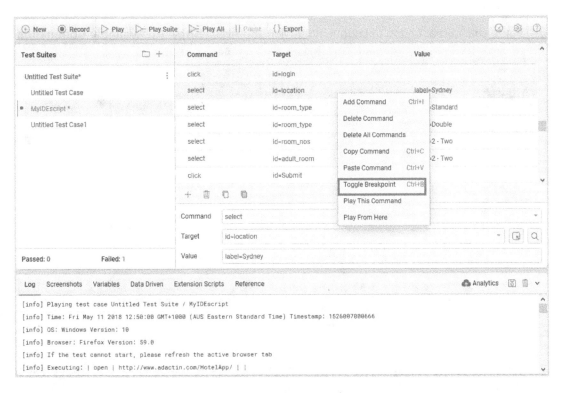

Figure 6.16 – Insert Breakpoint

4. Run a test via IDE, you will notice that the script runs until location, and it pauses.

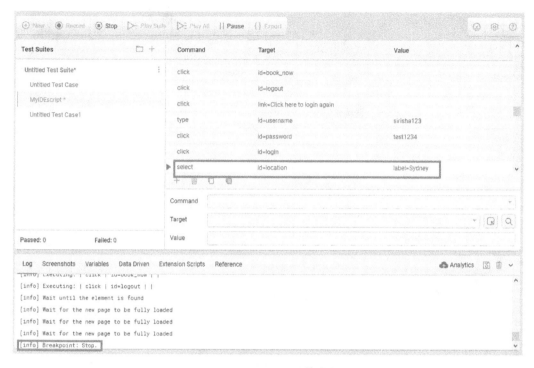

Figure 6.17 – Script Pause at Breakpoint

5. In the application, you will notice that the user is logging in. Now we want to verify if the logout link exists.

6. Place your cursor on top of Logout, right-click and select **Show All Available Commands**.

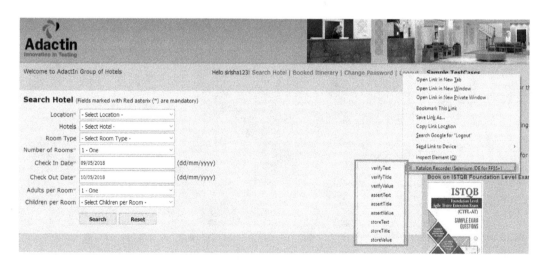

Figure 6.18 – Show Available Commands

7. Since we want to verify that the logout link is present and if the logout link is not present (which means we are not successfully logged in) we would want to abort the script. We will insert **"assertElementPresent link=logout"** command. Select this command from the list.

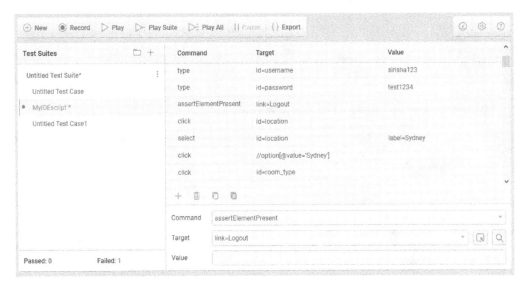

Figure 6.19 – Insert assertElementPresent Command

8. In the IDE script, you will notice a new statement added "assertElementPresent"

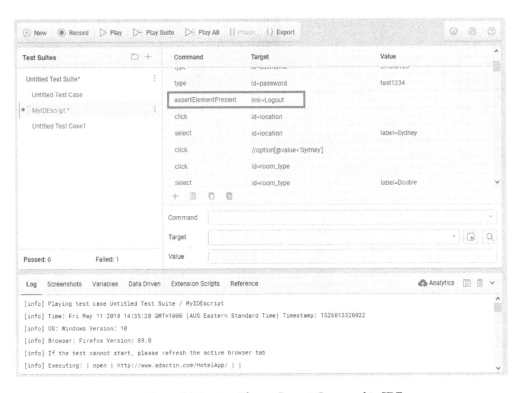

Figure 6.20 – assertElementPresent Command in IDE

9. You can rerun the test to confirm that the assertElementPresent statement got executed correctly and verifies logout link presence

Note: Also make a note of other verify and assert commands like VerifyTextPresent (verifies that text is present on the page) and VerifyTitle (which verifies the title of the page).

7. Managing User Interface Controls

Introduction

In the last chapter, we recorded a sample script and replayed it. You would be very curious to understand how Katalon actually replayed the whole script. How could it identify the location field and enter the value that we had earlier recorded in the previous chapter? Was it like a video recording that got replayed? In this chapter, we will understand test automation fundamentals of how a recorded script is replayed and how automation tools recognize objects on the application.

Key objectives:

- Understanding Object Recognition fundamentals and how Selenium replays.
- Understanding various locators to identify objects.

7.1. How Does Selenium Replay Scripts?

Let us take a simple example:

Assume that you parked your car on some level of a big shopping mall before going to a party. For the sake of this example, say you had too many drinks at the party and so took a cab to get home. Next morning, you come back to the mall to pick up your car but you do not remember the location of the car apart from knowing the level on which your car was parked. How will you find your car? Assume that you do not have a remote control for the car!

Figure 7.1 – Sample Car

If I were to find my car, I will go looking for my car in the first row and look for the Make and Color of my car. If I find a car with the same make and color, I will go closer to the car and try to identify my car based on the registration number. If I can match all these three properties, I am sure I will find my car. So the three properties I will look for will be:

- Make of the car.
- Color of the car.
- Registration No. of the car.

I do not really need to care about height, width or any other details about my car.

This is what Selenium as a tool does and as a matter of fact, this principle is followed by all other automation tools available in the market. They use some key properties of the objects to identify the user interface controls and then use those properties to identify the objects. For instance, if the user clicks on a button, Selenium uses the label of the button to identify the object.

So this is the process of how Katalon Recorder replays a script:

- While recording, Selenium stores object property information somewhere in the script.
- When we replay the script, Selenium will pick up the object properties and try to find the object in the application by matching the properties.
- Once it finds the object, it will perform the operation (click, select, etc.) on that object.

This is the basic automation fundamental required to understand how functional automation tools work. The key point to remember is that the Selenium script is not a video recording of functionality but a step-by-step execution of actions recorded in the script.

7.2. Locating the Elements on a Web page

Every Web page is nothing but a set of different UI web elements or objects. Before we work with an element on a page, we need Selenium to locate that element. The element on the Web page can be located by various locator types.

To understand the various locators one needs to have a basic understanding of HTML. *Id, name, input, type*, etc., are the HTML tags/attributes. Using these HTML tags, attributes like "xpath" can be constructed. We can use these tags or attributes to identify elements.

Let us follow these steps to understand tags and locators.

1. Launch Sample Application URL: www.adactin.com/HotelApp

2. Right-click on the home page and select **View Page Source.**

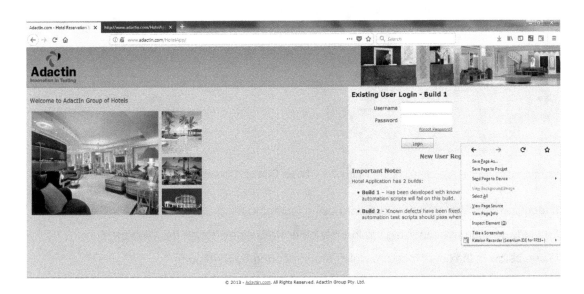

Figure 7.2 – View Page Source Option

3. You will find the source code as shown below.

```
40    <tr>
41        <td colspan="2" class="login_title">Existing User Login - Build 1</td>
42        </tr>
43    <tr>
44        <td width="150" align="right">Username </td>
45        <td><input type="text" name="username" id="username" class="login_input" value="" />&nb
46        </tr>
47    <tr>
48        <td align="right">Password </td>
49        <td><input type="password" name="password" id="password" class="login_input" value="" /:
50        </tr>
51    <tr>
52        <td> </td>
53        <td><div class="login_forgot"><a href="ForgotPassword.php">Forgot Password?</a></div></
54        </tr>
55    <tr>
56        <td></td>
57        <td><div class="auth_error"></div></td>
58        </tr>
59    <tr>
60        <td> </td>
61        <td><input type="Submit" name="login" id="login" class="login_button" value="Login"/></1
62        </tr>
```

Figure 7.3 – Page Source

The above source code is HTML-based with tags -- **type**, **name**, **class**, **href**-- which are used to define and identify elements.

4. Let us see our Selenium script again. Notice the **Target** field which is used to identify an element based on the locator.

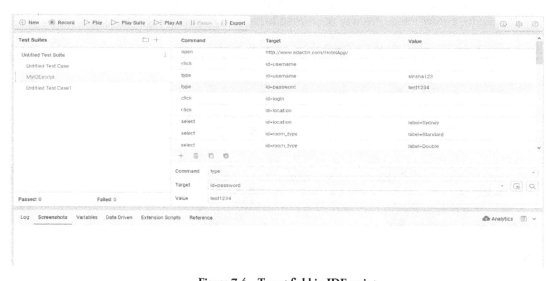

Figure 7.4 – Target field in IDE script

It identifies the Web element password using locator id as *id=password*.

Similarly, we can use other tags to identify other Web elements on the Web page.

Given below is the list of locators which are supported by Selenium:

- id
- name
- xpath
- tag name

- class name
- link text
- DOM
- CSS

We will understand each of these locators in detail in the next point.

5. Based on the following source code let us see how Selenium can recognize a few of the elements in our application.

```
<tr>
    <td colspan="2" class="login_title">Existing User Login - Build 1</td>
    </tr>
    <tr>
    <td width="150" align="right">Username </td>
    <td><input type="text" name="username" id="username" class="login_input" value="" >&nb
    </tr>
    <tr>
    <td align="right">Password </td>
    <td><input type="password" name="password" id="password" class="login_input" value="" /:
    </tr>
    <tr>
    <td> </td>
    <td><div class="login_forgot"><a href="ForgotPassword.php">Forgot Password?</a></div></
    </tr>
    <tr>
    <td></td>
    <td><div class="auth_error"></div></td>
    </tr>
    <tr>
    <td> </td>
    <td><input type="Submit" name="login" id="login" class="login_button" value="Login"/></
    </tr>
```

Figure 7.5 – Page Source

Locating by Name

The name locator type will locate the first element with a matching name attribute. For instance, to recognize username Web element we can use:

name=username

If multiple elements have the same value for a name attribute, then you can use filters to further refine your location strategy. The default filter type is *value* (matching the value attribute).

Locating by ID

The ID locator type will locate the first element with a matching id attribute. Use this when you know an element's id attribute.

id=username

There is one big difference between the "id" and "name" attributes though. The name attributes do not have to be unique on a page. If there are multiple elements with the same name, then the first element in the page is selected. In such a case, you can use filters to further refine your location strategy.

Unlike some other types of locators like XPath and DOM locators, ID and Name allow Selenium to test a UI element independent of its position on the page. So if the page structure and organization is altered, the test will still run. In cases where Web designers frequently alter the page display and if its functionality must be regression tested, testing via id and name attributes, or via any HTML property, becomes very important.

Note: Locating by ID is the most preferable way to locate elements if the element in your application has an id attribute assigned.

Even though id is a great locator, it is not realistic for all elements on a page to have ids. The developers add ids to key elements on the page to better control the look and feel or provide dynamic user interaction.

Locating by XPath

XPath is the language used for locating nodes in an XML document. As HTML can be an implementation of XML (XHTML), Selenium users can leverage this powerful language to target elements in their Web applications. XPath extends beyond (as well as supports) the simple methods of locating by id or name attributes, and opens up all sorts of new possibilities such as locating the third checkbox on the page.

One of the main reasons for using XPath is to locate an element when you don't have a suitable id or name attribute for the element. You can use XPath to either locate the element in absolute terms (not advisable) or relative to an element that does have an id or name attribute. XPath locators can also be used to specify elements via attributes other than id and name.

Absolute XPaths contain the location of all elements from the root (**html** tag) and are likely to change with only the slightest adjustment to the user interface of the web application. By finding a nearby element with an id or name attribute (ideally a parent element), you can locate your target element based on that relationship. This is much less likely to change and can make your element search more robust.

Locating Hyperlinks by Link Text

This is a simple method of locating a hyperlink in your Web page by using the text of the link. If two links with the same text are present, then the first match will be used.

For example, we can identify Logout link in our application by using

Link=Logout

See the snapshot below for IDE command using link locator.

Figure 7.6 – Locating by Link attribute in IDE

See the snapshot below for IDE command using the link locator.

```
| <a href="BookedItinerary.php">Booked Itinerary</a> | <a href="Logout.php">Logout</a></td>

? TEST CASES for this application. <span style="text-decoration:blink;">Enjoy automation!</span>
```

Figure 7.7 – View Source for Link

Locating elements by class

The class locator type will locate the first element with a matching class attribute. For instance, to recognize class name attribute

Class=login_forgot

```
         </tr>
47       <tr>
48         <td align="right">Password </td>
49         <td><input type="password" name="password" id="password" class="login_input" value="" />&n
50       </tr>
51       <tr>
52         <td> </td>
53         <td><div class="login_forgot"><a href="ForgotPassword.php">Forgot Password?</a></div></td>
54       </tr>
55       <tr>
```

Figure 7.8 – Locating by Class Attribute

Locating by DOM

The Document Object Model represents an HTML document and can be accessed using JavaScript. This location strategy uses a JavaScript that evaluates the location of an element on the page using the hierarchical dotted notation.

Since DOM locators start with "document", it is not necessary to include the dom=label when specifying a DOM locator. Let us see how we can locate the Username field in the following page source using DOM locators.

```
<html>
 <body>
  <form id="HotelAppLogin">
   <input name="username" type="text" />
   <input name="password" type="password" />
   <input name="login" type="submit" value="Login" />
  </form>
 </body>
<html>
```

Highlighted element (Username field) can be located by any of the following DOM locators.

Possible DOM locators

- document.forms[0].username
- document.forms[0].elements['username']
- document.forms[0].elements[0]

Locating by CSS

CSS (Cascading Style Sheets) is a language for describing the rendering of HTML and XML documents. CSS uses Selectors for binding style properties to elements in the document. These Selectors can be used by Selenium as another locating strategy. Let us see how we can locate the input field element in the following page source.

```
<table name="Booking Itinerary ">
  <tr id="item1">
    <td class="label">Order RE111</td>
    <td class="item"><input name="qty" class="formfield disabled" /></td>
  </tr>
  <tr id="item2">
    <td class="label"> Order RE112</td>
    <td class="item">
<input id="item2_quantity" name="qty" class="Select_text" type="text"/></td>
  </tr>
    ...
</table>
```

Possible CSS locators

- css= input [class= 'Select_text']
- css=input.Select_text [type='text']
- css=#item2_quantity
- css=input#item2_quantity

In this case, any of the above CSS locator variations will help us locate the highlighted input field.

7.3. Finding XPath on Firefox Add-on

In this section, we will see how to identify the Xpath on Firefox from the console

1. Open **Firefox** and open our AUT- **www.adactin/HotelApp/** home page.

2. Click on ≡ on the toolbar.

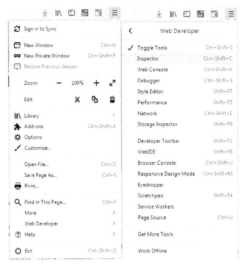

Figure 7.9 – Open Inspector

3. A console window opens up

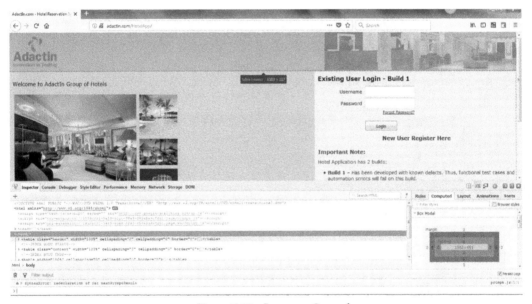

Figure 7.10 – Inspector Opened up

4. Click on the inspect element icon

Figure 7.11 – Inspect element icon

5.   Inspect on the required element on the webpage.

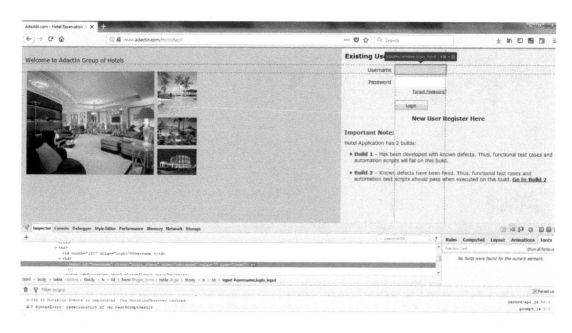

Figure 7.12 – Inspect on the required element

6.   On the console, right click on the highlighted text. Click on Copy→XPath

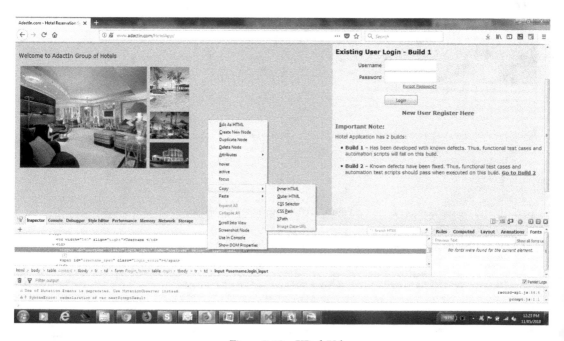

Figure 7.12 – XPath Value

7. Paste it in a notepad

Figure 7.13 – Copied Xpath Value

EXERCISE

1. Go back to our Login Script in IDE, perform Save As and replace all the locators by XPath. Rerun the script and see if it works.

   Hint - Use the Inspector to get the XPath. Then replace the Target field for each step with XPath value as seen in the snapshot below.

Figure 7.14 – XPath Value Replaced in Script

8. Creating First Selenium WebDriver Script

Now that we understand Selenium Basics (Katalon IDE and Locators) and basics of C#/.Net we are ready to jump into the real Selenium automation tool – Selenium WebDriver.

In this chapter, we will see how to create a WebDriver script. Also, we will configure Visual Studio environment.

Key objectives:

- Exporting Katalon IDE script as a C# Selenium WebDriver script.
- Configuration of project structure in Visual Studio and use Selenium WebDriver script.
- Running of Selenium WebDriver script.

8.1. Recording and Exporting Script from IDE

In this section, we will record the test case using Katalon IDE and then export the test case using *C#/NUnit /WebDriver* option. Follow the steps given below:

1. Open **Katalon Automation IDE** and verify that recording mode is **ON**.

2. Assuming that the application login page is already open in **Firefox browser** with login page visible, perform the following steps (in IDE recording mode):

   a. Login (Use the username/password with which you have registered earlier).

   b. Search for a Hotel.

      i. Select a location, e.g., Sydney.
      ii. Select number of rooms, e.g., 2-Two.
      iii. Select adults per rooms, e.g., 2-Two.
      iv. Click on Search button.

   c. Select a Hotel.

      i. Select one of the Hotel Radio buttons, e.g., select radio button next to Hotel Creek.

   d. Book a Hotel.

      i. Enter First Name.
      ii. Enter Last Name.
      iii. Enter Address.
      iv. Enter 16-digit Credit Card No.
      v. Enter Credit Card type.

      vi.   Enter Expiry Month.

      vii.   Enter Expiry Year.

     viii.   Enter CVV number.

      ix.   Click on Book Now.

    e.   After you see the Booking confirmation page, click on Logout link in the top right corner

    f.   Click on "Click here to Login again" link to go back to the Home page.

3.   Stop recording by clicking on the **Stop Recording** button in the record toolbar.

4.   Verify the steps below that are recorded in the Katalon IDE.

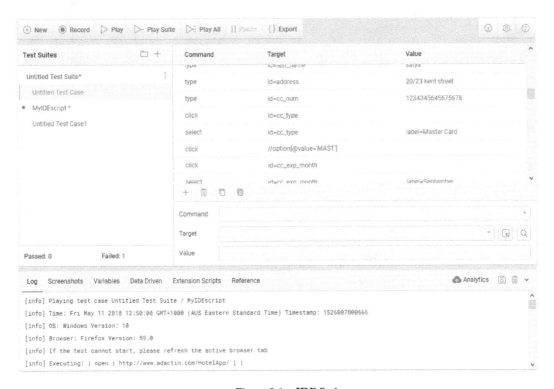

Figure 8.1 – IDE Script

5.   Click on **Export.** Select the format from the dropdown as **C#(WebDriver + NUnit)**.

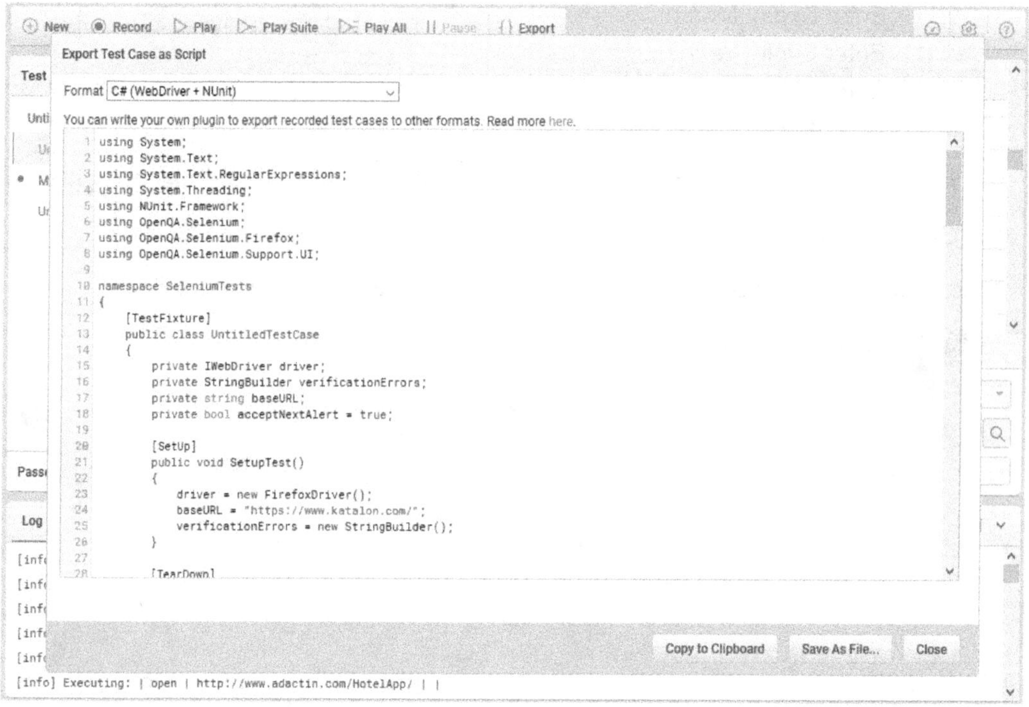

Figure 8.2 – Export IDE Test

Note: We will focus on Selenium WebDriver with C# but as you can see Selenium supports export as Java, Python and Ruby languages as well.

6. Save it as MyFirstWebDriverTest in C:\Selenium Folder. You will notice that the script is saved as MyFirstWebDriverTest.cs file.

7. Try to open the script you have saved in an editor like NotePad++ (you can download this freely from internet).

Next step will be to review this code and use it in Visual Studio.

1. Let us review the exported C# code. The exported test is NUnit test. NUnit is a unit testing framework for the .NET programming languages.

2. We will see a class "MyFirstWebDriverTest" shown in the snapshot below.

The highlighted lines in the snapshot below will acquire an instance of a new Firefox browser and assign it to the driver (WebDriver) object which we will use to perform all of our browser actions.

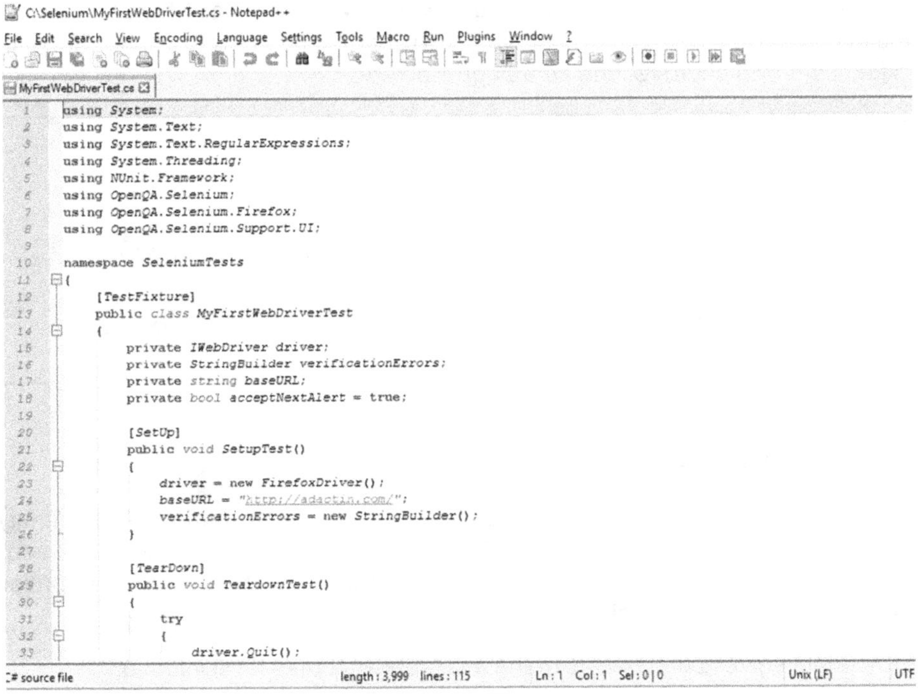

```
using System;
using System.Text;
using System.Text.RegularExpressions;
using System.Threading;
using NUnit.Framework;
using OpenQA.Selenium;
using OpenQA.Selenium.Firefox;
using OpenQA.Selenium.Support.UI;

namespace SeleniumTests
{
    [TestFixture]
    public class MyFirstWebDriverTest
    {
        private IWebDriver driver;
        private StringBuilder verificationErrors;
        private string baseURL;
        private bool acceptNextAlert = true;

        [SetUp]
        public void SetupTest()
        {
            driver = new FirefoxDriver();
            baseURL = "http://adactin.com/";
            verificationErrors = new StringBuilder();
        }

        [TearDown]
        public void TeardownTest()
        {
            try
            {
                driver.Quit();
```

Figure 8.3 – Code View

As shown in the image below, the code written next to [Test] annotation is performing all our test step actions. The first line fetches the Web page for us according to the given URL. Then we enter username, password and click the Login button, all using our driver instance.

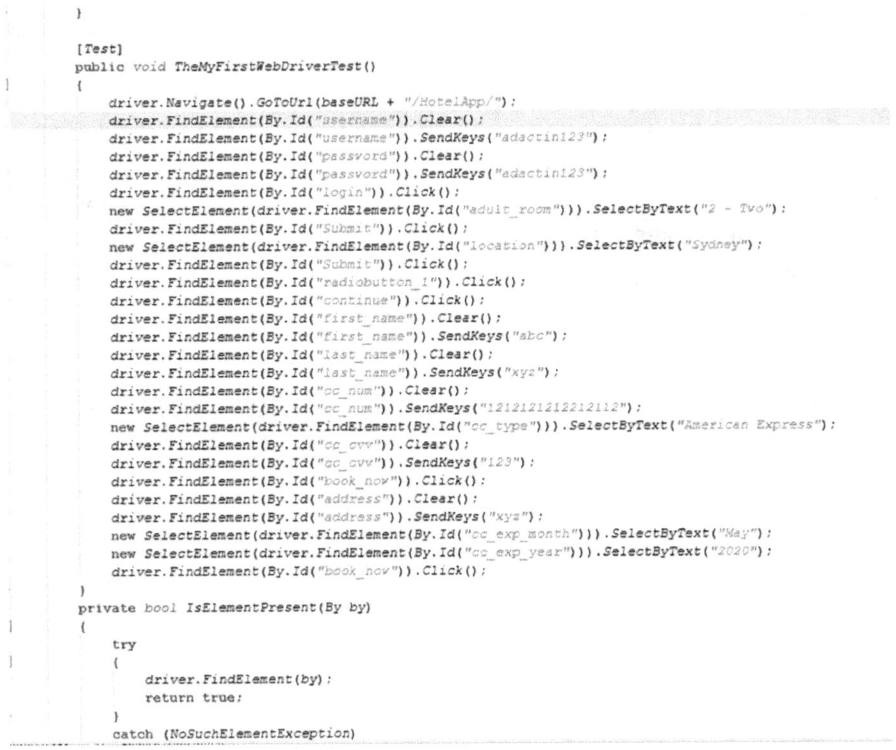

```
}

[Test]
public void TheMyFirstWebDriverTest()
{
    driver.Navigate().GoToUrl(baseURL + "/HotelApp/");
    driver.FindElement(By.Id("username")).Clear();
    driver.FindElement(By.Id("username")).SendKeys("adactin123");
    driver.FindElement(By.Id("password")).Clear();
    driver.FindElement(By.Id("password")).SendKeys("adactin123");
    driver.FindElement(By.Id("login")).Click();
    new SelectElement(driver.FindElement(By.Id("adult_room"))).SelectByText("2 - Two");
    driver.FindElement(By.Id("Submit")).Click();
    new SelectElement(driver.FindElement(By.Id("location"))).SelectByText("Sydney");
    driver.FindElement(By.Id("Submit")).Click();
    driver.FindElement(By.Id("radiobutton_1")).Click();
    driver.FindElement(By.Id("continue")).Click();
    driver.FindElement(By.Id("first_name")).Clear();
    driver.FindElement(By.Id("first_name")).SendKeys("abc");
    driver.FindElement(By.Id("last_name")).Clear();
    driver.FindElement(By.Id("last_name")).SendKeys("xyz");
    driver.FindElement(By.Id("cc_num")).Clear();
    driver.FindElement(By.Id("cc_num")).SendKeys("1212121212212112");
    new SelectElement(driver.FindElement(By.Id("cc_type"))).SelectByText("American Express");
    driver.FindElement(By.Id("cc_cvv")).Clear();
    driver.FindElement(By.Id("cc_cvv")).SendKeys("123");
    driver.FindElement(By.Id("book_now")).Click();
    driver.FindElement(By.Id("address")).Clear();
    driver.FindElement(By.Id("address")).SendKeys("xyz");
    new SelectElement(driver.FindElement(By.Id("cc_exp_month"))).SelectByText("May");
    new SelectElement(driver.FindElement(By.Id("cc_exp_year"))).SelectByText("2020");
    driver.FindElement(By.Id("book_now")).Click();
}
private bool IsElementPresent(By by)
{
    try
    {
        driver.FindElement(by);
        return true;
    }
    catch (NoSuchElementException)
```

Figure 8.4 – Test Annotation

On a Web page, *driver* finds an element by using its unique identifier which in this case is the id of the element. Every element is expected to have a unique id on the page. Selenium uses various identifiers/locators to recognize a page element.

driver.get(baseUrl + "/HotelApp/");

driver.findElement(By.id("username")).clear();

driver.findElement(By.id("username")).sendKeys("adactin123");
driver.findElement(By.id("password")).clear();
driver.findElement(By.id("password")).sendKeys("xxxxxxxx");
driver.findElement(By.id("login")).click();

Available NUnit Attributes

Attributes are part of syntax in NUnit tests. NUnit uses custom attributes to identify tests. All NUnit attributes are contained in the NUnit.Framework namespace. Each source file that contains tests must include a using statement for that namespace and the project must reference the framework assembly, nunit.framework.dll.

The following table gives an overview of the available attributes in NUnit. 3.0.

Annotations

Attribute	Description
TestFixture	The [TestFixture] Attribute marks a class that contains tests and optionally [Setup] or [Teardown] attributes.
Test	The [Test] Attribute marks a specific method of a TestFixture as a test method.
SetUp	The [Setup] Attribute is used inside a TestFixture when a common set of functions have to be performed before calling the test method.
TearDown	The [TearDown] Attribute is used inside a TestFixture when a common set of functions have to be performed after the test methods have been run.
Parallelizable	The [Parallelizable] attribute is used to indicate whether the tests and/or the descendants may be run in parallel with other tests. By default, no parallel execution takes place.
Ignore	The [Ignore] attribute helps to not run a test or test fixture for a period of time. This feature should be used to temporarily not run a test or fixture.

8.2. Configuring Visual Studio to Work with Selenium

1. Download and install Visual Studio Community version as per section 5.2 (Installing and configuring Microsoft Visual Studio).

2. Go to **File >New > Project > Test>Unit Test Project**.

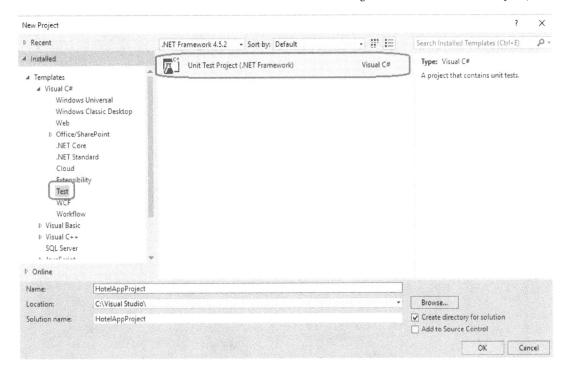

Figure 8.5 – New Unit Test Project

3. Click **Ok**.

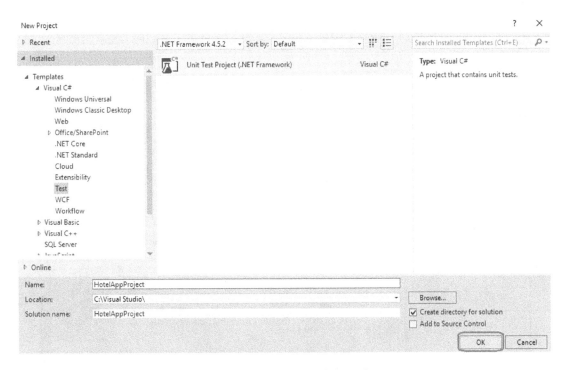

Figure 8.6 – New Unit Test Project Creation

4. In the Solution Explorer, right-click on the project. Click on Manage NuGet Packages.

Figure 8.7 – NuGet Package

5. Go to Manage NuGet Packages and click on the **Browse** tab to install **Selenium WebDriver**, **NUnit and Nunit3TestAdapter, the browser driver** (eg. Chrome Driver for chrome browser) **and Selenium Support**.

Note: Please install the latest version available. The book show cases the latest version at the time of publication.

6. In the browse tab, search for NUnit and you will be able to see all the options related to NUnit. Click on **NUnit by Charlie Poole**. On the right-hand side, the versions will be displayed. Choose **Version: 3.6.1.**

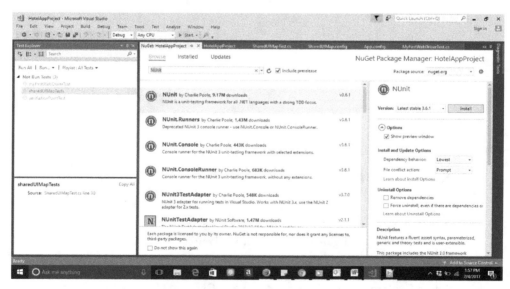

Figure 8.8 – NUnit Package

7. Click on **Install.** A pop-up window will appear.

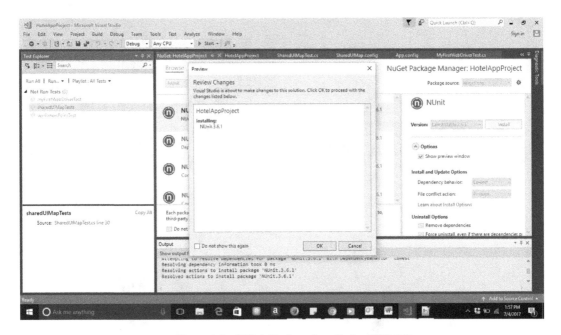

Figure 8.9 – NUnit Package Installation (V 3.6.1)

8. Scroll down on the browse tab, and search for **NUnit3TestAdapter**. Select the version 3.7.0. Click on Install.

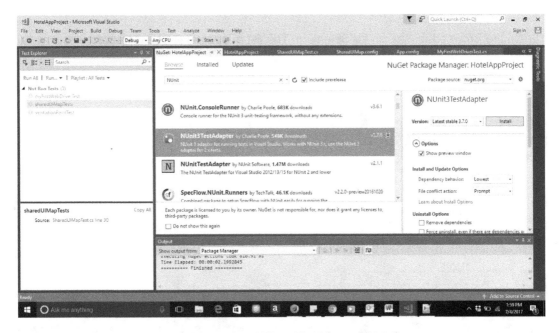

Figure 8.10 – NUnit3 Test Adapter (V 3.7.0)

9. A pop-up window will appear prompting about the changes to be made to the solution. Click **OK**.

Figure 8.11 – NUnit3 Test Adapter Installation

10. On the Browse tab, search for Selenium. The list of options will be displayed.

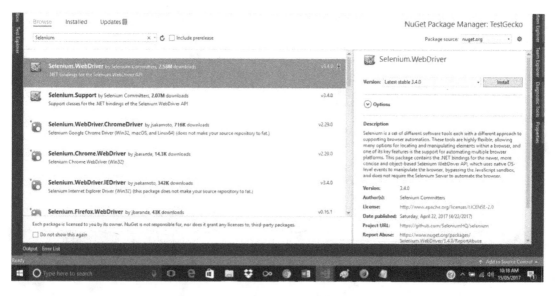

Figure 8.12 – Selenium WebDriver Installation

11. Select **Selenium.Support.** Choose version **3.4.0.** Click on Install.

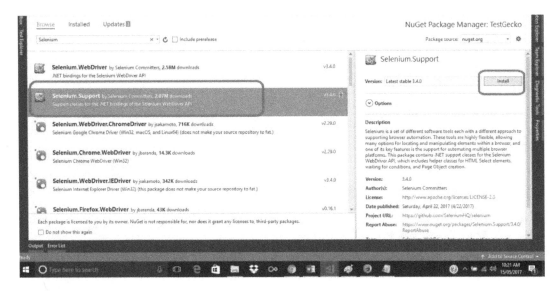

Figure 8.13 – Selenium Support Installation

12. A pop-up window will open prompting about the changes to be made to the solution. This installation will include both **Selenium**.**Support** as well as **Selenium WebDriver**. Click **OK**.

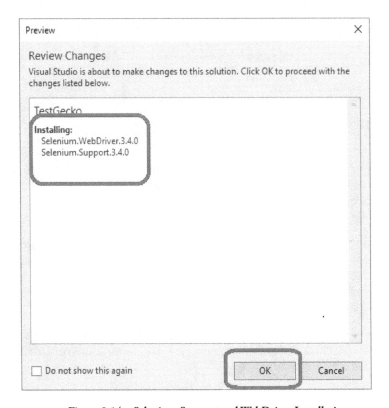

Figure 8.14 – Selenium Support and WebDriver Installation

13. To Install Selenium ChromeDriver, search for Selenium. The user will be able to find the ChromeDriver in the options. Click on **Install**.

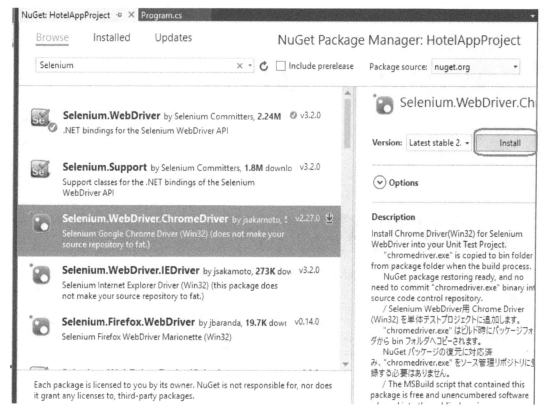

Fig 8.15 – Selenium ChromeDriver Installation

8.3. Introduction to Gecko Driver for the Firefox Browser

Gecko Driver is the link between your tests in Selenium and the Firefox browser. GeckoDriverGecko Driver is a proxy for using W3C WebDriver-compatible clients to interact with Gecko-based browsers, i.e., Mozilla Firefox in this case. As *Selenium 3* will not have any native implementation of Firefox, we have to direct all the driver commands through Gecko Driver. So Selenium 3 and above will use Gecko Driver.

GeckoDriver is an executable file that you need to have in one of the system paths before starting your tests. Firefox browser implements the *WebDriver* protocol using an executable called **GeckoDriver.exe**. This executable starts a server on your system. All your tests communicate to this server to run your tests. It translates calls into the Marionette automation protocol by acting as a proxy between the local and remote ends.

To Install Gecko Driver for Firefox, on the Browse tab search for the gecko driver. A list of options will be displayed. Scroll down the page and look for **Selenium.WebDriver.GeckoDriver. Win64, version 0.16.0.** Click on Install.

Fig 8.16 – Selenium GeckoDriver Installation

14. A pop-up window will open prompting the changes to be made to the solution. Click **Ok**.

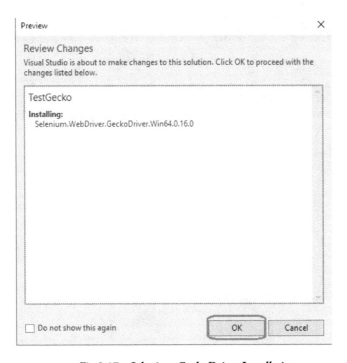

Fig 8.17 – Selenium GeckoDriver Installation

Note: Please use the latest version of Selenium that is 3.4.0 for Gecko Driver to work with Firefox. If you use the earlier versions you need to make changes in the code so that the Firefox browser uses GeckoDriver or changes the environment variable path in System settings.

8.4. Building the First Selenium Test

Once all the DLLs are installed, all the packages will be available under the Installed Tab. Now start creating test scripts.

1. Create a new Class File that will contain all the test cases. Right-click on the project name. Click on **Add > Class**.

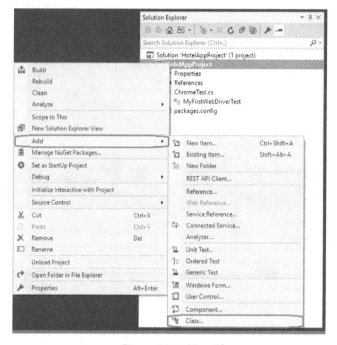

Figure 8.18 – New Class

2. A window will open prompting to give a class name. Provide the name of the class in **Name** textbox. Provide the name as "**MyFirstWebDriverTest**". Click on **Add.**

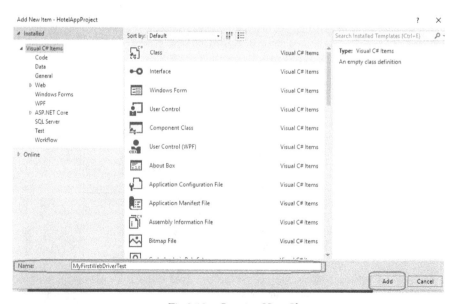

Fig 8.19 – Creating New Class

3. Project Structure

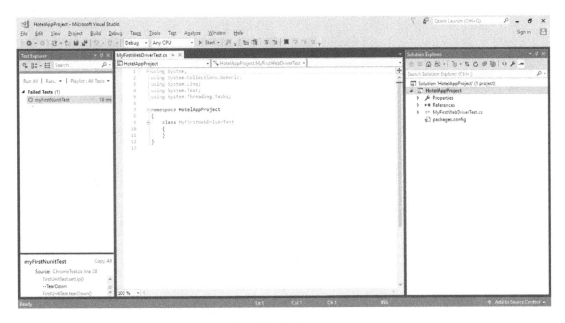

Fig 8.20 – Project Structure

4. A new Class file will be added to the Solution Explorer. Click on the class file. Copy the Code from the exported Selenium IDE script, **MyFirstWebDriverTest.cs** (open in Notepad and copy) and Overwrite existing code of VisualStudio **MyFirstWebDriverTest.cs**.

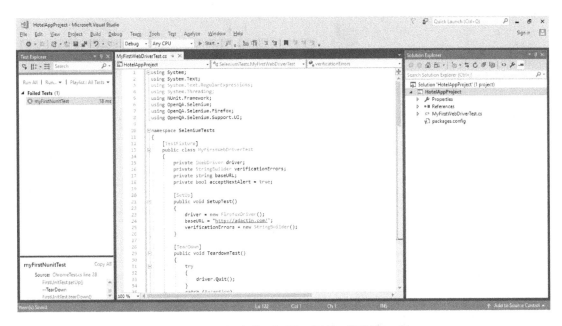

Fig 8.21 – Code for the New MyFirstWebDriverTest

5. Once the code has been copied, save the solution. You may need to add an additional wait statement under the [Setup] annotation.

```
driver.Manage().Timeouts().ImplicitWait = TimeSpan.FromSeconds(10);
```

This can be added to wait till the element appears on the page before the automation test code starts performing action on them. Otherwise, the test may fail. There are different types of wait like Implicit and Explicit wait. We will use Implicit wait in our project. We will discuss this in detail in the later chapters.

6. Click on **Build > Build Solution**. This helps in checking if there are any errors.

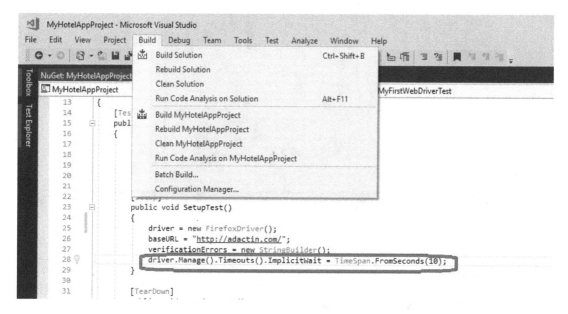

Fig 8.22 – Build Solution

7. The Output screen can be used to check if there are any errors in the build.

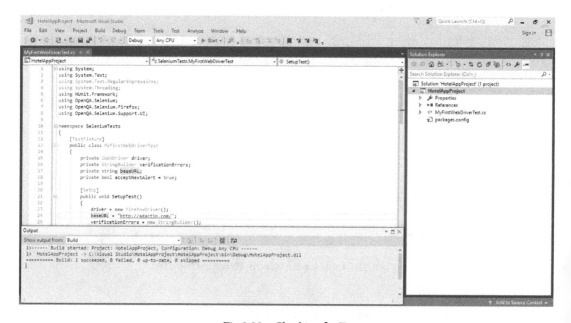

Fig 8.23 – Checking for Errors

8. If there are no errors, click on **Test > Windows > Test Explorer** to view all the tests written in the code section.

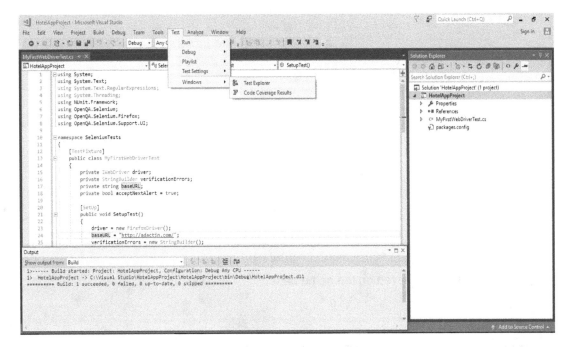

Fig 8.24 – Test Explorer

9. The Test Explorer screen will be displayed on the left-hand side of the screen. All the tests get displayed.

Fig 8.25 – Test Explorer Window with all Tests

10. Click on **Run** to execute the test cases. Choose **Run Not Run Tests.**

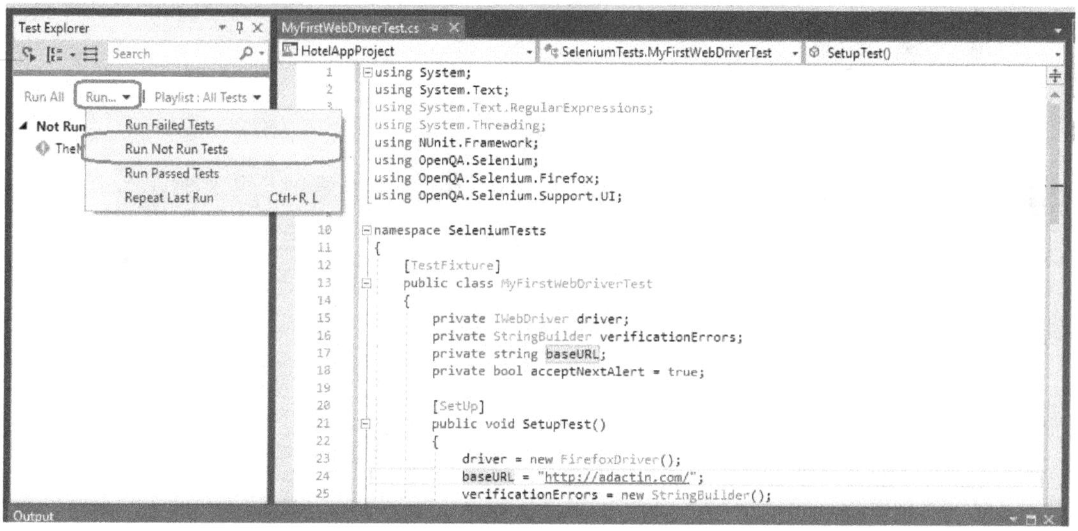

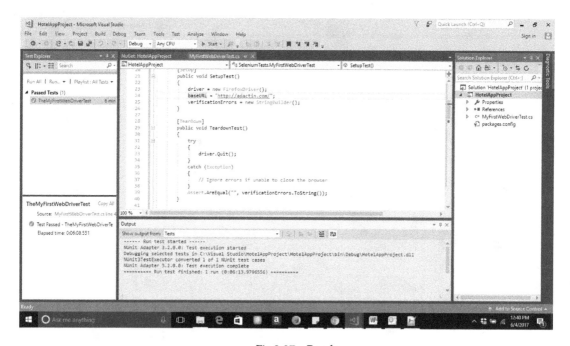

Fig 8.26 – Run Test

11. The result will be displayed on the same pane.

Fig 8.27 – Result

EXERCISE

1. Open your second Selenium IDE script "**IDEVerificationScript**".

   o Export the script as NUnit WebDriver test.

   o Create a new test in Visual Studio and use the exported script.

   o Review the exported code, classes and methods (especially review code exported verification method).

   o Run the test and view the results.

9. Selenium Methods

While working with Selenium we need to use C# as well as Selenium WebDriver functions. WebDriver provides various methods to perform different actions on Web elements. In this chapter, we'll have an insight into these.

Let us look at the script we previously exported from IDE and configured in Visual Studio. This script performs the following actions:

- Login.
- Search a hotel.
- Book a hotel room.
- Finally logout.

We will see the following code:

```
[Test]
        public void TheMyFirstWebDriverTest()
        {
            driver.Navigate().GoToUrl(baseURL + "/HotelApp/index.php");
            driver.FindElement(By.Id("username")).Clear();
            driver.FindElement(By.Id("username")).SendKeys("adactin123");
            driver.FindElement(By.Id("password")).Clear();
            driver.FindElement(By.Id("password")).SendKeys("adactin123");
            driver.FindElement(By.Id("login")).Click();
            new
SelectElement(driver.FindElement(By.Id("location"))).SelectByText("Sydney");
            new
SelectElement(driver.FindElement(By.Id("room_nos"))).SelectByText("2 - Two");
            new
SelectElement(driver.FindElement(By.Id("adult_room"))).SelectByText("2      -
Two");
            driver.FindElement(By.Id("Submit")).Click();
            driver.FindElement(By.Id("radiobutton_2")).Click();
            driver.FindElement(By.Id("continue")).Click();
            driver.FindElement(By.Id("first_name")).Clear();
            driver.FindElement(By.Id("first_name")).SendKeys("Abc");
            driver.FindElement(By.Id("last_name")).Clear();
            driver.FindElement(By.Id("last_name")).SendKeys("XYZ");
            driver.FindElement(By.Id("address")).Clear();
            driver.FindElement(By.Id("address")).SendKeys("12");
            driver.FindElement(By.Id("cc_num")).Clear();
            driver.FindElement(By.Id("cc_num")).SendKeys("1212121212121212");
            new
```

```
SelectElement(driver.FindElement(By.Id("cc_type"))).SelectByText("American
Express");
            new
SelectElement(driver.FindElement(By.Id("cc_exp_month"))).SelectByText("May");
            new
SelectElement(driver.FindElement(By.Id("cc_exp_year"))).SelectByText("2020");
            driver.FindElement(By.Id("cc_cvv")).Clear();
            driver.FindElement(By.Id("cc_cvv")).SendKeys("123");
            driver.FindElement(By.Id("book_now")).Click();
    }
```

Figure 9.1 – Selenium WebDriver Script Code

If we look carefully at these code lines we see that different methods are being used for performing different actions. For instance:

SendKeys( )	**To send keyboard input to** target **field.**
SelectByText( )	**To select a drop-down list item.**
Click( )	**To click a button or link.**

9.1. Common Selenium WebDriver Methods

The following lists show details of some of the methods that Selenium provides to perform actions on different Web elements (listbox, edit box, checkbox, radio button) depending upon their type.

Method	Purpose
Clear()	Clears the content of this element.
Click()	Simulates a mouse click on the element.
GetAttribute (string name)	Returns the value associated with the provided attribute name (if present) or null (if not present).
GetCssValue (string propertyName)	Gets the CSS property value of the given element. This accepts string as a parameter which is property name.
SendKeys(string text)	Simulates typing into an element.
Submit()	When called on an element within a form, WebDriver will walk up the DOM until it finds the enclosing form and then calls submit on that.

Property	Purpose
TagName	Gets the tag name of this element
Text	Gets the innerText of this element, without any leading or trailing whitespace, and with other whitespace collapsed .
Enabled	Gets a value indicating whether or not this element is enabled.
Size	Gets a Size object containing the height and width of this element.
Selected	Gets a value indicating whether or not this element is selected.

Note: **GetAttribute** is one of the most common methods used specifically to get property values and used to verify data in the fields.

Search Element methods

In addition to the above methods designed for interacting with the element in hand, WebDriver also provides two methods allowing you to search for elements within the current page's scope:

Method	Purpose
FindElement(By by)	Finds the first element located by the provided method (based on different location type).
FindElements(By by)	Finds all elements located by the provided method.

Select Web Element's Methods

WebDriver provides a support class named Select to greatly simplify interaction with select elements and their association options. It is mostly used with elements of type list boxes.

Method	Purpose
SelectByIndex(int index)/ SeselectByIndex(int index)	Selects/deselects the option at the given index.
SelectByValue(String value)/ DeselectByValue(String value)	Selects/deselects the option(s) that has a value matching the argument.
SelectByText (String text)/ DeselectByText(String text)	Selects/deselects the option(s) that displays text matching the argument.
DeselectAll()	Deselects all options.
Options()	Returns a List<WebElement> of all options.
isMultiple()	Returns true if this is a multi-select list; false otherwise.
AllSelectedOptions	Gets all of the selected options within the select element.

Actions class

Provides a mechanism for building advanced user interactions with the browser. This is under OpenQA.Selenium.Interactions namespace.

Example for mouse-hover event:

IWebElement element = driver.findElement(By.id("header"));
Actions action = new Actions(driver);
action.MoveToElement(element).Perform();

Actions class methods

Method	Purpose
DragAndDrop	Performs a drag-and-drop operation from one element to another.
MoveToElement (IWebElement)	Moves the mouse to the specified element.
Perform	Performs the currently built action.
ClickAndHold(IWebElement)	Clicks and holds the mouse button down on the specified element.

The following public members can be used for accessing specific items that are found on the page.

Property	Purpose
Location	Gets a Point object containing the coordinates of the upper-left corner of this element relative to the upper-left corner of the page.
Size	Gets a Size object containing the height and width of this element.
Displayed	Gets a value indicating whether or not this element is displayed.

Method	Purpose
GetCssValue	Gets the value of a CSS property of this element.
GetAttribute	Gets the value of the specified attribute for this element.

IWebDriver Methods

WebDriver methods are useful when you are working with the browser object itself and you would want to perform certain operations like close browser, get the title of the browser page or if working with an application which has multiple frames or Web pop-up windows.

Method	Purpose
Manage()	Instructs the driver to change its settings.
Navigate()	Instructs the driver to navigate the browser to another location.
Close()	Close the current window, quitting the browser if it is the last window currently open.
FindElement()	Finds the first IWebElement using the given method. (Inherited from ISearchContext.)
Quit()	Quits this driver, closing every associated window.
SwitchTo()	Instructs the driver to send future commands to a different frame or window.

Property	Purpose
CurrentWindowHandle	Gets the current window handle, which is an opaque handle to this window that uniquely identifies it within this driver instance.
PageSource	Gets the source of the page last loaded by the browser.
Title	Gets the title of the current browser window.
Url	Gets or sets the URL the browser is currently displaying.
WindowHandles	Gets the window handles of open browser windows.

We will understand the methods better as we use more of these methods in the coming chapters.

10. Verification Point in Selenium

10.1. Need for a Verification Point

A verification point is a specialized step that compares two values and reports the result. A verification point compares the actual results from the test run, with the expected results in the test case.

A basic test cannot be considered as a valid functional test without some form of validation.

You use a checkpoint to:

- Verify the state of an object.
- Confirm that an application performs as expected.

A verification point checks whether an application responds appropriately when a user performs tasks correctly while testing the application. A verification point ensures that a user is barred from performing certain tasks and confirms that invalid or incomplete data are flagged with appropriate messages.

- Examples of validation are specifying limits, conditions, or boundaries.

example We once tested an investment banking application where we could create varied instruments such as bonds, ADRs, etc. When creating an instrument, we would receive a "Save was successful" message and a unique instrument number. As part of our test case, we had to verify that "Save was successful" message appeared. We also had to verify that we could search using the same instrument number and verify that all details were saved correctly. As part of our automation scripts, we had to verify both these conditions, so we used a verification point to verify the same.

10.2. Inserting a Verification Point

A Verification point can be inserted in the WebDriver script. In this section, we will lay out a test scenario in which we have the expected result and we will try to automate that test scenario.

Test Scenario

Let us take a simple test case for automation from our Hotel Application.

Test Objective: To verify that when a location is selected in Search Hotel page, the same location is displayed in the Select Hotel page.

Test Steps:

1. Login to the application using User credentials.
2. Select Location as "Sydney" in Location field in Search Hotel Page.
3. Keep all the default selections.
4. Click on the Search Button.
5. Verify that in the next Select Hotel Page the correct Location is displayed.

Expected Result

1. Correct location "Sydney" should appear in the location column of select hotel search results.

How to insert a verification point

Let us see how to insert a verification point.

Pre-conditions

1. **Right-click** on your existing class and select **Copy**.

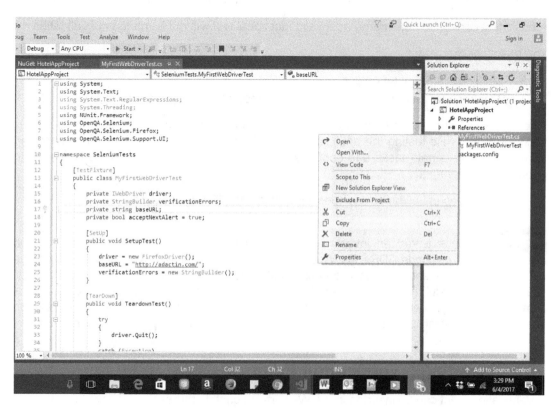

Figure 10.1 – Copy MyFirstWebDriverTest.cs

2. Select the **project** and click on paste.

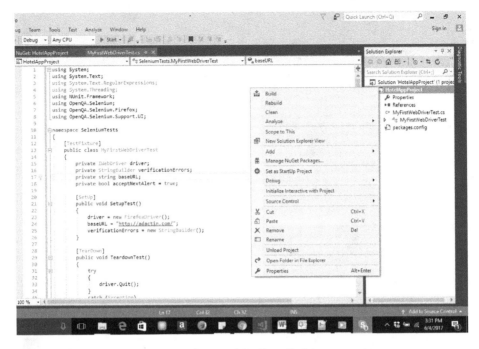

Figure 10.2 – Paste Script

3. A copy of the class file will be created. Right-click on the new class file to rename. Rename to **"VerificationPointTest"**. Click **OK**.

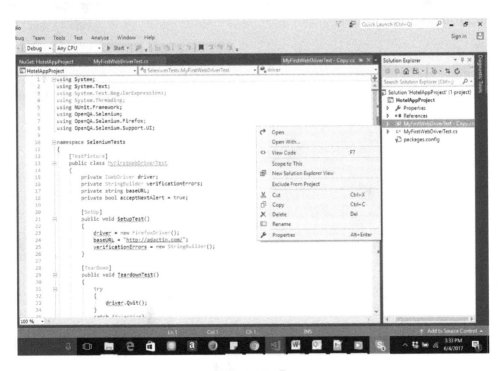

Figure 10.3 – Rename

4. Click on the newly created **"VerificationPointTest.cs" script** so that you can see the script.

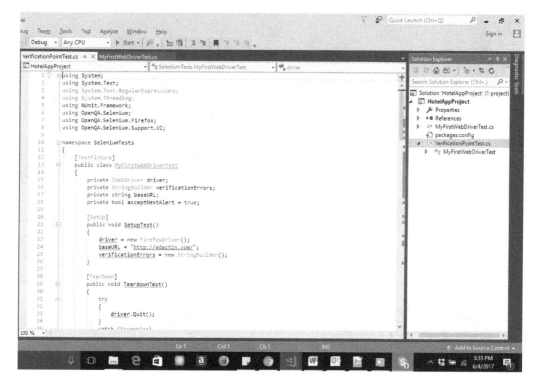

Figure 10.4 – VerificationPointTest

5. Rename the class name from MyfirstWebDriverTest to VerificationPointTest under TextFixture and save the file.

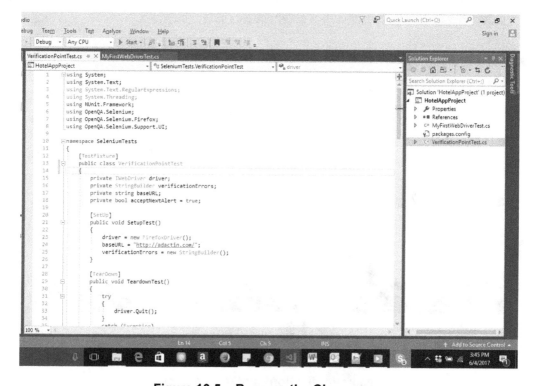

Figure 10.5 – Rename the Classname

Now we will insert a verification point.

Steps to insert a verification point

Objective – We need to verify that in Select Hotel Page we see location Sydney which we selected in the previous search step.

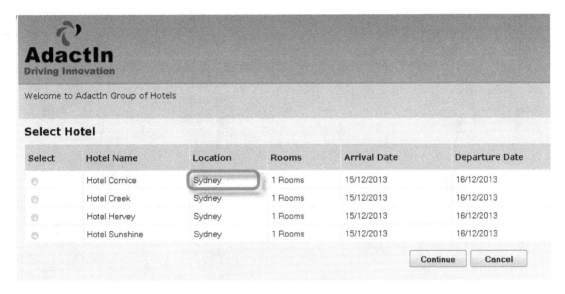

Figure 10.6 – Expected Location Value

1. In the script go to the step after which the user submits a search request for the location Sydney.

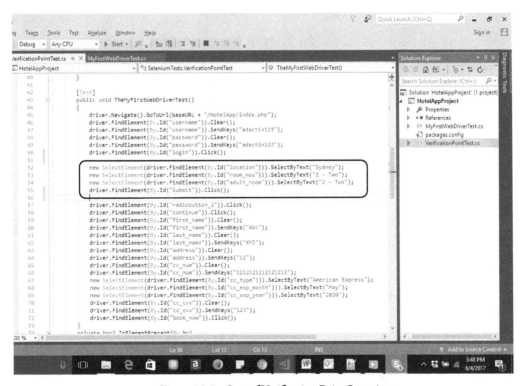

Figure 10.7 – Step of Verification Point Insertion

2. Now let us find out the XPath or id value for the Location field in the Select Hotel Page. To do this, open your Firefox browser, open application URL, login and navigate to the Select Hotel Page.

Note: We can ignore step 2 if the application is already open and we are on the Select Hotel page.

3. In Firefox broswer, open the Inspector and hover over the element. On the console, the element's properties get highlighted.

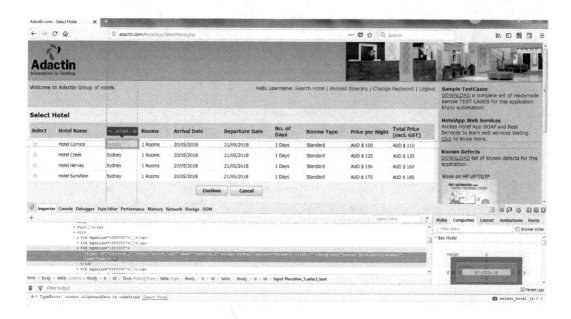

Figure 10.8 – XPath finder using Inspect Element

We notice in the above snapshot that the Xpath for location field is

Xpath = .//*[@id='location_1']

and

Id = location_1

Now we know the XPath or id of the object to locate the object.

We would also need to find out the property value for this object which stores the value "Sydney". We will again use Inspect element to find this out.

4. Right click on the highlighted text and choose Show DOM properties.

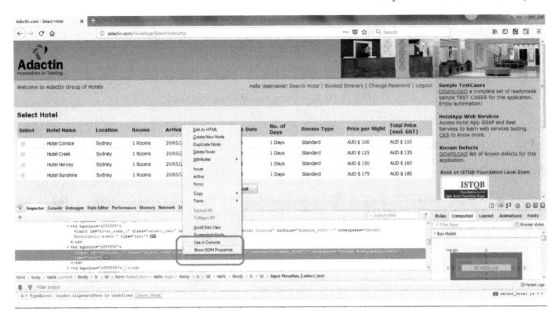

Figure 10.9 – DOM Tab

5. To get the property name:

   a. Click on the Highlight icon.

   b. Then click on the Location field "Sydney".

   c. Scroll down in the DOM tab to find out which property stores the value "Sydney".

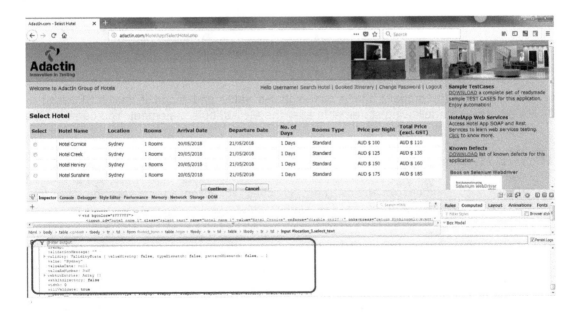

Figure 10.10 – Property Name in DOM

In the above snapshot, you will notice the property name **value** is storing "Sydney".

6. Now to insert a verification point in the script, we will insert the statement below:

```
String slocation =
driver.FindElement(By.XPath(".//*[@id='location_1']")).GetAttribute("value");
```

Figure 10.11 – Using GetAttribute Method

In the above statement

driver.findElement – Helps to find the element based on locator.

By.xpath(".//[@id='location_1']"))* – helps to locate the element based on xpath. This is the same xpath we got using Inspect element in the previous step.

GetAttribute – GetAttribute helps us to get the desired property value of the Web element.

value - is the property name which stores the actual value for location.

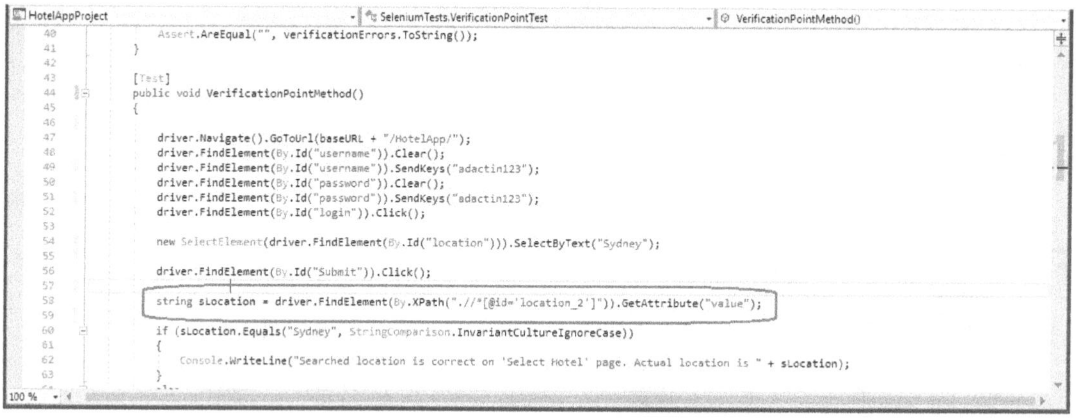

```
HotelAppProject                          SeleniumTests.VerificationPointTest              VerificationPointMethod()
    40              Assert.AreEqual("", verificationErrors.ToString());
    41          }
    42
    43          [Test]
    44          public void VerificationPointMethod()
    45          {
    46
    47              driver.Navigate().GoToUrl(baseURL + "/HotelApp/");
    48              driver.FindElement(By.Id("username")).Clear();
    49              driver.FindElement(By.Id("username")).SendKeys("adactin123");
    50              driver.FindElement(By.Id("password")).Clear();
    51              driver.FindElement(By.Id("password")).SendKeys("adactin123");
    52              driver.FindElement(By.Id("login")).Click();
    53
    54              new SelectElement(driver.FindElement(By.Id("location"))).SelectByText("Sydney");
    55
    56              driver.FindElement(By.Id("Submit")).Click();
    57
    58              string sLocation = driver.FindElement(By.XPath(".//*[@id='location_2']")).GetAttribute("value");
    59
    60              if (sLocation.Equals("Sydney", StringComparison.InvariantCultureIgnoreCase))
    61              {
    62                  Console.WriteLine("Searched location is correct on 'Select Hotel' page. Actual location is " + sLocation);
    63              }
100 %
```

Figure 10.12 – Get Attribute Value

7. Now we need to compare it with our expected value and report if the test Passed or Failed. Insert the following statements after the GetAttribute statement. You can type the statements.

```
if (sLocation.Equals("Sydney", StringComparison.InvariantCultureIgnoreCase))
        {
                Console.WriteLine("Searched location is correct on 'Select
Hotel' page. Actual location is " + sLocation);
        }
        else
        {
            Console.WriteLine("Searched location is incorrect on 'Select
Hotel' page. Actual location is " + sLocation);
        }
```

8. That's it! Now we can perform **Build > BuildSolution...** and **run all**.

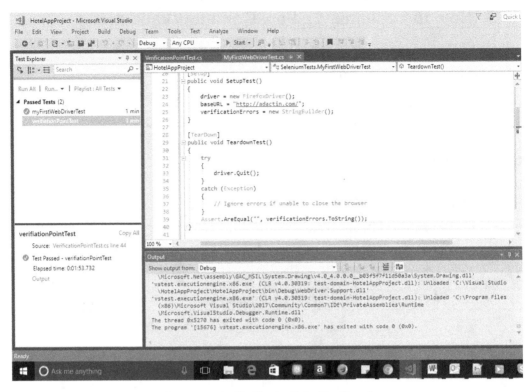

Figure 10.13 – VerificationPoint Test Passed

9. Click on Output in Test Explorer and you can see "Searched location is correct on 'Select Hotel' Page. Actual location is Sydney" which is the expected result.

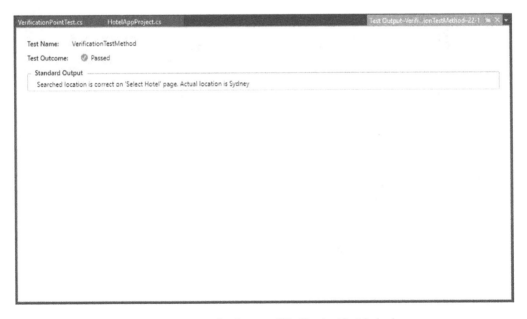

Figure 10.14 – Output of VerificationTestMethod

10.3. How to Implement a Few Common Validations

The common types of validations are:

- Is the page title as expected?
- Does text exist on the Page/WebElement and is it as expected?

Let us see how we can achieve each of these using the WebDriver API.

Get Page Title (using Title Method)

You can get the current page title simply by calling method *Title* on the WebDriver instance. Here is a simple test that would verify the title:

```
String pageTitle = driver.Title;
if (pageTitle.Equals("AdactIn.com - Select Hotel"))
Console.WriteLine("Page Title is correct. Actual page title is " +pageTitle);
else
Console.WriteLine("Page Title is incorrect. Actual page title is " +pageTitle);
```

Figure 10.15 – Get Page Title code sample

Validations against an element on the page (using Text method)

You can use the following approach for validating text within an element. Here we find the element using one of the locator strategies and then call *GetAttribute() or Text* on the element object returned.

For instance, if we do not select the Location field and click the Search button you get the following error message in the application:

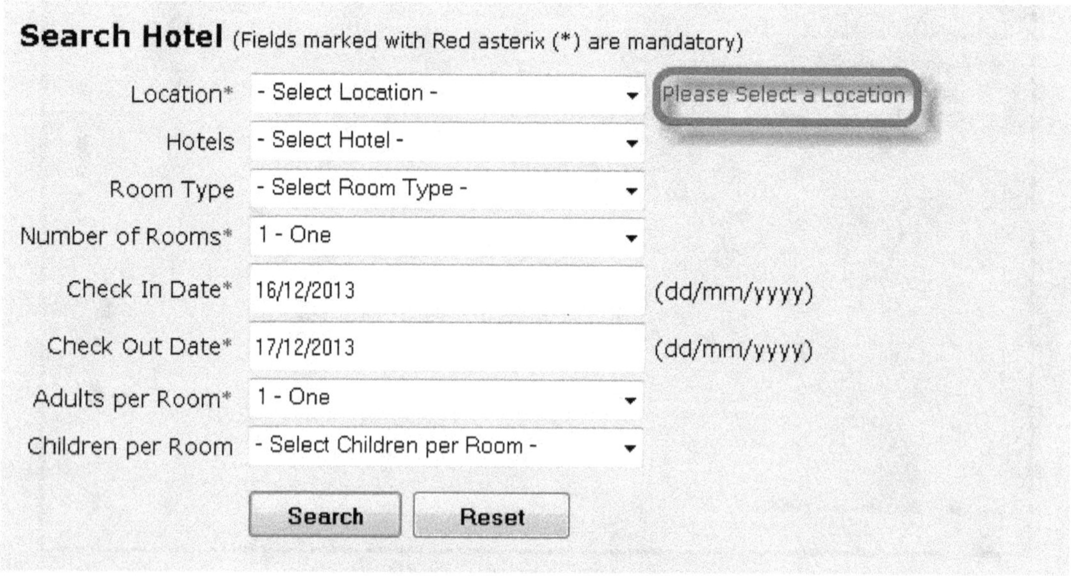

Search Hotel (Fields marked with Red asterix (*) are mandatory)

Location*	- Select Location - ▾	Please Select a Location
Hotels	- Select Hotel - ▾	
Room Type	- Select Room Type - ▾	
Number of Rooms*	1 - One ▾	
Check In Date*	16/12/2013	(dd/mm/yyyy)
Check Out Date*	17/12/2013	(dd/mm/yyyy)
Adults per Room*	1 - One ▾	
Children per Room	- Select Children per Room - ▾	

[Search] [Reset]

Figure 10.16 – Location Field blank Error

We can use *Text* method on the message field "Please Select a Location".

Using the inspector, verify the Xpath for the error message.Right click on the highlighted text.

Click on copy →Xpath and copy the Xpath

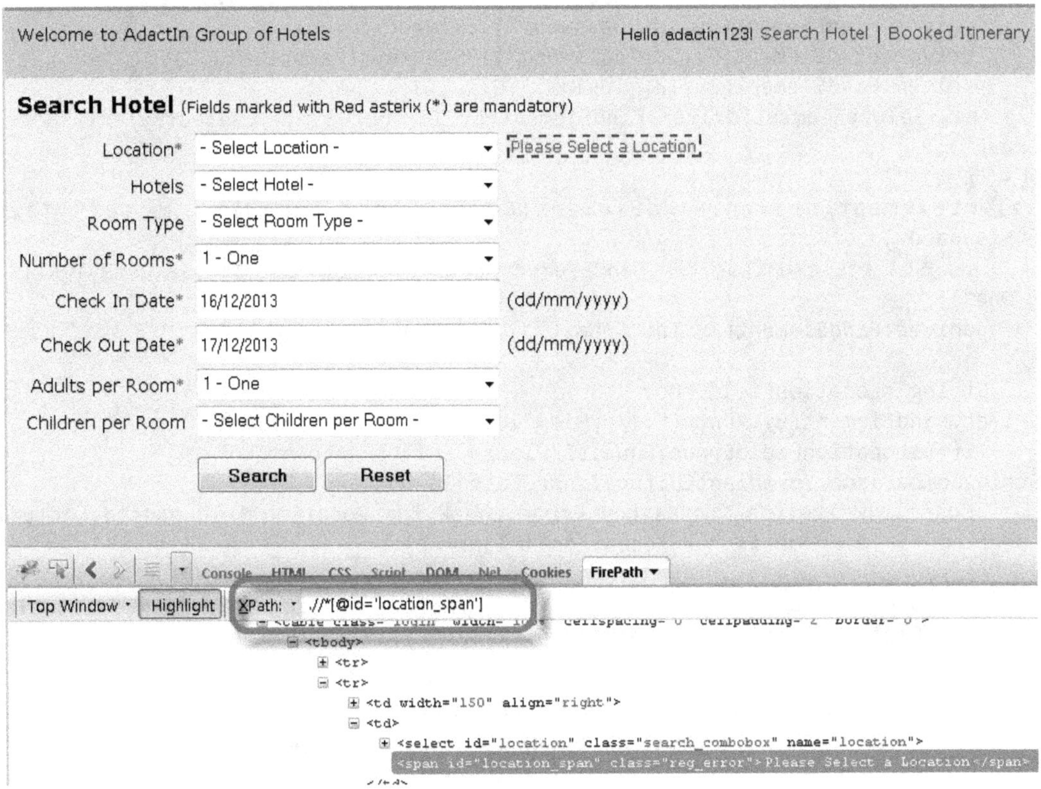

Figure 10.17 – XPath for Location Field Error

Xpath = .//*[@id='location_span']

Write another Test method to verify the error message. Here we do not select location *value* on the page to verify if the error message is shown correctly or not.

```
[Test]
 public void VerifyErrorMessage()
 {
     driver.Navigate().GoToUrl(baseURL + "/HotelApp/");
     driver.FindElement(By.Id("username")).Clear();
     driver.FindElement(By.Id("username")).SendKeys("adactin123");
     driver.FindElement(By.Id("password")).Clear();
     driver.FindElement(By.Id("password")).SendKeys("adactin123");
     driver.FindElement(By.Id("login")).Click();
    new SelectElement(driver.FindElement(By.Id("hotels"))).SelectByText("Hotel
Creek");
    new
SelectElement(driver.FindElement(By.Id("room_type"))).SelectByText
("Standard");
    new SelectElement(driver.FindElement(By.Id("child_room"))).SelectByText("1
- One");
     driver.FindElement(By.Id("Submit")).Click();

    String sLocationFieldError =
driver.FindElement(By.XPath(".//*[@id='location_span']")).Text;
    if (sLocationFieldError.Equals("Please Select a Location",
StringComparison.InvariantCultureIgnoreCase))
    Console.WriteLine("Mandatory Error check for Location field passed. Actual
Location Field Error is " + sLocationFieldError);
    else
    Console.WriteLine("Mandatory Error check for Location field failed.Actual
Location Field Error is " + sLocationFieldError);

}
```

Figure 10.18 – Verification Point for Text on Page

Now **Build > Build Solution** and Run this particular test case and check if it passes.

10.4. Assert Statements in NUnit

NUnit provides a rich set of assertions as static methods of the Assert class.

If an assertion fails, the method call does not return and an error is reported. If a test contains multiple assertions, any method that follows the one that failed will not be executed. For this reason, it's usually best to try for one assertion per test.

Each method may be called without a message, with a simple text message or with a message and arguments. In the last case, the message is formatted using the provided text and arguments. An *assertion method* compares the actual value returned by a test to the expected value and throws an AssertionException if the comparison test fails.

When we use the Assert statement we do not have to use an "If-Else" logical statement as the Assert statement will verify the result for us and return the correct value.

But it is important to note that in case of a failure, the Assert statement will **Abort** and exit the script. There are ways of implementing the Assert statement to avoid stopping and exiting the script. We will see a sample implementation in the script below.

The following table gives an overview of these methods. Parameters in [] brackets are optional.

Test methods

Statement	Description
fail(String)	Let the method fail. Might be used to check that a certain part of the code is not reached. Or to have a failing test before the test code is implemented. The String parameter is optional.
Assert.True(bool condition, string mesasge);	Checks if the boolean condition is true.
Assert.False(bool condition, string message);	Checks if the boolean condition is false.
Assert.AreEqual (expected, actual)	Checks whether the two arguments are equal.
Assert.AreNotEqual (expected, actual)	Checks whether the two arguments are not equal.
Assert.Null(object anObject, string message);	Verifies that the object that is passed in is equal to null. If the object is not null then an AssertionException is thrown.
Assert.NotNull(object anObject, string message);	Verifies that the object that is passed in is not equal to null. If the object is null then an AssertionException is thrown.
StringAssert.Contains (string expected, string actual);	Asserts that a string is found within another string.
StringAssert. AreEqualIgnoringCase (string expected, string actual);	Asserts that two strings are equal, without regard to case.

Let us see an example where we had earlier used the Assert statement.

1. Go to your Katalon Automation IDE and make sure the script "IDEVerificationScript" is Open.

Figure 10.19 – Verification Point IDE Script

2. Click on **Export** → **C#(WebDriver + NUnit)**

3. Open the exported WebDriver test in NotePad++.

```
[Test]
public void TheIDEVerificationScriptTest()
{
    driver.Navigate().GoToUrl(baseURL + "/HotelApp/");
    driver.FindElement(By.Id("username")).Clear();
    driver.FindElement(By.Id("username")).SendKeys("adactin123");
    driver.FindElement(By.Id("password")).Clear();
    driver.FindElement(By.Id("password")).SendKeys("adactin123");
    driver.FindElement(By.Id("login")).Click();
    new SelectElement(driver.FindElement(By.Id("adult_room"))).SelectByText("2 - Two");
    new SelectElement(driver.FindElement(By.Id("room_type"))).SelectByText("Standard");
    driver.FindElement(By.Id("Submit")).Click();
    Assert.IsTrue(IsElementPresent(By.LinkText("Logout")));
    new SelectElement(driver.FindElement(By.Id("location"))).SelectByText("Sydney");
    driver.FindElement(By.Id("Submit")).Click();
    driver.FindElement(By.Id("radiobutton_1")).Click();
    driver.FindElement(By.Id("continue")).Click();
    driver.FindElement(By.Id("first_name")).Clear();
    driver.FindElement(By.Id("first_name")).SendKeys("Abc");
    driver.FindElement(By.Id("last_name")).Clear();
    driver.FindElement(By.Id("last_name")).SendKeys("XYZ");
    driver.FindElement(By.Id("address")).Clear();
    driver.FindElement(By.Id("address")).SendKeys("12345678");
    driver.FindElement(By.Id("cc_num")).Clear();
    driver.FindElement(By.Id("cc_num")).SendKeys("12312423435");
    new SelectElement(driver.FindElement(By.Id("cc_type"))).SelectByText("VISA");
    driver.FindElement(By.Id("cc_cvv")).Clear();
    driver.FindElement(By.Id("cc_cvv")).SendKeys("123");
    driver.FindElement(By.Id("book_now")).Click();
    driver.FindElement(By.Id("cc_num")).Clear();
```

Figure 10.20 – Exported Verification Point Script

If you notice a new statement, **Assert.IsTrue** has been added which validates that the logout link is present.

Now note that in the above implementation if the logout link does not appear the script will abort. But there would be scenarios where we would not want to abort the script on verification failure. To avoid aborting the script we can include the assert command in the Try-Catch block. See sample code below.

```
try {
    Assert.IsTrue(IsElementPresent(By.LinkText("Logout")));
} catch (Exception e) {
    verificationErrors.Append(e.ToString());
}
```

Figure 10.21 – Assert Statement in Try-Catch Block

In the sample code above, the exception thrown by the failed assert statement will be captured in the catch block and the script will move to the next step and will not abort.

EXERCISE

1. According to the functional requirements of our sample application, the user should see a message saying "Hello *username!*" on a successful login as shown in the highlighted text in the figure below.

Welcome to AdactIn Group of Hotels   Hello adactin123! Search Hotel

Search Hotel (Fields marked with Red asterix (*) are mandatory)

Location*	- Select Location - ▾	Please Select a Location
Hotels	- Select Hotel - ▾	
Room Type	- Select Room Type - ▾	
Number of Rooms*	1 - One ▾	
Check In Date*	16/12/2013	(dd/mm/yyyy)
Check Out Date*	17/12/2013	(dd/mm/yyyy)
Adults per Room*	1 - One ▾	
Children per Room	- Select Children per Room - ▾	

Search   Reset

Figure 10.22 – Welcome User Message

Create a new script with a verification point which verifies a successful login with the correct message "Hello username".

 Hint

1. Using the Inspector, inspect the element. Right click on the highlighted text on the console and we can copy the Xpath for the highlighted area of the page where the expected message is displayed

2. Code snippet should appear as shown below:

```
String sWelcometext =
driver.FindElement(By.XPath(".//*[@id='username_show']")).GetAt-
tribute("value");
if (sWelcometext.Equals("Hello adactin123",
StringComparison.InvariantCultureIgnoreCase))
        Console.WriteLine("Login Test Pass");
else
        Console.WriteLine("Login Test Fail");
```

Figure 10.23 – Verification Test for Successful Login

3. Now we can run this test again for the same user, i.e., "adactin123". For a successful run we get a console message: *Login Test Pass*.

If we want to run the same test for different users we have to parameterize our test.

11. Shared UI Map

Introduction

We now know how Selenium works as a tool, and recognizes Web elements based on properties and its values. In a WebDriver script, the Web element property values are located within the script. For instance, when we login, the username Web element's Xpath property gets added locally within the script statement.

> driver.findElement(By.*xpath*(".//*[@id='username']")).clear();

In the above statement, the property value for Xpath (Xpath=.//*[@id='username']) is located within the script.

What if due to business requirements, the developer changes the property value of these Web elements? For instance, change 'username' to 'customername'. This would result in all of our scripts that use this Web element to fail. In order to fix this issue, we will need to go to each and every script, and change its properties information. This can be a nightmare to maintain!

Worst can be if the object is being used multiple times within the same script. We would need to make the same change multiple times in every script.

A better solution would be if we keep all the required Web elements and their properties in an external location/file and all the scripts could just use Web element properties from this shared location. This will certainly avoid redundancy. Also, if any Web element changes, we would only need to change the Web element once and the script will be working again.

example

At one of our clients, where we had to implement automation, we were given 100 existing automation scripts. We were told that the scripts used to work 3 months earlier, but now, they fail on new builds. We were asked to fix the scripts. Guess what we found? All the scripts were using local Web element properties. When we identified the Web elements that were causing the script to fail, we discovered that the same Web element was used in all 100 scripts. So the Web element had to be modified at least 100 times as it was being used in all the scripts. But there were at least 100 Web elements, which had changed. Adding to this, they informed us that UI (user interface) changes were still happening and that the Web elements will change again. Our recommendation to them was to hold on and to re-do the scripts using a Shared UI Map. The advice stemmed from the fact that the same effort invested now would be required again when we get a new application build, with updated Web elements. Yes, it did mean that most of the previous efforts already made had been wasted. But our re-scripting approach, using a Shared Web Element Map, ensured that script maintenance was future proofed.

In this chapter we will discuss how to create and add objects to a shared UI Map, and how to use objects from a shared UI Map.

Key objectives:

- What is a Shared UI Map
- Create a Shared UI Map
- Add Web element and properties in a Shared UI Map
- Using a Shared UI Map in the WebDriver script

11.1. What is a Shared UI Map?

What makes a Shared UI Map helpful?

Its primary purpose is to make test script management easier. When a locator needs to be edited, there is a central location from where you easily find that object, rather than having to search through the entire script code. Also, it allows changing the Identifier in a single place, rather than having to make the change in multiple places within a test script, or for that matter, in multiple test scripts.

In a nutshell, a Shared UI Map has two significant advantages:

- Using a centralized location for UI Web elements instead of having them scattered throughout the script. This makes script maintenance more efficient.

- Cryptic HTML Identifiers and names can be given more human-readable names, improving the readability of test scripts.

Consider the following example of our Login Test that is difficult to understand:

```
public void Login()
{
    try
    {
        driver.Navigate().GoToUrl(baseURL + "/HotelApp/");
        driver.FindElement(By.XPath(".//*[@id='username']")).Clear();
                        driver.FindElement(By.XPath(".//*[@
id='username']")).SendKeys("adactin123");
        driver.FindElement(By.XPath(".//*[@id='password']")).Clear();
            driver.FindElement(By.XPath(".//*[@id='password']")).
SendKeys("xxxxxx");
        driver.FindElement(By.XPath(".//*[@id='login']")).Click();
    }
    catch (Exception e)
    {
        throw e;
    }
}
```

Figure 11.1 – Login Script with local Web Element Properties

This script would be hard to follow for anyone not familiar with the AUT's (Application Under Test) page source especially when the locator references are of more complex XPath or CSS types. Even regular users of the application might have difficulty understanding the script. A better script could be

```
public void Login()
{
                try
                {
                    driver.Navigate().GoToUrl(baseURL + "/HotelApp/");
driver.FindElement(By.XPath(ReadMap("login.userName"))).Clear();
driver.FindElement(By.XPath(ReadMap("login.userName"))).SendKeys("adactin123");
driver.FindElement(By.XPath(ReadMap("login.password"))).Clear();
driver.FindElement(By.XPath(ReadMap("login.password"))).SendKeys("xxxxxx");

driver.FindElement(By.XPath(ReadMap("login.submit"))).Click();
                }
                catch (Exception e)
                {
                    throw e;
                }
}
```

Figure 11.2 – Login Script with Shared Web Element Properties

ReadMap() could be a method we use to read the element locator from our Shared UI Map. Now, using some comments and whitespace along with the UI Map identifiers makes a very readable script.

```
public void Login()
{
                try
                {
                    //Open the application url
                    driver.Navigate().GoToUrl(baseURL + "/HotelApp/");

                    //Provide admin Username
driver.FindElement(By.XPath(ReadMap("login.userName"))).Clear();
driver.FindElement(By.XPath(ReadMap("login.userName"))).
SendKeys("adactin123");

                    //Provide admin Password
driver.FindElement(By.XPath(ReadMap("login.password"))).Clear();
driver.FindElement(By.XPath(ReadMap("login.password"))).SendKeys("xxxxxx");

                    //Click on Login button
driver.FindElement(By.XPath(ReadMap("login.submit"))).Click();
                }
                catch (Exception e)
                {
                    throw e;
                }
}
```

Figure 11.3 – Login Script with Shared Web Element Properties with Comments

There are various ways a Shared UI Map can be implemented. One, we could create a class which only has public String variables each storing a locator. Alternatively, a text/properties file storing key value pairs could be used. In C#, a properties file containing key/value pairs is probably a convenient and efficient method as this uses built-in C# functions.

11.2. Add a Shared UI Map to Selenium Project

Let's add a UI Map to our project.

1. *Select the Project Folder **HotelAppProject. Right-click** and select **Add > New Item**.*

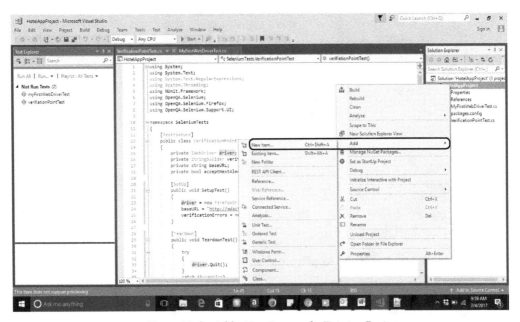

Figure 11.4 – Add a New Item to the Existing Project

2. Click on **Application Configuration File** and provide the name of the file name is **App. config.** Click **OK**.

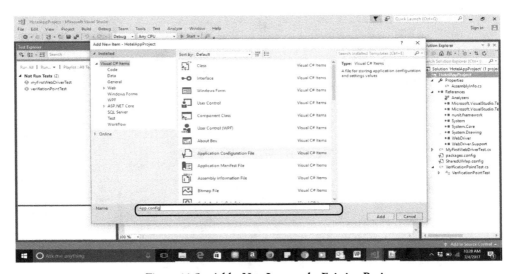

Figure 11.5 – Add a New Item to the Existing Project

3. A new App.config file will be added to the project.

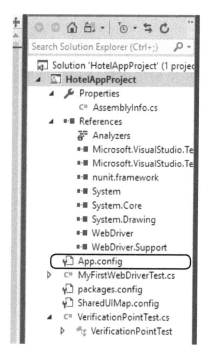

Figure 11.6 – App.Config

4. Now again, click on the **HotelAppProject and Add > New Item**.

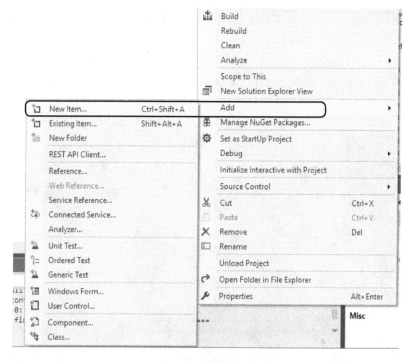

Figure 11.7 – New Item

5. In the **Add New Item** window, click on Application Configuration File and provide the name as **SharedUIMap**. Click on **Add**.

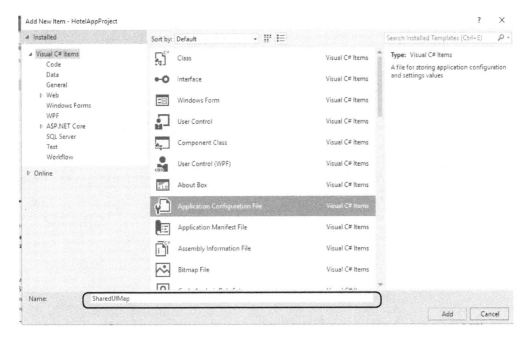

Figure 11.8 – New Config File

6. A new config file **SharedUIMap.config** will be added to the project.

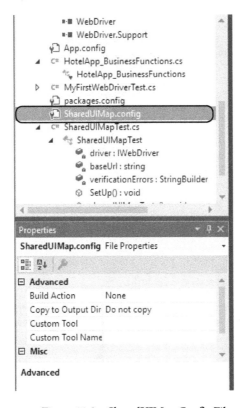

Figure 11.9 – SharedUIMap Config File

7. Click on the **SharedUIMap.config** file and the script will appear as shown.

Figure 11.10 – SharedUIMap.Config Script

8. Remove the xml reference and the configuration tags and add the following.

Note: We suggest strictly following some naming conventions while naming Web Elements. For example:• ElementType_PageName_ElementName

```
<appSettings>

  <!-- Login Page Elements-->
  <add key="Txt_Login_Username"  value=".//*[@id='username']"/>
  <add key="Txt_Login_Password"  value="password"/>
  <add key="Btn_Login_Login"  value="login"/>

  <!-- Search Hotel Page Elements-->
  <add key="Lst_SearchHotel_Location"  value="location"/>
  <add key="Btn_SearchHotel_Search"  value="Submit"/>
  <add key="Lbl_SearchHotel_WelcomeMessage"  value="username_show"/>

  <!--Select Hotel Page Elements-->
  <add key="Rad_SelectHotel_RadioButton_1"  value="radiobutton_1"/>
  <add key="Btn_SelectHotel_Continue"  value="continue"/>

  <!-- Booking Hotel Page Elements-->
  <add key="Txt_BookingHotel_FirstName"  value="first_name"/>
  <add key="Txt_BookingHotel_LastName"  value="last_name"/>
  <add key="Txt_BookingHotel_Address"  value="address"/>
  <add key="Txt_BookingHotel_CCNumber"  value="cc_num"/>
  <add key="Lst_BookingHotel_CCType"  value="cc_type"/>
  <add key="Lst_BookingHotel_CCExpMonth"  value="cc_exp_month"/>
  <add key="Lst_BookingHotel_CCExpYear"  value="cc_exp_year"/>
  <add key="Txt_BookingHotel_CCCvvNumber"  value="cc_cvv"/>
  <add key="Btn_BookingHotel_BookNow"  value="book_now"/>

<!--Booking Confirmation Page Elements-->

  <add key="Txt_BookingHotel_OrderNo"  value="order_no"/>
  <add key="Btn_BookingHotel_Logout"  value="logout"/>
  <add key="Lnk_BookingHotel_Logout"  value="Logout"/>
  <add key="Btn_BookingHotel_MyItinerary"  value="my_itinerary"/>


  <!-- Booked Itinerary Elements-->
  <add key="Txt_BookedItinerary_SearchOrderid"  value="order_id_text"/>
  <add key="Btn_BookedItinerary_Go"  value="search_hotel_id"/>
  <add key="Lnk_Logout_ClickHeretoLoginAgain"  value="Click here to login again"/>

  <!-- Logout Elements-->

</appSettings>
```

Figure 11.11 – Configuration File

9. So we have our configuration file **SharedUIMap.config** as shown below. Here we assign "aliases" reader-friendly identifiers for UI elements.

```
 7
 8   <!-- Login Page Elements-->
 9   <add key="Txt_Login_Username"  value="username"/>
10   <add key="Txt_Login_Password"  value="password"/>
11   <add key="Btn_Login_Login"  value="login"/>
12
13   <!--Search Hotel Page elements-->
14   <add key="Lst_SearchHotel_Location" value="location"/>
15   <add key="Lst_SearchHotel_RoomNos" value="room_nos"/>
16   <add key="Lst_SearchHotel_AdultRoom" value="adult_room"/>
17   <add key="Lst_SearchHotel_ChildRoom" value="child_room"/>
18   <add key="Btn_SearchHotel_Search" value="Submit"/>
19   <add key="Lbl_SearchHotel_WelcomeMessage" value="username_show"/>
20
21   <!--Select Hotel Page-->
22   <add key="Rad_SelectHotel_RadioButton_1" value="radiobutton_1"/>
23   <add key="Btn_SelectHotel_Continue" value="continue"/>
24
25   <!--Booking Hotel Page Elements-->
26   <add key="Txt_BookingHotel_FirstName" value="first_name"/>
27   <add key="Txt_BookingHotel_LastName" value="last_name"/>
28   <add key="Txt_BookingHotel_Address" value="address"/>
29   <add key="Txt_BookingHotel_CcNum" value="cc_num"/>
30   <add key="Lst_BookingHotel_CcType" value="cc_type"/>
31   <add key="Lst_BookingHotel_ExpMonth" value="cc_exp_month"/>
32   <add key="Lst_BookingHotel_ExpYear" value="cc_exp_year"/>
```

Figure 11.12 – SharedUIMap Script

Note: The locators will still refer to HTML objects, but we have introduced a layer of abstraction between the test script and the UI elements. Values are read from the Config file and used in the Test Class to implement the Shared UI Map.

10. Create a folder called Configuration and move the **SharedUIMap.config** to that folder. This helps in better user readability and cleaner code.

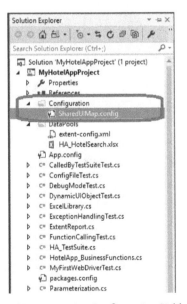

Figure 11.13 – Configuration Folder

11. Click on App.config file and add the following xml reference.

```xml
<?xml version="1.0" encoding="utf-8" ?>
<configuration>
  <appSettings configSource ="Configuration\SharedUIMap.config">
  </appSettings>
</configuration>
```

Figure 11.14 – Visual Studio View of App.config

11.3. Using a Shared UI Map file in Script

Now that we have created our external Shared UI map file, we would want to use it in our script. Let us follow these steps to create a script using a Shared UI map.

Pre-conditions:

1. **Right-click** on your existing MyFirstWebDriverTest.cs script and select **Copy.**

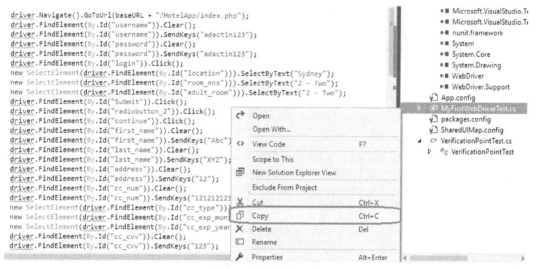

Figure 11.15 – Copy Script

2. **Right-click** on the project and select **Paste**.

Figure 11.16 – Paste Script

3. A copy of the existing class file will be generated on the Solution Explorer.

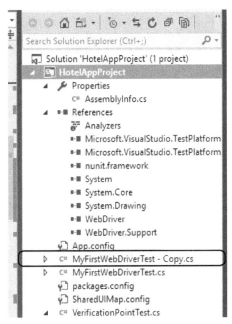

Figure 11.17 – Copy of the Class file

4. **Right -click** on it and click on **rename it to SharedUIMapTest**.

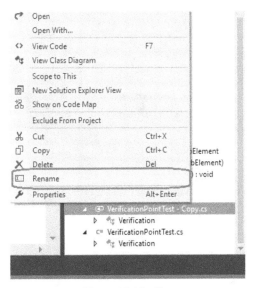

Figure 11.18 – Rename

5. Double click on the **SharedUIMapTest.cs** and we can see the copied script on the new file.

6. Let us design our script to read locators from our Shared UI Map file. Add the following code to the SharedUIMapTest.cs.

7. Right-click on the **Reference**. **Add > Reference**.

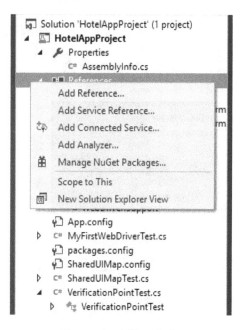

Fig 11.19 – Adding Reference

8. In the Reference Manager, click on **Assemblies > Framework.** Search for **System. Configuration** and click on the check box. Click on OK.

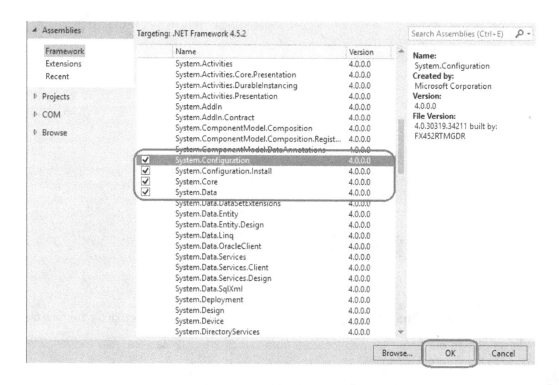

Fig 11.20 – Adding Reference - System.Configuration

9. In the script, we will use **ConfigurationManager.AppSettings** to access the Locators. Update the Test section with the following code.

ConfigurationManager.AppSettings Property gets the AppSettingsSection data for the current application's default configuration.

```
[Test]
public void sharedUIMapTests()
{
driver.Navigate().GoToUrl(baseUrl + "/HotelApp/");

driver.FindElement(By.XPath(ConfigurationManager.AppSettings["Txt_Login_Username"])).Clear();
driver.FindElement(By.XPath(ConfigurationManager.AppSettings["Txt_Login_Username"])).
SendKeys("adactin123");
driver.FindElement(By.Id(ConfigurationManager.AppSettings["Txt_Login_Password"])).Clear();
driver.FindElement(By.Id(ConfigurationManager.AppSettings["Txt_Login_Password"])).
SendKeys("adactin123");
driver.FindElement(By.Id(ConfigurationManager.AppSettings["Btn_Login_Login"])).Click();
        new
SelectElement(driver.FindElement(By.Id(ConfigurationManager.AppSettings["Lst_SearchHotel_
Location"]))).SelectByText("Sydney");
driver.FindElement(By.Id(ConfigurationManager.AppSettings["Btn_SearchHotel_Search"])).Click();
driver.FindElement(By.Id(ConfigurationManager.AppSettings["Rad_SelectHotel_RadioButton_1"])).
Click();
driver.FindElement(By.Id(ConfigurationManager.AppSettings["Btn_SelectHotel_Continue"])).
Click();
driver.FindElement(By.Id(ConfigurationManager.AppSettings["Txt_BookingHotel_FirstName"])).
Clear();
driver.FindElement(By.Id(ConfigurationManager.AppSettings["Txt_BookingHotel_FirstName"])).
SendKeys("test");
driver.FindElement(By.Id(ConfigurationManager.AppSettings["Txt_BookingHotel_LastName"])).
Clear();
driver.FindElement(By.Id(ConfigurationManager.AppSettings["Txt_BookingHotel_LastName"])).
SendKeys("test");
driver.FindElement(By.Id(ConfigurationManager.AppSettings["Txt_BookingHotel_Address"])).
Clear();
driver.FindElement(By.Id(ConfigurationManager.AppSettings["Txt_BookingHotel_Address"])).
SendKeys("test");
driver.FindElement(By.Id(ConfigurationManager.AppSettings["Txt_BookingHotel_CCNumber"])).
Clear();
driver.FindElement(By.Id(ConfigurationManager.AppSettings["Txt_BookingHotel_CCNumber"])).
SendKeys("1212121212121212");
        new
SelectElement(driver.FindElement(By.Id(ConfigurationManager.AppSettings["Lst_BookingHotel_
CCType"]))).SelectByText("American Express");
        new
SelectElement(driver.FindElement(By.Id(ConfigurationManager.AppSettings["Lst_BookingHotel_
CCExpMonth"]))).SelectByText("March");
        new
SelectElement(driver.FindElement(By.Id(ConfigurationManager.AppSettings["Lst_BookingHotel_
CCExpYear"]))).SelectByText("2015");
driver.FindElement(By.Id(ConfigurationManager.AppSettings["Txt_BookingHotel_CCCvvNumber"])).
Clear();
driver.FindElement(By.Id(ConfigurationManager.AppSettings["Txt_BookingHotel_CCCvvNumber"])).
SendKeys("111");
driver.FindElement(By.Id(ConfigurationManager.AppSettings["Btn_BookingHotel_BookNow"])).
Click();
driver.FindElement(By.LinkText(ConfigurationManager.AppSettings["Lnk_BookingHotel_Logout"])).
Click();
driver.FindElement(By.LinkText(ConfigurationManager.AppSettings["Lnk_Logout_
ClickHeretoLoginAgain"])).Click();
}
```

Figure 11.21 – Test Script with Reference to Shared UI Map

10. The Visual Studio is a smart IDE and hence you should include **System.Configuration** namespace. Double click on it.

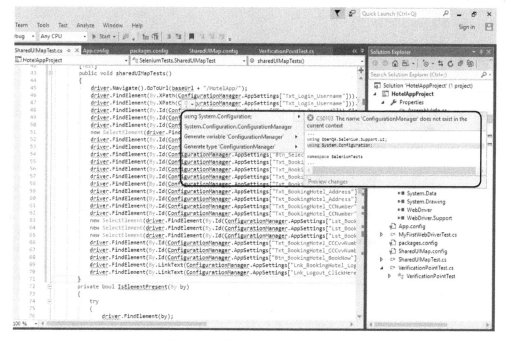

Fig 11.22 – Using System.Configuration

11. Once all the required changes have been made, the script will look like this.

12. Click on **Build->Build Solution** to check for any errors.

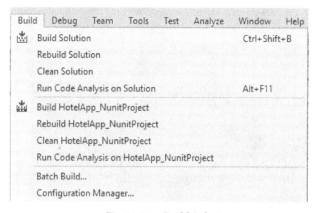

Fig 11.23 – Build Solution

13. Select the test and Run the test using **Run** on the TestExplorer. Confirm that the test can run fine.

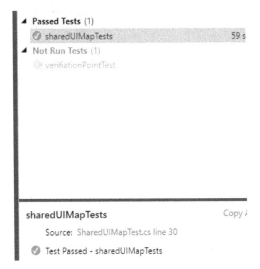

Figure 11.24 – Test Results

Note: If there's any error in the **System.Configuration.ConfigurationErrorsException: Unable to Open configSource File "SharedUIMap.config"**. It is possible that the configuration file may not be copied to the output release folder.

The following steps should fix the issue:

1. Right-click on the SharedUIMap.Config file and click on properties.

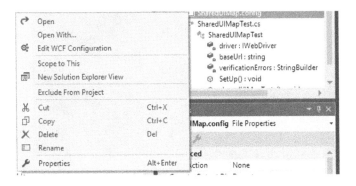

Figure 11.25 –Right-click on Properties

2. Under Advanced, Copy to Output Directory, change the value as Copy always. This ensures that the configuration file is copied to the Debug/Release folder during the build so that it is available at the time of execution. You have to use this option whenever the code depends on a particular file to execute.

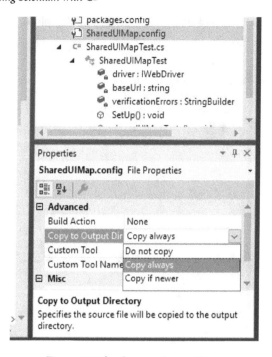

Figure 11.26 – Copy to Output Directory

1. Replace VerificationPointTest.cs script with UI elements from the Shared UI Map file.

12. Using Functions

Functions help divide your test into logical units, such as areas of key functionalities of the application. Functions help make our scripts modular and reusable, which will save our maintenance effort and also help us improve productivity. These functions can then be reused in different scripts.

For example, all of our scripts will have to login to the application. Now, instead of recording login steps repeatedly in every script, we can keep an external login function and reuse that function in all of our scripts.

example Let us see another practical example here:

At one of our client engagements, we were automating an investment banking application. As a first step of every test case, we had to create investment instruments after which we had to validate and add details in later steps (we had more than 100 test cases for each instrument type). Creating an instrument was a tedious step with up to 50 field values to be entered. Based on the test scenario, input data would change. Now recording the steps of investment instrument creation in each and every script would have been a nightmare and time-consuming. It would also be a maintenance issue, if in later development stages the application workflow is changed or new fields were added.

So we created functions to create instruments and for each of the test cases that were automated, we just invoked the same function in every script. This helped us reduce the overall time to automate. This also assisted in maintenance down the line, when the investment instrument creation workflow changed.

Key objectives:

- Create Functions.
- Calling Functions in WebDriver script.

12.1. Creating Functions in WebDriver

Key steps in creating Functions in WebDriver using Visual Studio IDE include:

1. Create a separate Class for Functions.
2. Create Function definition and add steps to functions based on function's objective.
3. Replace any data within functions with arguments from that function.
4. Within the script, extend class to use function within your scripts.

PreConditions: Select **HotelAppProject** solution, right-click and select **Add ->Class..**

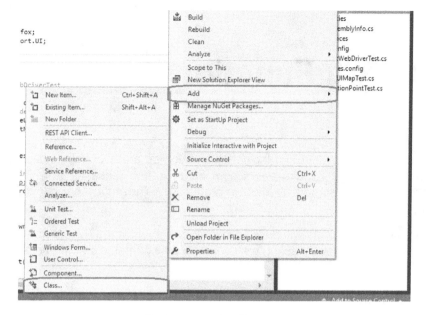

Figure 12.1 – New Class Creation

1. Give the name as HotelApp_BusinessFunctions and click on **Add**.

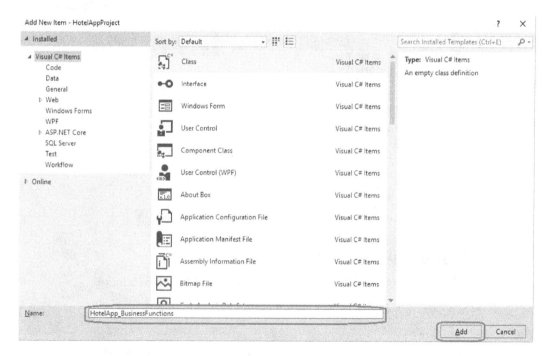

Figure 12.2 – Class File Name

2. A new class file is created in the Solution.

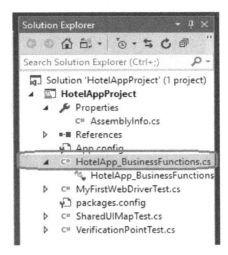

Figure 12.3 – BusinessFunctions Class

3. Click on HotelApp_BusinessFunctions.cs file and you will see the following script.

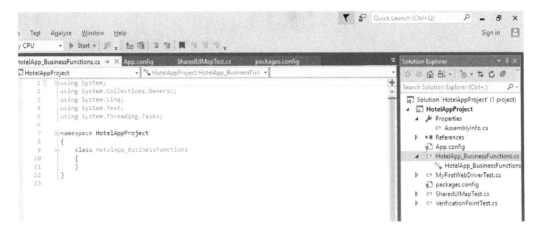

Figure 12.4 – Default Script

4. **Right-click** on your existing SharedUIMap.cs script, click on **Copy**.

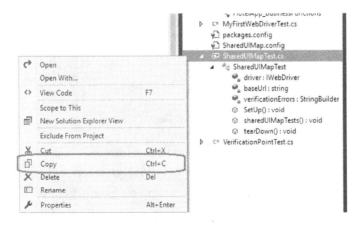

Figure 12.5 – Copy Script

5. Right-click on the project name and click on paste.

Figure 12.6 – Paste Script

6. A copy of ShareddUIMap will be created.

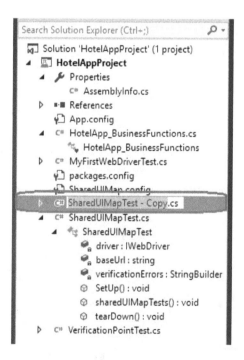

Figure 12.7 – Copy of the Class File

7. Right-click on the SharedUIMapTest-Copy.cs and click on **Rename**.

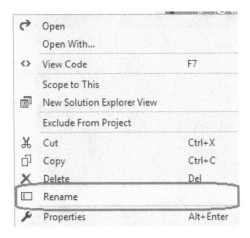

Figure 12.8 – Rename

8. Give the name as "FunctionCallingTest" and click Enter.

9. Double click on "FunctionCallingTest.cs" script so that you can see the script.

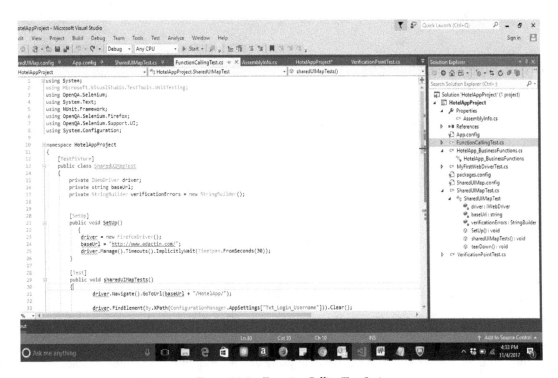

Figure 12.9 – FunctionCallingTest Script

Note: Change the class name to FunctionCallingTest to avoid conflicting classnames.The script will look as shown below.

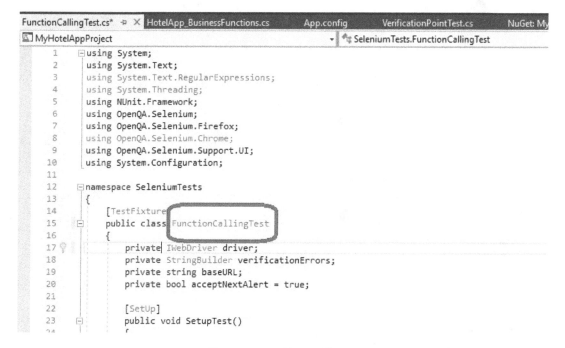

Figure 12.10 – Change Class Name

Create Function Definitions

Now let us create the Login Function first.

As discussed in the Basic C# chapter, syntax for creating a method or function is below.

Here is an example of a typical function declaration:

```
<Access Specifier> <Return Type> <Method Name> (<List of Parameters>)
  {//Method Body
}
```

Figure 12.11 – C# Method Syntax

The following are the various elements of a method:

Access Specifier: This determines the visibility of a variable or a method from another class.

Return type: A method may return a value. The return type is the data type of the value the method returns. If the method is not returning any values, then the return type is void.

Method name: Method name is a unique identifier and it is case sensitive. It cannot be the same as any other identifier declared in the class.

Parameter list: Enclosed between parentheses, the parameters are used to pass and receive data from a method. The parameter list refers to the type, order, and number of the parameters of a method. Parameters are optional, i.e., a method may contain no parameters.

Method body: This contains the set of instructions needed to complete the required activity.

10. Based on the above syntax, let us create the following Function for Login. We will copy steps to login to the application from our **FunctionCallingTest.cs** script and create the Login function definition with its arguments in **HotelApp_BusinessFunctions.cs**.

```
public void HA_BF_Login(IWebDriver driver, string sUsername, string sPassword)

driver.FindElement(By.XPath(ConfigurationManager.AppSettings["Txt_Login_
Username"])).Clear();
driver.FindElement(By.XPath(ConfigurationManager.AppSettings["Txt_Login_
Username"])).SendKeys(sUsername);

driver.FindElement(By.Id(ConfigurationManager.AppSettings["Txt_Login_
Password"])).Clear();
driver.FindElement(By.Id(ConfigurationManager.AppSettings["Txt_Login_
Password"])).SendKeys(sPassword);
driver.FindElement(By.Id(ConfigurationManager.AppSettings["Btn_Login_Login"])).
Click();
}
```

Figure 12.12 – Login Method

Note: We are trying to follow a few naming conventions on how to name methods:

- HA – HotelApp

- BF – Business Function

- Login – Name of the function

We are going to cover more on naming conventions in further chapters.

11. Once you copy the steps you will notice quite a few errors popping up in the Visual Studio interface.

Figure 12.13 – Errors in Visual Studio Interface

If you look at the errors (place your cursor above the red underlined keywords), you will notice quite a few logical reasons for the errors.

- The type or namespace name IWebDriver could not be found.
- The name ConfigurationManager does not exist in the current context.
- The name Thread does not exist in the current context.

12. To resolve the errors we need to include the following (Choose from the "***Show potential fixes"***):

- Using OpenQA.Selenium.
- Using System.Configuration.
- Using System.Threading.

Your script should appear as follows after resolving the Visual Studio errors:

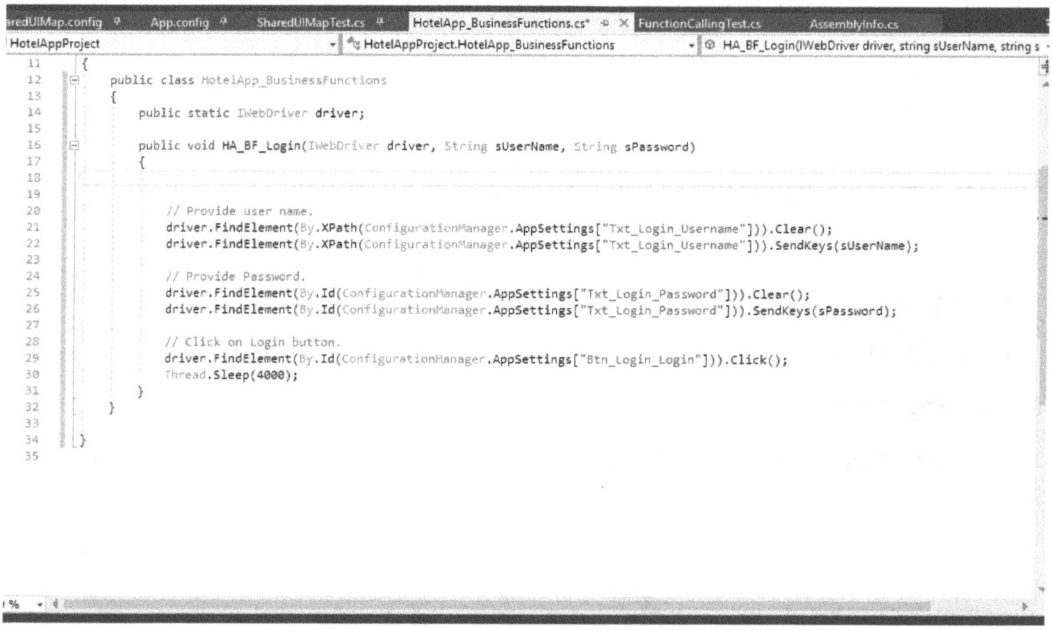
App.config
SharedUIMapTest.cs
HotelApp_BusinessFunctions.cs*
FunctionCallingTest.cs
AssemblyInfo.cs
HotelAppProject
HotelAppProject.HotelApp_BusinessFunctions
HA_BF_Login(IWebDriver driver, string sUserName, string s
{
public class HotelApp_BusinessFunctions
{
public static IWebDriver driver;
public void HA_BF_Login(IWebDriver driver, String sUserName, String sPassword)
{
// Provide user name.
driver.FindElement(By.XPath(ConfigurationManager.AppSettings["Txt_Login_Username"])).Clear();
driver.FindElement(By.XPath(ConfigurationManager.AppSettings["Txt_Login_Username"])).SendKeys(sUserName);
// Provide Password.
driver.FindElement(By.Id(ConfigurationManager.AppSettings["Txt_Login_Password"])).Clear();
driver.FindElement(By.Id(ConfigurationManager.AppSettings["Txt_Login_Password"])).SendKeys(sPassword);
// Click on Login button.
driver.FindElement(By.Id(ConfigurationManager.AppSettings["Btn_Login_Login"])).Click();
Thread.Sleep(4000);
}
}
}

Figure 12.14 – Resolve Visual Studio Errors

13. We can now replace the values of arguments within the function

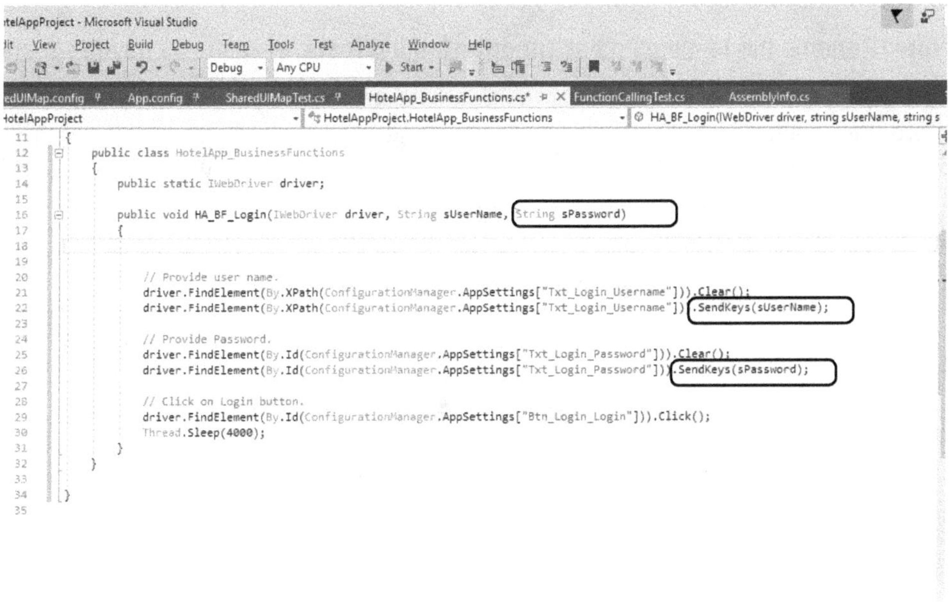

Figure 12.15 – Replace Arguments

Note: You would have noticed that we are not returning any value as part of this function; hence the return type is **void.** If we were to return any variable value, we could have used appropriate return type (int, String, etc.) and used the **return** statement to return the value.

12.2. Calling a Function in WebDriver Script

1.   Double click on copied script **"FunctionCallingTest.cs"** to see the script.

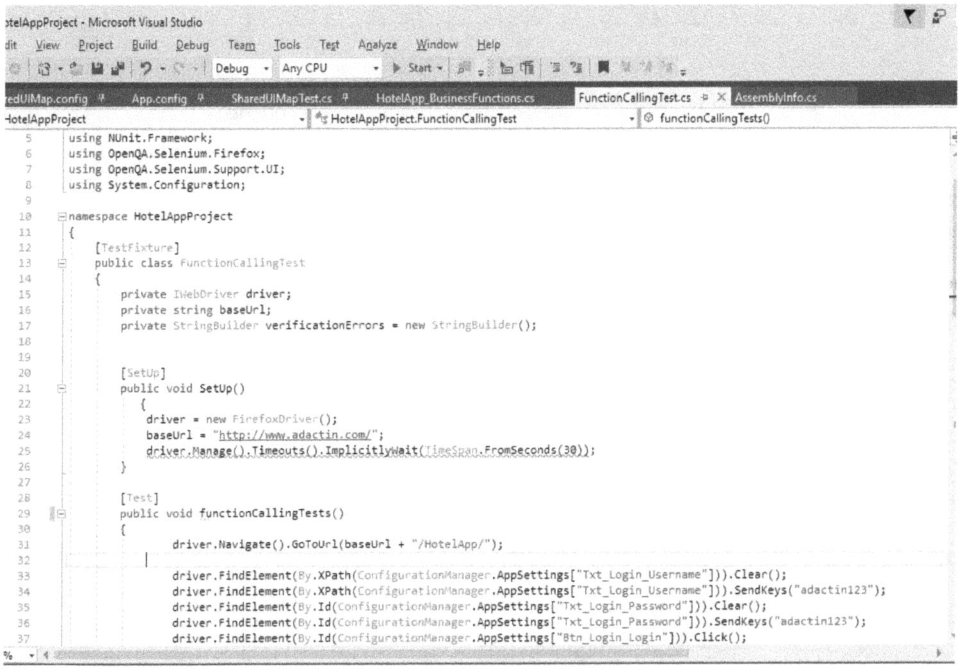

Figure 12.16 – FunctionCallingTest Script

Note: Rename the test method as **functionCallingTests**, in case you haven't changed it earlier.

2. In order to use the function just created, we will need to inherit function class in the script. Use the statement below to import the class HotelApp_BusinessFunctions.

```
class FunctionCallingTest : HotelApp_BusinessFunctions
```

Figure 12.17 – Inheriting the Function Class

3. The script will look like

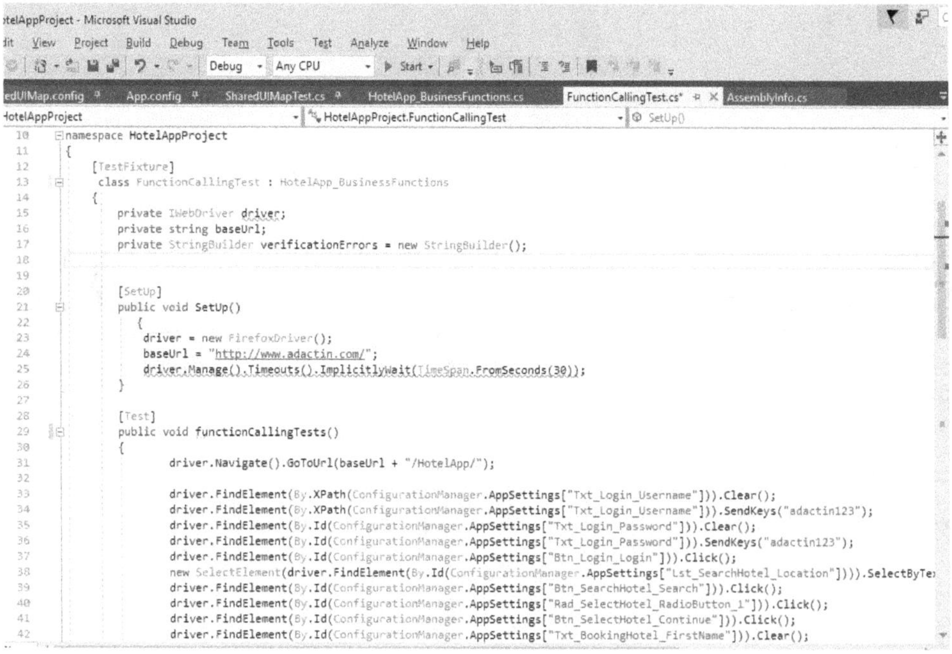

Figure 12.18 – Extend Test Class to Inherit Functions

4. The next step is to make the existing test case to inherit functions from our function library file **HotelApp_BusinessFunctions**.

5. Update the declarations for variables driver which has already been declared in Functions file.

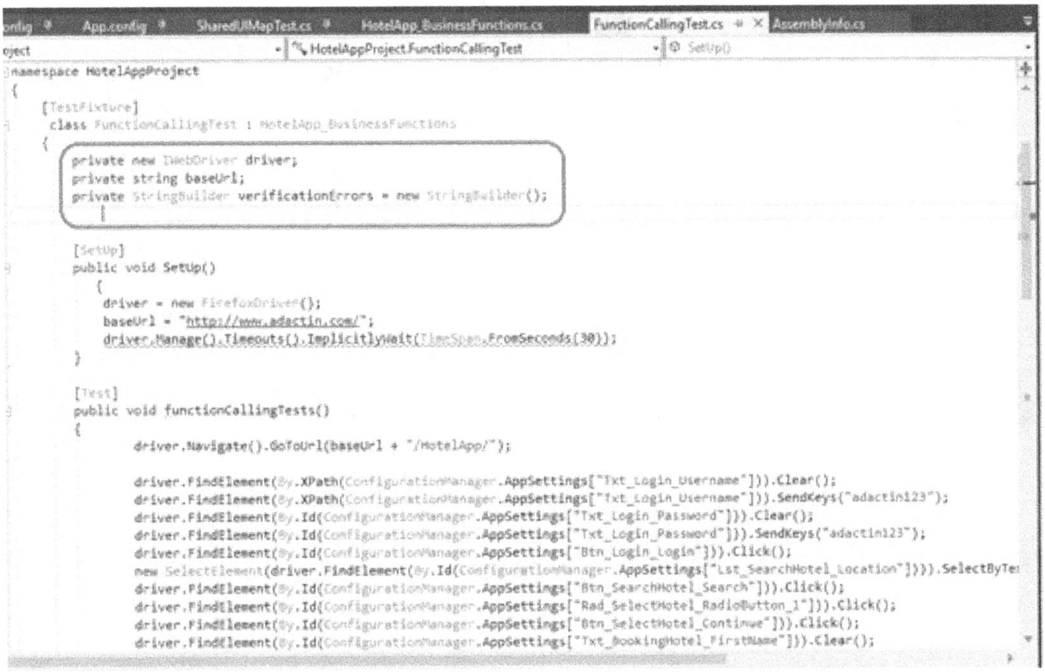

Figure 12.19 – Update Already Defined Variables

6. Make a call to **HA_BF_Login** function and comment out the existing steps from the script.

Figure 12.20 – Call Function

7. Save and click on **Build>Build Solution**.

8. Select the test and Run the test by clicking on **Run the selected test**. Confirm the test can run fine.

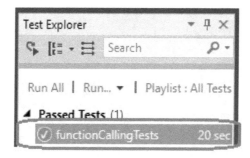

Figure 12.21 – Run Results

 Important Step:

We need to take into account this particular step whenever we are creating Test Suites or NUnit projects.

In the **HotelApp_BusinessFunctions** we need to add a code snippet to kill the **geckodriver** process. Since this is a common class used by many test scripts, we have added our code here. If the test executes correctly and the driver is closed in the Teardown function, Selenium automatically kills the process but in case of an incorrect driver shutdown due to exception or something, the geckodriver process remains open. In such a scenario, we need to explicitly kill the process in our code as shown below. Otherwise, the build fails when you try to run the tests again.

Use **SetupFixture** annotation for any setup which needs to be applied globally. The Fixtures inside this class is executed before any other fixtures when the tests start running.

```
[SetUpFixture]
public class GlobalSetup
{
    //To Kill Any existing geckodriver processes
    [OneTimeSetUp]
    public void KillGeckoDriver()
    {
        foreach (var proc in Process.GetProcessesByName("geckodriver"))
        {
            proc.Kill();
        }
    }
}
```

Figure 12.22 – Kill Geckodriver Process

Assembly wide initialization -- If you don't put the class in any namespace, it will apply to all tests in the assembly. In the above code, we are putting the code under OneTimeSetup so that it executes just once when the tests in the test suite start running.

EXERCISE

1. Create a function for each of the modules below and save them in the HotelApp_ BusinessFunctions file.

    - Search Hotel.
    - Select Hotel.
    - Hotel Booking.
    - Logout.

Replace existing script with function calls to these functions.

13. Using a Configuration File

During automation, we work with various parameters which are dynamic in nature. For instance, application path or the URL may vary based on the environment we are running the scripts (stage or test environment) on. This would mean we would need to change parameter values based on our execution needs.

Secondly, if we have a lot of scripts, we would need to change these parameter values in each and every script.

example

In the previous script that we created, we had the application URL (www.adactin.com/HotelApp/) defined within our script. Now assume we have automated 100+ scripts and our project manager wants us to execute these test cases in the staging environment or Build2 (which has a different URL, www.adactin.com/HotelAppBuild2). In order to run our scripts in different environments, we would need to go into each of the scripts and modify the URL value.

And guess what, if next time our project manager wants us to rerun the scripts in a different test environment, we would need to update the scripts again. That can be a nightmare!

A better solution would be to keep these dynamic values in a configuration file which is centrally located and shared between all scripts. So we make a change at a single place and it will help all of the scripts get updated parameter values.

Another fundamental automation rule is we would want to avoid making code/script changes for these parameter related changes as these can cause regression issues in the script. So making changes in a configuration file will be a safer way to update parameter values.

Key objectives:

- Create a configuration file.
- Using a configuration file parameter within the WebDriver script.

13.1. Create a Configuration File

Let's add a UI Map to our project.

1. Select the Project Folder **HotelApp_TestAutomation**, Right-click and select **Add > New Folder**.

Figure 13.1 – Add New Folder

2. A new folder will get added.

Figure 13.2 – New Folder

3. Rename the Folder as **Configuration**.

Figure 13.3 – Configuration Folder

4. Click and drag the existing **SharedUIMap.config** and move it to the new **Configuration** folder. The folder will look like this.

Figure 13.4 – Configuration Folder

5. Double click and open the **SharedUIMap.config file** and add all the dynamic parameters that can affect our script.

So our property file SharedUIMap.config should look like this.

```
#//////////Application URL//////////

<add key="sAppURL"  value="http://www.adactin.com/HotelApp/"/>
```

Figure 13.5 – Web Elements Name Value Pair

Note: We will add more parameters in the coming chapters.

6.   Save the file using **File → Save** or **Ctrl + S**.

13.2. Using Configuration File Parameters in a Script

Now that we have created an external configuration file, we want to use it in our script. Let us follow these steps to create a script which uses a Configuration file.

1.   **Right-click** on your existing FunctionCallingTest.cs script and select **Copy.**

2.   Select the **project**, **right-click** and select **Paste.**

3.   Rename the new script as **ConfigurationFileTest.cs** and click **OK.**

4.   Let us design our script to read parameters from our Configuration file. We will follow these steps to modify the script:

   a.   Click on **App.config**. Update the SharedUIMap file path.

```xml
<?xml version="1.0" encoding="utf-8" ?>
<configuration>
  <appSettings configSource ="Configuration\SharedUIMap.config">
  </appSettings>
</configuration>
```

Figure 13.6 – SharedUIMap File Path

5.   Double click on the new **"ConfigurationFileTest.cs"** script so that you can see the script.

 Note: The classname and the test method names should be updated accordingly.

6.   In the test method, update the script where the URL is passed on as

```
driver.Navigate().GoToUrl(ConfigurationManager.AppSettings["sAppURL"]);
```

Figure 13.7 – URL

Your script should appear as in the figure below:

```
SharedUIMap.config   App.config    SharedUIMapTest.cs    ConfigurationFileTest.cs ×  FunctionCallingTest.cs
HotelAppProject                  HotelAppProject.ConfigurationFileTest        configurationFileTest()
  4    using System.Text;
  5    using NUnit.Framework;
  6    using OpenQA.Selenium.Firefox;
  7    using OpenQA.Selenium.Support.UI;
  8    using System.Configuration;
  9
 10    namespace HotelAppProject
 11    {
 12        [TestFixture]
 13        class ConfigurationFileTest : HotelApp_BusinessFunctions
 14        {
 15            private new IWebDriver driver;
 16            private string baseUrl;
 17            private StringBuilder verificationErrors = new StringBuilder();
 18
 19
 20            [SetUp]
 21            public void SetUp()
 22            {
 23                driver = new FirefoxDriver();
 24                baseUrl = "http://www.adactin.com/";
 25                driver.Manage().Timeouts().ImplicitlyWait(TimeSpan.FromSeconds(30));
 26            }
 27
 28            [Test]
 29            public void configurationFileTest()
 30            {
 31                // driver.Navigate().GoToUrl(baseUrl + "/HotelApp/");
 32
 33                driver.Navigate().GoToUrl(ConfigurationManager.AppSettings["sAppURL"]);
 34
 35                // Calling the Login Function
 36                HA_BF_Login(driver, "adactin123", "adactin123");
 37
100 %
```

Figure 13.8 – Script Changes

7. Save the changes and Click on **Build > Build Solution**.

8. Select the test and Run the test using **Run → Run the Selected Test**. Confirm that the test can run fine.

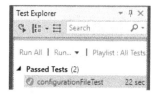

Figure 13.9 – Test Results

EXERCISE

1. Create a new function which will load a configuration file and a SharedUIMap file in a function library file.

2. Create a copy of an existing script and call this function in your script.

14. Data Driven Testing - Parameterization

Introduction

In many instances, when we perform regression testing, we need to repeat the same test case with different sets of data. This can be a monotonous and time-consuming task, depending on how many different data sets are required for the test case.

 Let us take an example:

I worked for one of our retail domain clients as part of the testing and automation team which had more than 2000 stores in the country. They had developed a point of sales system. Once this was manually tested, they gave us a list of more than 10000 usernames and password pairs and asked us to set them up in the system. As a testing team, our task was to verify if all usernames and passwords were set up correctly. We were given a target of .01% failure threshold. If we had to verify all this manually, assuming we would verify 1 username/password combination every 1 minute (as there were a couple of validations we had to do once logged in), it would have taken us 5000 minutes or approximately 20-24 days of man effort. Imagine how laborious and time-consuming that task would have been.

Solution: Wouldn't it be great if you had an automated script that could pick up the first username and password entered from an Excel sheet, log the user in and perform all the validations without any manual intervention?

An even better solution would be to create a script to iterate across all the 10000 usernames and passwords. It took us less than 4 hours to develop the script, ran it overnight, got the failed records, again re-tested the records once fixed and delivered it to the customer with 0% issues. The concept of running the same script with multiple dataset values is called **Parameterization**.

Any test case which needs to be executed multiple times with different data values is an ideal candidate for automation.

Another objective of Data Driven tests is to keep all of the test data in one central location.

example Let us take an example.

Suppose you have 200+ scripts and all the scripts start with login which needs a username and password. Where should you be keeping this test data? If this data is residing within the script, and for some reason your username or password changes, you would need to go in each script and make these changes.

Is there a better solution?

Wouldn't it be nice if you could have all of this data in one central file so that all of the scripts which need username/password refer to just one file? If any of the usernames/passwords change, then we just make the change(s) at one location and all of the scripts will be good to go.

Key objectives:

- Data driving the script to read specific data from a central location.
- How to parameterize a Selenium WebDriver script to execute the same steps for multiple sets of data.

14.1. <u>Data Drive a Script with a Single Value from an Excel Sheet</u>

Selenium does not provide any out-of-the-box solution for data driven testing but leaves it up to the user to implement this on his/her own. To implement data driven tests in Selenium we can take multiple approaches which include:

- Reading test data from an Excel file using NUnit.
- Creating a data driven test using NUnit.
- Reading test data from a CSV file using NUnit.
- Reading test data from a database using NUnit and ODBC.
- Creating a data driven test in JUnit, Ruby or Python.

As part of this chapter, we will discuss how to read test data from an Excel file using NUnit for parameterization.

To use Excel sheets as our data source we need to do the following:

1. Create a Data file in MS Excel.
2. Create a c# function to fetch the data from the file.
3. Parameterize our script to use the data.

We store test data in the form of tables within an Excel sheet. One table can have any number of columns. A table always begins with a column header row. This column header, along with the row number, is used for accessing the data.

Problem Description: Let us try to create a script which will read data from the first row of the data sheet and search hotel based on the retrieved value.

Let us see how to implement this.

<u>Step 1 – Add ExcelReader from NuGet Package</u>

1. Right-click on the **HotelAppProject**. Click on **Manage NuGet Packages**.

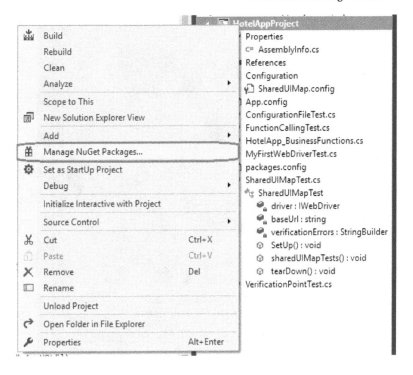

Figure 14.1 – Manage NuGet Packages

2. Under the **Browse** tab, search for **Excel**. Click on **ExcelDataReader** and click on **Install**.

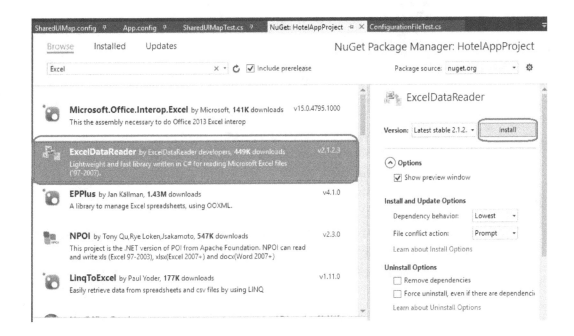

Figure 14.2 – ExcelDataReader

3. A preview window will pop-up intimating the user about the intended changes. Click on **Ok**.

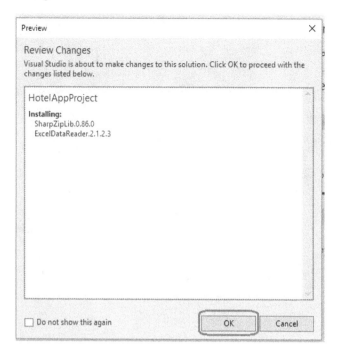

Figure 14.3 – Preview

4. An Excel reference will get added to the **Reference**.

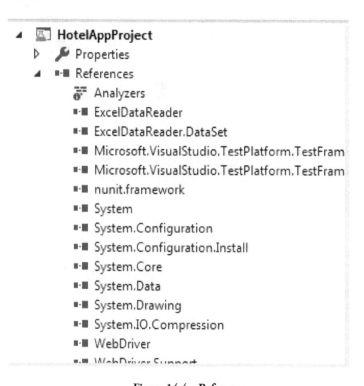

Figure 14.4 – Reference

Step 2 - Create a Data file in MS Excel

1. Select C# Project **HotelAppProject** and right-click and select **Add > New Folder**.

2. Add a new folder called *DataPools* to our project.

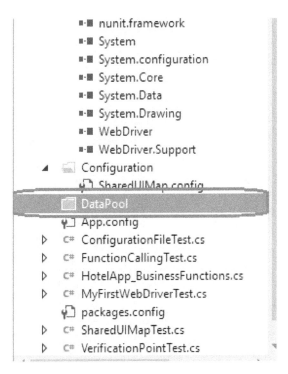

Figure 14.5 – DataPool Folder

This is the folder in which we keep all of our data files for the project.

3. Create an Excel file named **HA_HotelSearch.xls** and store data in the following format

ID	Location
1	Sydney
2	Brisbane
3	Melbourne
4	Adelaide
5	ENDOFROW

Figure 14.6 – Excel Sheet Content

Note that we have entered "ENDOFROW" in the last row to indicate there is no more data left to be read in the datasheet. Rename the Sheet name as HA_HotelSearch.

Save this file in the *DataPool* folder of our project and close the sheet

(C:\Visual Studio\HotelAppProject\HotelAppProject\DataPools).

Note: The relative path to our file is ".*DataPools*\ HA_HotelSearch.xlsx". Save the excel file as HA_HotelSearch.xlsx.

4. Within your visual studio project, select your **HotelAppProject**. **Right-click** on **DataPools.** Click on **Add > Existing Item**.

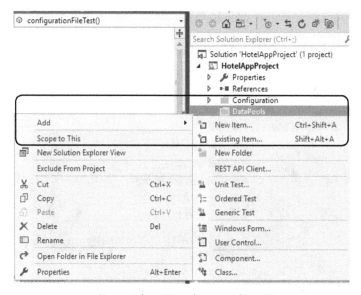

Figure 14.7 – Datasheet in Eclipse View

5. Click on the **HA_HotelSeach.xlsx** file and click on **Add**.

6. The Excel file will be added to the DataPools folder.

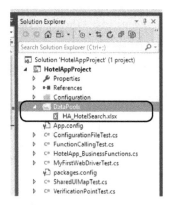

Figure 14.8 – Datasheet in Visual Studio View

Step 3 - Create a C# function to fetch the data from the Excel file

Now that we have created our external datasheet file, we would want to use it in our script. Before that we need to create a new class file that will read the data from the Excel sheet.

1. Right-click on the **HotelAppProject. Add>class**.

2. Give the name as ExcelLibrary and click on Add.

3. A new class ExcelLibrary.cs will be added to the project.

4. Now insert the following script in the class file.

```
  public static List<Datacollection> dataCol;
  private static DataTable ExcelToDataTable(string fileName)
  {
    //open file and returns as Stream
    string localPath = new Uri(fileName).LocalPath;
    FileStream stream = File.Open(localPath, FileMode.Open, FileAccess.Read);
    //Createopenxmlreader via ExcelReaderFactory
    IExcelDataReader excelReader = ExcelReaderFactory.
CreateOpenXmlReader(stream); //.xlsx

//Set the First Row as Column Name
  //Return as DataSet
    DataSet result = excelReader.AsDataSet(new ExcelDataSetConfiguration()
                                            {
    ConfigureDataTable = (_) => new ExcelDataTableConfiguration()
                                            {
    UseHeaderRow = true

                                            }
                                            });

    //Get all the Tables
    DataTableCollection table = result.Tables;
    //Store it in DataTable
    DataTable resultTable = table["Sheet1"];
    //return
    return resultTable;
  }
  public static void PopulateInCollection()
  {
    dataCol = new List<Datacollection>();
    string filepath = Path.GetDirectoryName(Assembly.GetExecutingAssembly().
CodeBase);
    DataTable table = ExcelToDataTable(filepath + "\\DataPools\\HA_HotelSearch.
xlsx");
  }
  public class Datacollection
  {
    public int rowNumber { get; set; }
    public string colName { get; set; }
    public string colValue { get; set; }
  }
}
```

Figure 14.9 – Code Snippet for ExcelLibrary Class File

5. You will find that there are a lot of errors in the script. It can be fixed by adding the following:

- Using Excel.

- Using System.Reflection.

- Using.Data.

6. The **ExcelLibrary.cs** file will look like this.

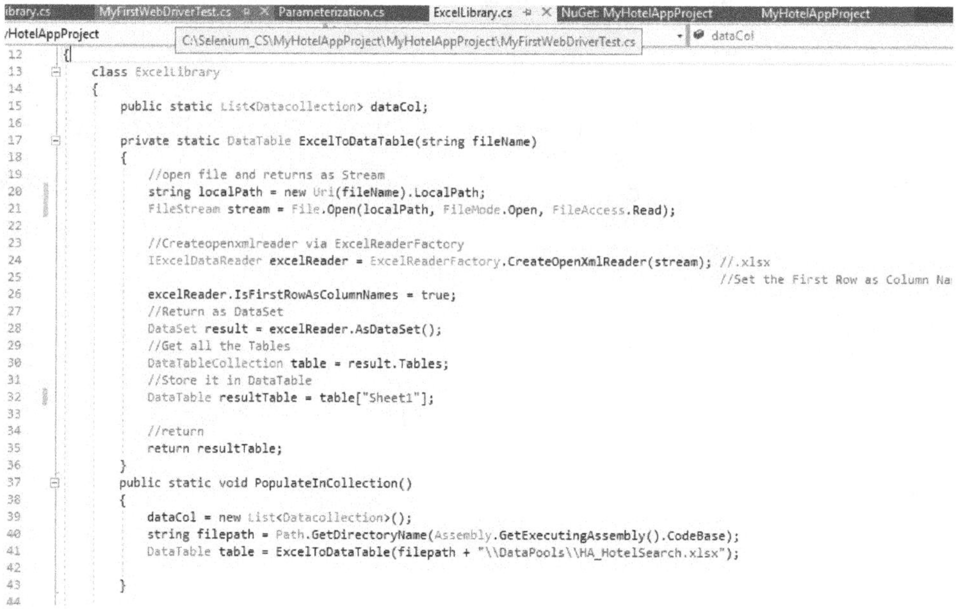

Figure 14.10 – ExcelLibrary Script

Step 4 – Calling the function in C# Class file

1. **Right-click** on your existing **ConfigurationFileTest.cs** script, select **Copy**.

2. Select the **project**, **right-click** and select **Paste**.

3. Rename the new script as **Parameterization.cs** and click **OK**.

4. In the test method, insert the following script.

```
//Comment - Call to Login Function
HA_BF_Login(driver, "adactin123", "adactin123");
ExcelLibrary.PopulateInCollection();
```

Figure 14.11 – Code Snippet for ParameterizationTest Script

Your script should appear as in the figure below:

```
ParameterizationTest.cs  ×   ExcelLibrary.cs      ConfigurationFileTest.cs      FunctionCallingTest.cs
HotelAppProject                          HotelAppProject.ParameterizationTest        parameterizationTest()

18
19          [SetUp]
20          public void SetUp()
21          {
22              driver = new FirefoxDriver();
23              driver.Manage().Timeouts().ImplicitlyWait(TimeSpan.FromSeconds(30));
24          }
25
26          [Test]
27          public void parameterizationTest()
28          {
29              driver.Navigate().GoToUrl(ConfigurationManager.AppSettings["sAppURL"]);
30              driver.Manage().Window.Maximize();
31
32              //Call to Login Function
33              HA_BF_Login(driver, "adactin123", "adactin123");
34
35
36              ExcelLibrary.PopulateInCollection();
37
38
39              new SelectElement(driver.FindElement(By.Id(ConfigurationManager.AppSettings["Lst
40              driver.FindElement(By.Id(ConfigurationManager.AppSettings["Btn_SearchHotel_Searc
41              driver.FindElement(By.Id(ConfigurationManager.AppSettings["Rad_SelectHotel_Radio
42              driver.FindElement(By.Id(ConfigurationManager.AppSettings["Btn_SelectHotel_Conti
43              driver.FindElement(By.Id(ConfigurationManager.AppSettings["Txt_BookingHotel_Firs
44              driver.FindElement(By.Id(ConfigurationManager.AppSettings["Txt_BookingHotel_Firs
45              driver.FindElement(By.Id(ConfigurationManager.AppSettings["Txt_BookingHotel_Lastl
46              driver.FindElement(By.Id(ConfigurationManager.AppSettings["Txt_BookingHotel_Lastl
47              driver.FindElement(By.Id(ConfigurationManager.AppSettings["Txt_BookingHotel_Addr
48              driver.FindElement(By.Id(ConfigurationManager.AppSettings["Txt_BookingHotel_Addr
49              driver.FindElement(By.Id(ConfigurationManager.AppSettings["Txt_BookingHotel_CCNu
50              driver.FindElement(By.Id(ConfigurationManager.AppSettings["Txt_BookingHotel_CCNu
51              new SelectElement(driver.FindElement(By.Id(ConfigurationManager.AppSettings["Lst
```

Figure 14.12 – ParameterizationTest Script

5. Save the changes and Click on **Build > Build Solution**.

6. Select the test and Run the test using **Run → Run the Selected Test**. Confirm that the test can run fine.

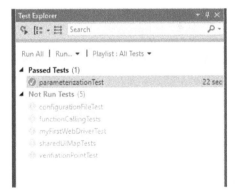

Figure 14.13 – Run Test

EXERCISE

1. Run the above script for row value 2 and verify it reads the second location correctly.

14.2. <u>Parameterize the Script with Multiple Values from an Excel Sheet</u>

In the previous example, we read data from an Excel data sheet. The advantage we got was to keep all data files at a central location and share them among all of the scripts. If data values need to change, we can change them at one central location instead of repeatedly changing them in all of the scripts.

Another aspect of data driven testing is parameterization when we can run the same script for multiple sets of data values.

Problem Description: Let us try to create a script which will create multiple bookings for different locations (Sydney, Brisbane, Melbourne, and Adelaide) in the Search Hotel page.

Solution: Based on our previous script, we now know how to read data from an Excel datasheet. If we know how many rows of data are available in the Excel sheet, we can use any looping statement (like for, while) to loop the script for the number of rows available in the datasheet.

So as a solution we can create a function which will return the maximum number of valid rows in an Excel sheet and use its return value to loop through the script.

Let us see the steps given below to parameterize the script to run for multiple values:

1. Double click on **"ExcelLibrary.cs"** to see the code in the functions file.

2. In the **PopulateInCollection** method, add the following script. It fetches the data from each row and column in the Excel sheet.

```csharp
for (int row = 1; row <= table.Rows.Count; row++)
        {
                for (int col = 0; col <= table.Columns.Count - 1; col++)
                {
                    Datacollection dtTable = new Datacollection()
                    {
                        rowNumber = row,
                        colName = table.Columns[col].ColumnName,
                        colValue = table.Rows[row - 1][col].ToString()
                    };
                    //Add all the details for each row
                    dataCol.Add(dtTable);
```

Figure 14.14 – Code Snippet for PopulateInCollection Method

 Note: Table.Rows.Count() gives the count of the maximum number of rows.

Table.ColumsColumns.Count() gives the count of the maximum number of columns.

3. Add the following method. ReadData() retrieves data from each row and column and passes the value to the object dtTable.

```
public static string ReadData(int rowNumber, string columnName)
        {
        try
        {

            string data = (from colData in dataCol
                            where colData.colName == columnName && colData.
rowNumber == rowNumber

                                select colData.colValue).SingleOrDefault();


            return data.ToString();
        }
        catch (Exception)
        {
            return null;
        }
    }
```

Figure 14.15 – Code Snippet for Readdata() in ExcelLibrary Class File

4. Verify that there are no syntax errors. Try to resolve syntax errors if any exist. **Save** the ExcelLibrary.cs file.
5. Right-click on your existing **ParameterizationTest.cs** script, select **Copy**.
6. Select the tests package folder, right-click and select **Paste**.
7. In the Name Conflict dialog box, enter the name of the script as **ParameterizationLoopTest. cs** and click OK.

 Note: Rename the class file according to the naming conventions.

8. Double click the **ParameterizationLoopTest**.cs file and add the code in [Test] below the ExcelLibrary.PopulateInCollection to read from the Excel sheet.

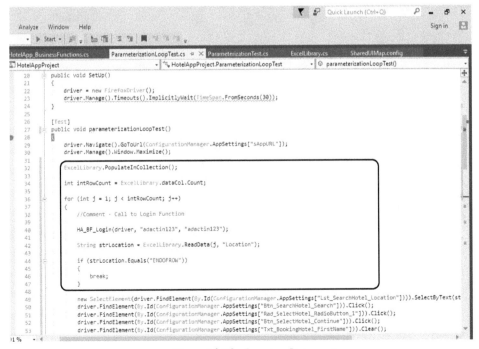

Figure 14.16 – Looping Statement

The key things to modify include:

- Use a for loop to loop through the maximum number of rows.

- Pass the value as SelectByText(strLocation) instead of hardcoding.

- Do not forget to close the for loop with a closing parenthesis.

9. Save the test and perform **Build > Build Solution**.

10. Select and run the test using **Run** > **Run the Selected Test.** Confirm that the test can run fine with the correct location value.

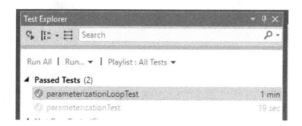

Figure 14.17 – Run Test

15. Synchronizing WebDriver Scripts

In any Web automation project, the automation success depends upon the robustness of your scripts; whether that's adaptation of your code to project or software changes or synchronization of the script with the site's performance.

Many a time, your application performance will vary which will require you to manipulate your WebDriver script's execution speed.

In one of the applications that we tested, it took more than 60 seconds for an application form to save and confirm that save was successful. How does WebDriver support these situations?

Synchronization is a critical issue for any test automation script. You may think that synchronization of test script actions is a built-in ability of today's functional testing tools. Reality shows that many unexpected test script failures are related to synchronization issues generating false negative results. These false negatives make it hard to detect real application problems as each test script failure may be related to a test script synchronization issue. Synchronization errors are timing issues, therefore, they are non-deterministic, heavily dependent on the HW/SW, the network, and their utilization. The biggest challenge in automating a Web application is the loading of a Web page which is always at the mercy of certain conditions, such as:

- Load on the server.
- Network speed.
- Performance of AUT.
- Ajax call to load an element.

Key objectives:

- What is Synchronization?
- Approaches to script synchronization.
- Synchronizing a script.

15.1. What is Synchronization?

What is script synchronization?

Test scripts need to be synchronized in a way that the script driving the application **waits** until the AUT is ready to accept the next user input.

The following are some situations where synchronization is required:

- The creation of a window (more general control) must be completed before it can receive messages/commands.
- A page is completely loaded before you can click on a link on the page.
- A button must be activated before you can click on it.
- A data grid has loaded a row before you can verify the row.
- A data grid has loaded completely before you can verify the row count of the grid.
- A tree is expanded before you can select one of its children.
- Selecting a tree node, the details pane of the node needs to be completely loaded before you can verify text on it.

Ajax-specific synchronization problems

Ajax is shorthand for Asynchronous JavaScript and XML. With Ajax, Web applications can retrieve data from the server asynchronously in the background without interfering with the display and behavior of the existing page. The use of Ajax techniques has led to an increase in interactive or dynamic interfaces on Web pages. Data is usually retrieved using the XMLHttpRequest object. The asynchronous nature of Ajax makes it hard to detect when an Ajax request is fulfilled and when the application is ready to proceed with the next UI interaction (as the UI is not blocked while executing the request).

Even worse, the current browsers do not indicate the execution and the end of the execution of Ajax-based requests. Processing normal HTML pages is indicated visually by an animated icon in the browser and programmatically by an event that is fired when processing is completed. This means that there is no easy way to decide when the application is ready to process the next UI action. Usually, this is not a problem for humans because we have multiple cognitive techniques to detect if an application is ready to proceed. Humans are also not that fast when working with an application compared to "computer programs" like test automation tools that are driving the application. So many of the synchronization problems do not appear when a human is accessing the application. But asynchronous behavior as seen in Ajax applications is a real nightmare for a testing tool.

15.2. Approaches Used for Script Synchronization

So the major task in automating Web applications is to wait for the HTML element to appear in the page before your automation test code starts performing an action on them. You need to make sure that the Web element is present before the code begins working on it. This can be achieved by waiting for the element to appear in the page. For synchronization, we can implement three different execution control mechanisms:

1. Implicit wait – Used to set the default wait time throughout the program.
2. Explicit wait – Used to set the wait time for a particular instance only.
3. The global controlling of wait times.

Implicit Wait

An implicit wait is to tell WebDriver to poll the DOM for a certain amount of time when trying to find an element or elements if they are not immediately available. The default setting is 0. Once set, the implicit wait is set for the life of the WebDriver object instance.

```
driver.Manage().Timeouts().ImplicitWait = TimeSpan.FromSeconds(10);
```

This means that you are setting 10 seconds to be your default wait time whenever the driver comes across a situation where it can't find the required element or condition.

Explicit Static Wait

The simplest and easiest way to handle synchronization is to use the **Explicit static wait** statement in scripts. If you know that the application can take up to 60 seconds to respond, you can enter a *Thread.Sleep* statement after the step where you want WebDriver to wait which will **"pause"** the script for 60 seconds. See the statement below.

Thread.Sleep(timeToSleep);

The disadvantage of using static wait statements is that the script will **wait for the entire 60 seconds,** even though the application might respond quicker.

Automation testers should be careful while adding wait statements, as this increases the overall test execution time of the automation suite.

Note: You can define time to wait as a global variable. The benefit of this is that we can control the wait time centrally according to our AUT performance.

public int expectedWaitTime = 10;

And then we use this global variable as an argument for **all** our explicit wait methods.

Thread.Sleep(expectedWaitTime);

Explicit Dynamic Wait

We noticed in the above Static Wait statement that the script will wait for the entire time mentioned in the Wait statement. A better option would be for the WebDriver script to smartly wait or forge ahead based on an expected visual cue which will save overall script execution time.

Explicit Dynamic wait can be achieved in multiple ways:

- Using a WebDriverWait Class.
- Using a custom function to wait for an element's existence.

Using a WebDriverWait Class

A **WebDriverWait** class is used in combination with an **ExpectedCondition** class, which provides an elegant way to implement Explicit Wait.

The Selenium WebDriver provides WebDriverWait and ExpectedConditions classes for implementing an Explicit wait.

The ExpectedConditions class provides a set of predefined conditions to wait for using WebDriverWait before proceeding further in the code. The following table shows some common conditions that we frequently come across when automating Web browsers supported by the ExpectedCondition class:

Selenium method	Detail
ElementToBeClickable (By locator)	An expectation for checking an element is visible and enabled such that you can click it.
ElementToBeSelected (IWebElement element)	An expectation for checking if the given element is selected.
ElementExists (By locator)	An expectation for checking that an element is present on the DOM of a page. This does not necessarily mean that the element is visible.
PresenceOfAllElements LocatedBy (By locator)	An expectation for checking that all elements present on the Web page that match the locator.
TextToBePresentInElement (By locator)	An expectation for checking if the given text is present in the specified element.
TextToBePresentInElementValue (By locator,String text)	An expectation for checking if the given text is present in the specified elements value attribute.
TitleContains(String title)	An expectation for checking that the title of a page contains a case-sensitive substring.
ElementIsVisible(WebElement element)	An expectation for checking that an element, known to be present on the DOM of a page, is visible.
InvisibilityOfElementLocated (By locator)	An expectation for checking that an element is either invisible or not present on the DOM.
VisibilityOfAllElementsLocatedBy (By locator)	An expectation for checking that all elements present on the Web page that match the locator are visible. Visibility means that the elements are not only displayed but also have a height and width greater than 0.

Table-15.1 – ExpectedConditions Class

Note: More details on ExpectedConditions Class can be found at the link: https://msdn. microsoft.com/en-us/library/gg131072.aspx.

For the following example, we shall wait up to 10 seconds for an element whose id is "Logout" to become visible before proceeding to the next command.

WebDriverWait and ExpectedConditions are a part of the OpenQA.Selenium.Support.UI namespace. So, we have to include this namespace in our class if it is not already present.

Use myWait with ExpectedConditions on portions where you need the explicit wait to occur. In this case, we will use explicit wait to wait on for logout button appears after you book a hotel and get an order number for the order (AdactIn Hotel App Booking Confirmation Page) before we click onto it. See the code snippet below:

```
WebDriverWait myWait = new WebDriverWait(driver, TimeSpan.FromSeconds(10));
myWait.Until(ExpectedConditions.ElementIsVisible(By.Id(ConfigurationManager.
AppSettings[
"Btn_BookingHotel_Logout"])));
driver.FindElement(By.LinkText(ConfigurationManager.AppSettings["Lnk_BookingHo-
tel_Logout"
])).Click();
```

Figure 15.1 – Code Snippet for Explicit Wait

Using a Custom function

Function to explicitly wait for WebElement Presence

We can even create a custom function to wait for the presence of a WebElement using WebDriver FindElement method.

```
//Function to dynamically wait for element presence
        public void HA_GF_WaitForElementPresent(IWebDriver driver, By by, int
iTimeOut)
            {
            try
            {
                int iTotal = 0;
                int iSleepTime = 5000;
                while (iTotal < iTimeOut)
                {
                    IReadOnlyCollection<IWebElement> iWebElements = driver.
FindElements(by);
                    if (iWebElements.Count > 0)
                        return;
                    else
                    {

                        Thread.Sleep(iSleepTime);
                        iTotal = iTotal + iSleepTime;
                        Console.Write(String.Concat("Waited for " + iTotal +
" milliseconds " + by));


                    }
                }
            }
            catch (ElementNotVisibleException)
            {
                return;
            }

        }
```

Figure 15.2 - Sample Code for Explicit Wait for Element Present

Include this Custom function in **HotelApp_BusinessFuncitons.cs** class which we created earlier to hold all the common functions.

Note: Above code and other script snippets can be copied from www.adactin.com/stores section.

The above code uses the following logic:

- Input arguments: driver object, locator and timeout.
- Function FindElements returns a list of objects as defined by the locator argument.
- If the WebElement is found, then the function returns to the main script.
- If the Webelement is not found, then the function waits for iSleepTime (defined in the function) and again searches for the element.
- iSleeptime repeats until either the Webelement is found or the Wait time exceeds iTimeout.

Note: You will need to include namespace OpenQA.Selenium and System.Collections. Generic; Visual Studio will automatically suggest this after you paste the code into the Visual Studio IDE. If Visual Studio throws any other error try to resolve it using basic .Net knowledge.

The above custom function can also be enhanced to wait until a specific object property value is achieved using the GetAttribute method.

Function to explicit wait for WebElement property value matches expected value

```csharp
//Function to dynamically wait for Webelement to achieve its property value
        public void HA_GF_WaitForPropertyValue(IWebDriver driver, By by,
String ExpPropertyVal, String PropertName, int iTimeOut)
        {
            try
            {
                int iTotal = 0;
                int iSleepTime = 5000;
                while (iTotal < iTimeOut)
                {
                    IReadOnlyCollection<IWebElement> oWebElements = driver.
FindElements(by);
                        if (oWebElements.Count > 0)
                            foreach (IWebElement weOption in oWebElements)
                            {
                                if (ExpPropertyVal.Equals(weOption.
GetAttribute(PropertName), StringComparison.InvariantCultureIgnoreCase))
                                return;

                    else

                        {
                            Thread.Sleep(iSleepTime);
                            iTotal = iTotal + iSleepTime;
                            Console.Write(String.Concat("Waited for "
+ iTotal + " milliseconds " + by));
                        }
                    }

                else
                {

                    Thread.Sleep(iSleepTime);
                    iTotal = iTotal + iSleepTime;
                    Console.Write(String.Concat("Waited for " + iTotal
+ " milliseconds " + by));
                }
            }
        }
        catch (NoSuchElementException)
        {
            return;
        }
    }
```

Figure 15.3 – Sample Code for Explicit Wait for Property Value Existence

Include this Custom function in **HotelApp_BusinessFuncitons.cs** class which we created earlier to hold all the common functions.

Note: The above code and other script snippets can be copied from www.adactin.com/stores section.

15.3. Using Script Synchronization in a Script

Let us take a practical scenario to illustrate script synchronization.

Problem Description – As part of our Hotel booking workflow, when a user clicks on **Book Now** an order number is generated. We need to write this order number in the result.

The challenge here is that when a user clicks on the "Book Now" button it takes approximately 6-8 seconds before the order number is generated. So, to resolve this we need script synchronization.

Solution – We can follow multiple solutions to this problem.

- Use Static Wait, which is the easiest and simplest of all, before you fetch the value from the order number field.
- Use Explicit Wait to wait for the existence of the Logout Button. The Logout button only appears after the order number has been generated.

Solution – 1 – Using Static Wait

Use the following steps to get the order number using a Static Wait:

1. **Right- click** on your existing class FunctionCallingTest.cs and select **Copy**.

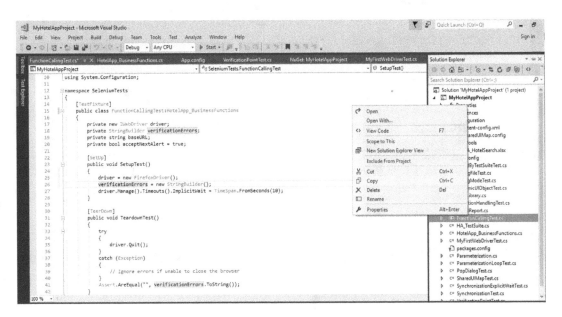

Figure 15.4 – Copy of Existing Class

2. Select the **project** and click on paste.

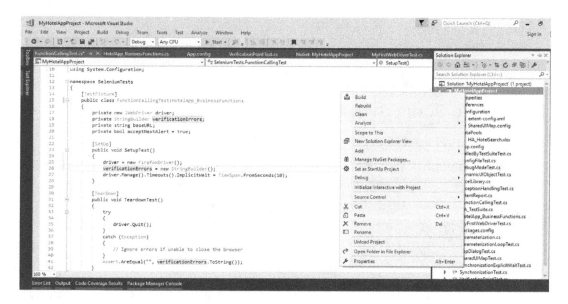

Figure 15.5 – Paste Script

A copy of the class file will be created. Right-click on the new class file to rename. Rename to **"SynchronizationTest.cs"**. Click **OK**.

Figure 15.6 – Rename

3. Click on the newly created **"SynchronizationTest.cs" script** so that you can see the script.

Figure 15.7 – SynchronizationTest

4. Rename the class name from FunctionCallingTest to SynchronizationTest under TestFixture and save the file.

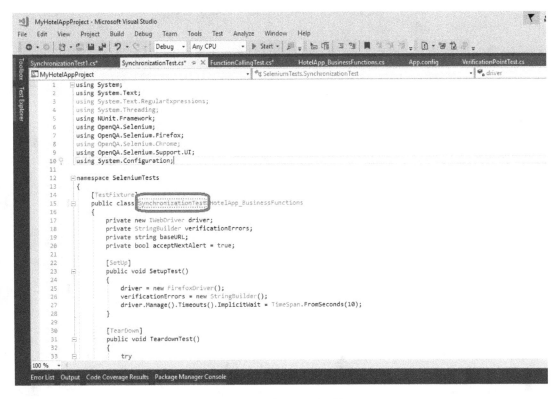

Figure 15.8 – Rename the Classname

Note that after we click on the Book Now button, we will need to add a Static Wait statement using the Thread.Sleep(timeout) method and use GetAttribute to fetch the value from the Order Number. field.

Before we do this, we need to add Locator details for the Order No. field and Logout button in our SharedUIMap file.

5. Use the Inspector to inspect the element and get the locator value for the Order No.field.

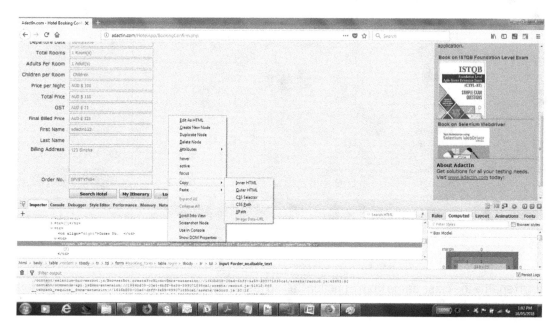

Figure 15.9 - Locator Value for Order No. Field

6. Use the inspector to inspect the element and get the locator values for Logout button.

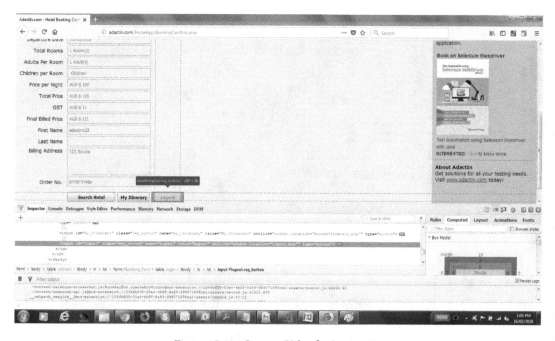

Figure 15.10 – Locator Value for Logout Button

7. Add these locator values to the **SharedUIMap.config** file.

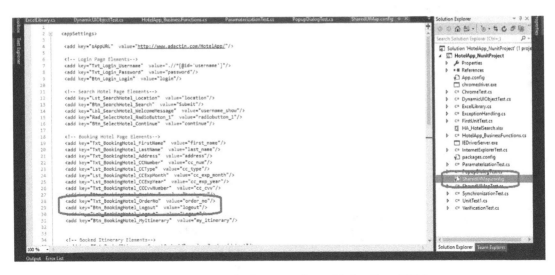

Figure 15.11 – Web Elements Values Added to SharedUIMap

8. Add this code snippet into the **SynchronizationTest.cs** file.

```
//Step added after Book Now button click
Thread.Sleep(10);
String strOrderNo =
driver.FindElement(By.Id(ConfigurationManager.AppSettings["Txt_
BookingHotel_OrderNo"])).GetAttribute("value");
Console.WriteLine("Order Number generated is " + strOrderNo;
```

Figure 15.12 – Code snippet

Figure 15.13 – Code for Static Wait

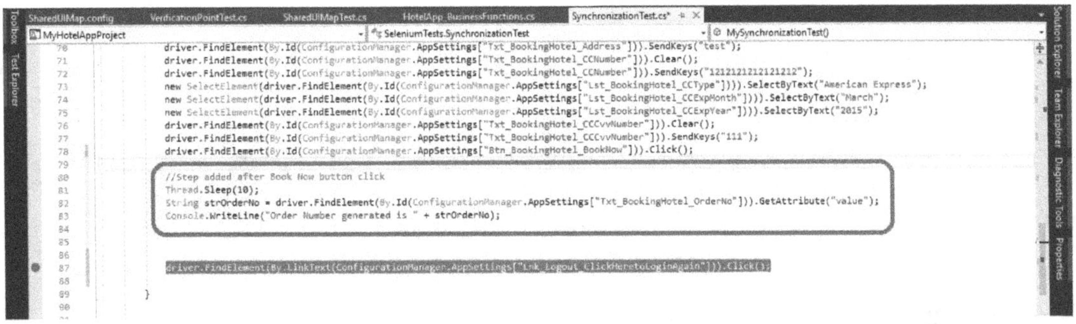

In the above script, we are using Thread.Sleep to wait for 10 seconds for the order to be inserted. After the order is inserted we use the GetAttribute method to retrieve the value from the Order No. field.

Simple and easy!

The only drawback of the above process is that the system will wait all of 10 seconds even though actual order insertion might take 6-7 seconds.

9. Once all the required changes have been made, Save the class.

10. Click on **Build>Build Solution** to check for any errors.

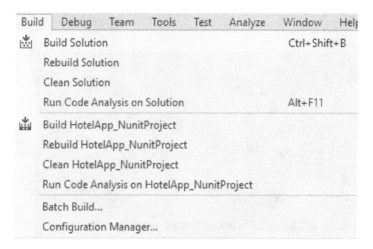

Figure 15.14 – Build Solution

11. Select the test and Run the test using **Run** on the TestExplorer. Confirm that the test can run fine. The order number is displayed in the output window.

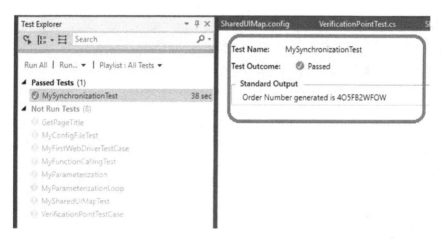

Figure 15.15 – Test Results

Solution – 2– Using Explicit Wait

Let us see how to get the order number using Explicit Wait-

1. **Right-click** on your SynchronizationTest.cs class and select **Copy**.

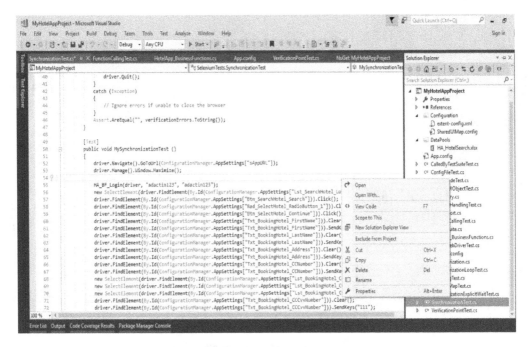

Figure 15.16 – Copy of SynchronizationTest.cs

2. Select the **project** and click on paste.

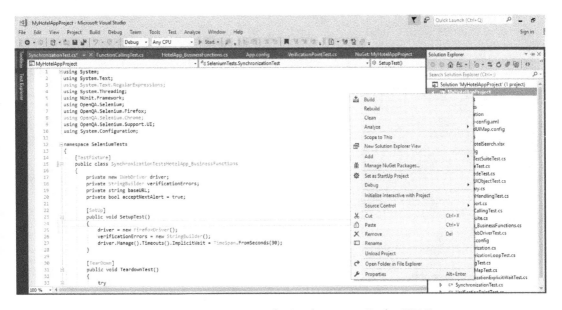

Figure 15.17 – Paste Script for SynchronizationExplicitWaitTest

3. A copy of the class file will be created. Right-click on the new class file to rename. Rename to **"SynchronizationExplicitWaitTest.cs"**. Click **OK**.

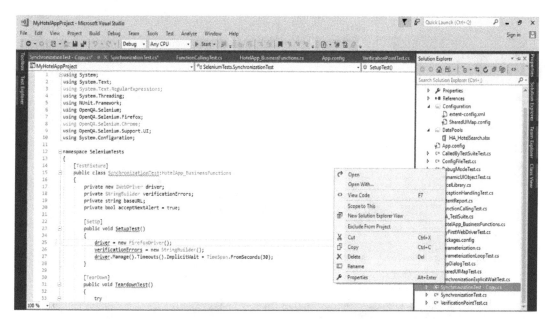

Figure 15.18 – Rename to SynchronizationExplicitWaitTest

4. Click on the newly created **"SynchronizationExplicitWaitTest.cs" script** so that you can see the script.

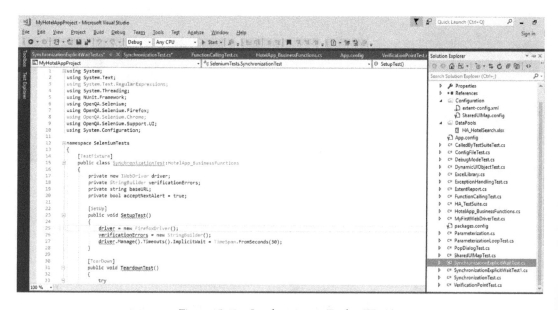

Figure 15.19 – SynchronizationExplicitWaitTest

5. Rename the class name from SynchronizationTest to SynchronizationExplicitWaitTest under TestFixture and save the file.

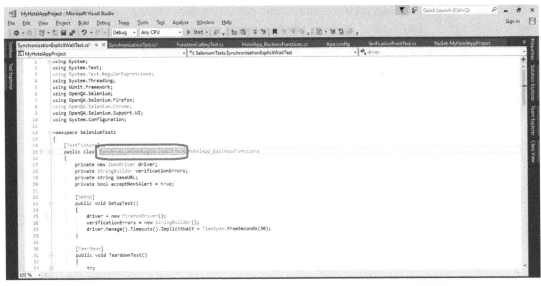

Figure 15.20 – Rename in the Class to SynchronizationExplicitWaitTest

6. Double click on the newly created **"SynchronizationExplicitWaitTest.cs"** file so that you can see the script.

Note: After we click the "Book Now" button we will need to use the Explicit Custom Wait function ("HA_GF_WaitForElementPresent" as discussed in the previous section) to wait until the order is inserted and then use GetAttribute to fetch the value from the Order No. field.

Before we do this, we need to add Locator details for the Order No. field and the Logout Button in our SharedUIMap.config file.

7. You can skip this step if you have already added Order No. and Logout Button in the previous solution.

8. Use the Inspector to inspect the element and get the locator value for the Order No.field.

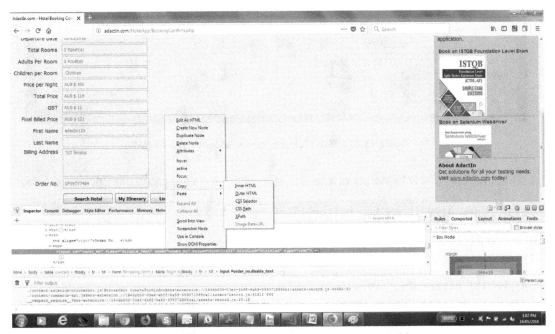

Figure 15.21 – Locator Value for Order No. Field

9. Use the inspector to inspect the element and get the locator values for Logout button.

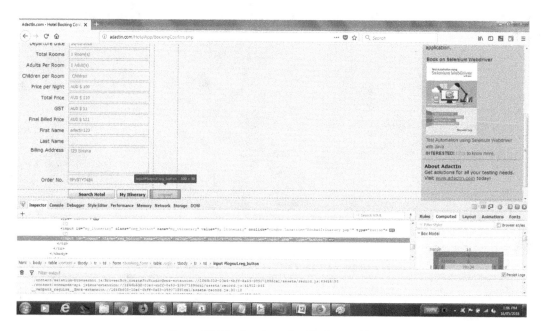

Figure 15.22 – Locator value for Logout Button

10. Add these locator values to the **SharedUIMap.config** file.

Figure 15.23 – Web Elements Values Added to SharedUIMap

11. Add the code below to the script after the step where the user clicks the Book Now button.

```
//Step added after Book Now button click
HA_GF_WaitForElementPresent(driver,
By.Id(ConfigurationManager.["Btn_BookingHotel_Logout"]), 10);
String strOrderNo =
driver.FindElement(By.Id(ConfigurationManager.AppSettings["Txt_BookingHotel_
OrderNo"])).GetAttribute("value");
 Console.WriteLine("Order Number Generated is " + strOrderNo);
```

Figure 15.24 – Script Code Added to Script for Explicit Wait

Note: This code assumes we have added the explicit function *HA_GF_ WaitForElementPresent* as part of the previous section in our function library file.

Figure 15.25 - Script Code for Explicit Wait in Visual Studio

In the above script, we are not using Thread.Sleep to wait for the order to be inserted. Instead we perform a dynamic wait and as soon as the order is inserted the script moves to the next step to fetch the order number value.

12. Once all the required changes have been made, Save the Test.

13. Click on **Build>Build Solution** to check for any errors.

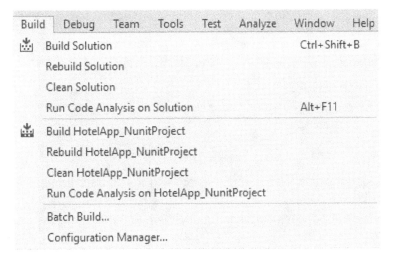

Figure 15.26 – Build Solution

14. Select the test and Run the test using **Run** on the TestExplorer. Confirm that the test can run fine and the order number is displayed in the output window.

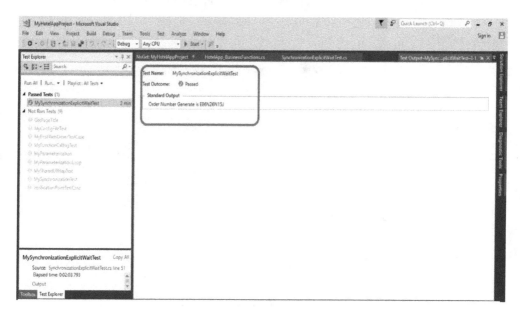

Figure 15.27 – Test Results for SynchronizationExplicitWait

Note: We can also use WebDriverWait and ExpectedConditions Class to perform the explicit wait instead of the custom function. The test results will be the same.

EXERCISE

1. Use the knowledge gained in this chapter and try automating the workflow below:

    a) Book a Hotel.

    b) Grab Order Number from Booking page.

    c) Click on Book Itinerary link.

    d) Search for your newly created Order Number.

    e) Logout.

Hint

a) Do not forget to add Web element locators in the SharedUI map file in the booked Itinerary page.

b) Copy/paste the previous step and modify them to perform actions as required in the booked Itinerary page.

16. Handling Pop-up Dialogs and Multiple Windows

Most of the modern-day applications come with various pop-up messages and multiple windows.

For instance, if you would like to delete a record in your application, many applications will throw a JavaScript-based confirmation pop-up dialog before deletion.

Also applications these days have child pop-up windows.

example We were once automating a mortgage-based Web application, which had search customer functionality. When a user clicks on the search link it opens a new pop-up window in which the user can search and select any customer. After the customer was selected, the pop-up window would close and the user would go back to the main Web page.

How would Selenium work in these scenarios?

In this chapter, we will see

- How WebDriver works with Alert dialogs.
- How WebDriver works with multiple windows.

16.1. Handling Alerts or Prompts

Test Scenario – Follow the steps below in the Hotel Application:

- Login.
- Search for the hotel.
- Select Hotel.
- In the Booking form enter required details but enter Credit Card expiry year as 2011.
- Click on Book Now. You will see a pop-up window.

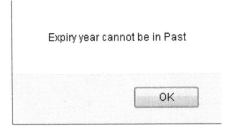

Expiry year cannot be in Past

OK

Figure 16.1 – Pop-up Dialog

- While the pop-up dialog is open, try to click on the Logout link or any other link. You would notice that all other links are disabled since the focus is on the pop-up dialog.

157

Now we will see how to handle this pop-up dialog using Selenium.

1. Right-click on your existing **MyFirstWebDriverTest.cs** script, select **Copy**.
2. Select the **project**, **right-click** and select **Paste.**
3. Rename the new script as **PopDialogTest.cs** and click **OK.**
4. Double click on the newly created **"PopDialogTest.cs"** script so that you can see the script.
5. Rename the class name from **MyFirstWebDriverTest** to **PopDialogTest** under TestFixture and save the file.
6. Modify the CreditCard Expiry Year from "2018" to **"2011"** to simulate the scenario.

```
84    driver.FindElement(By.Id("last_name")).SendKeys("sdsd");
85    driver.FindElement(By.Id("address")).Clear();
86    driver.FindElement(By.Id("address")).SendKeys("dsdfvcfdf");
87    driver.FindElement(By.Id("cc_num")).Clear();
88    driver.FindElement(By.Id("cc_num")).SendKeys("1234567123456234");
89    new SelectElement(driver.FindElement(By.Id("cc_type"))).SelectByText("American Express");
90    new SelectElement(driver.FindElement(By.Id("cc_exp_month"))).SelectByText("March");
91    new SelectElement(driver.FindElement(By.Id("cc_exp_year"))).SelectByText("2018");
```

Figure 16.2 – Credit Card Expiry Year – Previous

```
85    driver.FindElement(By.Id("address")).Clear();
86    driver.FindElement(By.Id("address")).SendKeys("dsdfvcfdf");
87    driver.FindElement(By.Id("cc_num")).Clear();
88    driver.FindElement(By.Id("cc_num")).SendKeys("1234567123456234");
89    new SelectElement(driver.FindElement(By.Id("cc_type"))).SelectByText("American Express");
90    new SelectElement(driver.FindElement(By.Id("cc_exp_month"))).SelectByText("March");
91    new SelectElement(driver.FindElement(By.Id("cc_exp_year"))).SelectByText("2011");
```

Figure 16.3 – Credit Card Expiry Year – Updated

7. Save the changes and Click on **Build > Build Solution**.

8. Select the test and Run the test using **Run → Run the Selected Test**. Check that the script runs   without error but the functionality does not work.

   Note: If there is a code which includes redirection and functionality in another page, exception is thrown that the element is not found.

9. In order to fix the script, let us add these lines of code in the script after the user clicks the "Book Now" Button. Enclose it in try and catch block to catch any errors.

   Alert Dialog uses the **IAlert** interface to handle alerts.

```
try
{
        string javascriptAlert = driver.SwitchTo().Alert().Text;
        Console.WriteLine(javascriptAlert); // Get text on alert box
        driver.SwitchTo().Alert().Accept();
}
catch (NoAlertPresentException)
{
        Console.WriteLine("No Alert");
}
```

Figure 16.5 – Alert Handler Script

In the above script-

We are using **SwitchTo()** to switch the focus from the driver to the alert pop-up.

Accept() is used to Accept the Alert pop-up or Click Ok on the Alert Pop.

 Note: Alternatively, we could use the functions below on the alert dialog.

SendKeys("Keys to Send");	To enter data into the Alert pop-up (in case it has an edit field).
Dismiss();	To click on Cancel in the alert pop-up.

10. We will see the script below in Visual Studio.

```
86      drive
87      driver.FindElement(By.Id("cc_num")).Clear();
88      driver.FindElement(By.Id("cc_num")).SendKeys("1234567123456234");
89      new SelectElement(driver.FindElement(By.Id("cc_type"))).SelectByText("American Express");
90      new SelectElement(driver.FindElement(By.Id("cc_exp_month"))).SelectByText("March");
91      new SelectElement(driver.FindElement(By.Id("cc_exp_year"))).SelectByText("2011");
92      driver.FindElement(By.Id("cc_cvv")).Clear();
93      driver.FindElement(By.Id("cc_cvv")).SendKeys("214");
94      driver.FindElement(By.Id("book_now")).Click();
95      //After user clicks on Book Now
96      try
97      {
98          string javascriptAlert = driver.SwitchTo().Alert().Text;
99          Console.WriteLine(javascriptAlert); // Get text on alert box
100         driver.SwitchTo().Alert().Accept();
101     }
102     catch (NoAlertPresentException)
103     {
104         Console.WriteLine("No Alert");
105     }
106
107     driver.FindElement(By.LinkText("Logout")).Click();
108     driver.FindElement(By.LinkText("Click here to login again")).Click();
109
110 }
111 private bool IsElementPresent(By by)
112 {
113     try
114     {
```

Figure 16.6 – Alert Handler Script in Visual Studio

11. Save the changes and Click on **Build > Build Solution**.

12. Select the test and Run the test using **Run → Run the Selected Test**. The test passes showing the text on the alert in the output window.

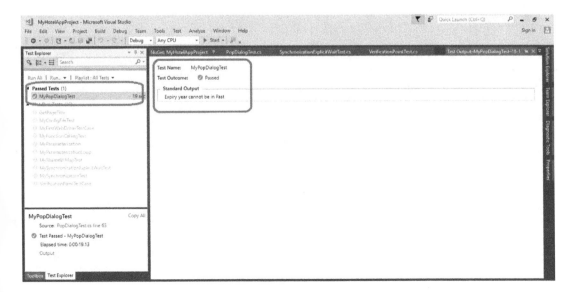

Figure 16.7 – Test Results

Note: Another traditional way of handling pop-ups in Selenium is using AutoIT script. You can find more details on AutoIT at www.autoitscript.com/.

Steps used to handle pop-up with AutoIT:

a. Install AutoIT script editor tool.
b. Create an AutoIT script to handle the pop-up.
c. Compile AutoIT script to create a .exe file.
d. Run the .exe file in Selenium using Runtime.*getRuntime*().exec command when required.

16.2. Working with Multiple Windows

An important part when working with multiple windows using WebDriver is to keep switching the focus between parent and child Web pop-up windows.

Key steps to working with multiple windows are:

1. Keep a handle on the existing parent window

Before we switch to the child window it is always appropriate to keep a handle on the existing parent window. We use the method **driver.CurrentWindowHandle** to keep a handle on the existing parent window.

```
String parentWindowHandle = driver.CurrentWindowHandle;
```

The `CurrentWindowHandle` gets the current window handle, which is an opaque handle to this window that uniquely identifies it within this driver instance.

2. Switch to the child or alternate window.

WebDriver supports moving between named windows using the "**SwitchTo**" method.

```
driver.SwitchTo().Window("WindowName");
```

Note: But how do you know the window's name? Take a look at the javascript or link that opened it:

<a href="somewhere.html" target="windowName">Click here to open a new window</a>

Alternatively, if the name is not known you can use **WebDriver.WindowHandles** to obtain the window handles of open browser windows. You can pass a "window handle" to the **SwitchTo(). Window()** method. Knowing this, use foreach loop to iterate through each of the open window handles like this:

```
foreach (String handle in driver.WindowHandles)
{
    driver.SwitchTo().Window(handle);
}
```

3. Perform operations on the child/alternate window

4. Switch the focus back to the Parent window.

```
driver.SwitchTo().Window(parentWindowHandle);
```

See below a sample script to work with multiple windows using window handles

```
Boolean bfound = false;
String strExpectedWindowtitle = "AdactIn Group";

//save the window handle of parent window for future reference
String parentWindowHandle = driver.CurrentWindowHandle;

//Use for loop to iterate through all the window handles found
foreach (String handle in driver.WindowHandles)
{
    //Switch focus to window with Handle handle
    driver.SwitchTo().Window(handle);

    // use gettitle method to get title of window
    String stractualtitle = driver.Title.Trim();

    //check if the current window has title match
    if
(stractualtitle.Equals(strExpectedWindowtitle,StringComparison.
InvariantCultureIgnoreCase))
    {
        Console.WriteLine(" Window with Title Match found: " +
stractualtitle);
        bfound = true;

        //close the driver window if needed
        driver.Close();
        Thread.Sleep(2000);

        //break from for loop since we have found the window
         break;
    }

}
//giving focus back to parent window
driver.SwitchTo().Window(parentWindowHandle);
```

Figure 16.8 – Sample of Multiple Windows Script

Explanation – The above code looks into the list of existing opened windows and matches the title of those windows with the expected Title.

It starts with the keep handle of the parent window for reference.

```
        String parentWindowHandle = driver.CurrentWindowHandle;
```

Using the foreach loop, it gets the handle to all of the open windows.

```
        foreach (String handle in driver.WindowHandles)
```

Using SwitchTo statement it switches focus to the current window given by the for loop:

```
        driver.SwitchTo().Window(handle);
```

Uses "driver.Title" statement to get the window title and if the title matches with the expected string then the user continues the for loop or break.

In the end, the focus is switched back to the Parent window handle.

Note: You can also switch from frame to frame:

```
driver.SwitchTo().Frame("frameName");
```

It's possible to access subframes by its index and frameElement too. See below:

```
Switches the frame based on its index:

driver.SwitchTo().Frame(frameIndex);

Selects a frame using its previously located IWebElementIwebElement:

driver.SwitchTo().Frame(frameElement);
```

17. Working with Dynamic UI Objects

In most real-life applications, we find objects whose properties change at runtime. For instance, a Web browser will have a variable date/time stamp in the title or the window title will contain the id number of the latest order you have booked. These types of objects whose properties change at run-time are called dynamic objects.

Since we are using a Shared UI Map and save the object properties statically in our map file, the WebDriver script will fail since the objects' properties are being generated at runtime.

In this chapter, we will see how WebDriver can handle these dynamic objects.

While testing a banking application which had account numbers generated at runtime, hyperlinks to those newly generated account numbers were created. As part of the test case steps, we had to click on the newly created account number link and modify the account details. So how do we deal with such objects like account number links which are dynamic and whose property values are generated at runtime?

We will learn how to work with objects whose properties change dynamically in this chapter.

Key objectives:

- Understand Dynamic Objects: Create a Test Scenario.
- Handling Dynamic Objects using programming.
- Regular Expression alternative to handling Dynamic Objects.

17.1. Handling Dynamic Objects using Programming

WebDriver Script for Cancelling a Booked Order

Let us enhance our existing WebDriver script to code for the steps for Cancelling a Booked order:

1. **Right-click** on your existing **SynchronizationTest.cs** script, select **Copy**.
2. Select the **project**, **right-click** and select **Paste.**
3. Rename the new script as **DynamicUIObjectTest.cs** and click **OK**.
4. Double click on the newly created **"DynamicUIObjectTest.cs"** script so that you can see the script.
5. Rename the class name from **SynchronizationTest** to **DynamicUIObjectTest** under TestFixture to remove conflicts and save the file.
6. Double click on SharedUI map file **SharedUIMap.config** to see the configuration settings.

Let us add new WebElements into our Shared UI Map file. The list of objects we need to add include (assuming we already have existing objects in our SharedUIMap.config file):

Hotel Booking Page

- My Itinerary Button

Booked Itinerary Page

- Search Order ID text field.
- Go Button.

See the snapshot below of the updated Shared UI Map file.

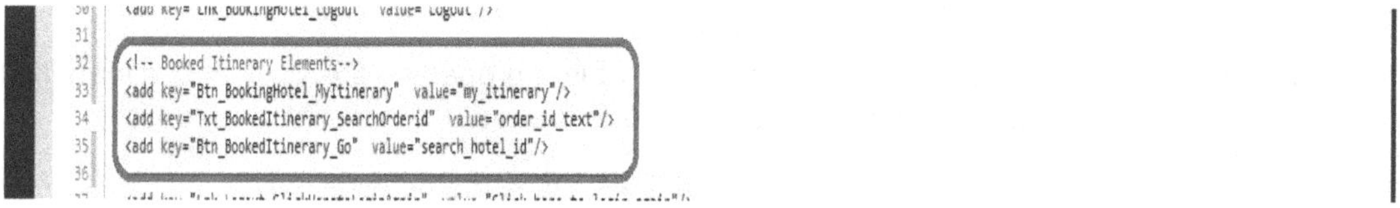

```
30    <add key="Lnk_BookingHotel_Logout"  value="Logout"/>
31
32    <!-- Booked Itinerary Elements-->
33    <add key="Btn_BookingHotel_MyItinerary"  value="my_itinerary"/>
34    <add key="Txt_BookedItinerary_SearchOrderid"  value="order_id_text"/>
35    <add key="Btn_BookedItinerary_Go"  value="search_hotel_id"/>
36
37    <add key="Lnk_Logout_ClickHeretologin..."  value="Click here to login again"/>
```

Figure 17.1 – Updated Shared UI Map

7. **Save** the Shared UI Map file.

8. We need to insert the additional steps mentioned below in the **DynamicUIObjectTest.cs** script after the Book now button click, so open the class file and insert the code below -

- Click on the **My Itinerary** button.

```
driver.FindElement(By.Id(ConfigurationManager.AppSettings["Btn_BookingHotel_
MyItinerary"])).Click();
```

Figure 17.2 – My Itinerary Button

- Enter the value into the **Search Order No.** field.

```
driver.FindElement(By.Id(ConfigurationManager.AppSettings["Txt_BookedItinerary_
SearchOrderid"])).SendKeys(strOrderNo);
```

Figure 17.3 – Search Order No. Field

- Click on the **Go** button.

```
driver.FindElement(By.Id(ConfigurationManager.AppSettings
["Btn_BookedItinerary_Go"]))

.Click();
```

Figure 17.4 – Go Button

9. Now we need to click the **Cancel <Order No>** button. Using the Inspector we've found Xpath for Cancel <Order No> = //*[@id="btn_id_253185"].

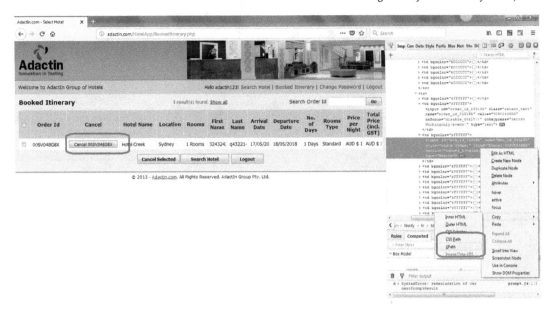

Figure 17.5 – XPath for Cancel Order Button

Notice that the id value "253185" is dynamic and we do not have any control on it. But property "value" has the value "Cancel 00SV048G8X" which we can use to uniquely identify the object.

So the XPath value that we will use is .//*[@ value='Cancel 00SV048G8X'].

Note: You can confirm whether the XPath values is correct or not by going to Firefox browser and on the console type $x(".//*[@value='Cancel 00SV048G8X']") and then Press Enter. If you can see the object highlighted it means that your XPath expression is correct. If you see document Interface shown without any specific object, then it means that the XPath is incorrect and it does not match any objects in the application.

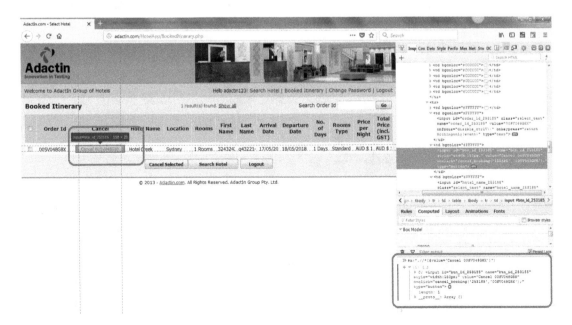

Figure 17.6 – Correct XPath

Figure 17.7 – XPath Mismatch

Now as you know the Order No. value is changing constantly so we will replace the hardcoded Order No with the value fetched using GetAttribute method from the Order Number.

The statement we will use in the script will be:

```
driver.FindElement(By.XPath(".//*[@value='Cancel " + strOrderNo + "']")).
Click();
```

10. Press OK on the Confirmation Prompt.

```
//Confirmation Prompt
string javascriptAlert = driver.SwitchTo().Alert().Text;
Console.WriteLine(javascriptAlert); // Get text on alert box
driver.SwitchTo().Alert().Accept();
```

The final script will look like this:

```
76    driver.FindElement(By.Id(ConfigurationManager.AppSettings["Txt_BookingHotel_CCCvvNumber"])).Clear();
77    driver.FindElement(By.Id(ConfigurationManager.AppSettings["Txt_BookingHotel_CCCvvNumber"])).SendKeys("111");
78    driver.FindElement(By.Id(ConfigurationManager.AppSettings["Btn_BookingHotel_BookNow"])).Click();
79
80    Thread.Sleep(10);
81    //Get order no
82    String strOrderNo = driver.FindElement(By.Id(ConfigurationManager.AppSettings["Txt_BookingHotel_OrderNo"])).GetAttribute(
83    Console.WriteLine("Order Number generated is " + strOrderNo);
84
85    //My Itenary button click
86    driver.FindElement(By.Id(ConfigurationManager.AppSettings["Btn_BookingHotel_MyItinerary"])).Click();
87    //Search for booked itenary for the given order id
88    driver.FindElement(By.Id(ConfigurationManager.AppSettings["Txt_BookedItinerary_SearchOrderid"])).SendKeys(strOrderNo);
89    driver.FindElement(By.Id(ConfigurationManager.AppSettings["Btn_BookedItinerary_Go"])).Click();
90
91    //Cancel the itenary
92    driver.FindElement(By.XPath(".//*[@value='Cancel " + strOrderNo + "']")).Click();
93
94    //Confirmation Prompt
95    string javascriptAlert = driver.SwitchTo().Alert().Text;
96    Console.WriteLine(javascriptAlert); // Get text on alert box
97    driver.SwitchTo().Alert().Accept();
98
99    driver.FindElement(By.LinkText(ConfigurationManager.AppSettings["Lnk_BookingHotel_Logout"])).Click();
100   driver.FindElement(By.LinkText(ConfigurationManager.AppSettings["Lnk_Logout_ClickHeretoLoginAgain"])).Click();
```

Figure 17.8 – Final Script

11. Save the changes and Click on **Build > Build Solution**.

12. Select the test and Run the test using **Run → Run the Selected Test**. The test passes showing the text on the alert in the output window.

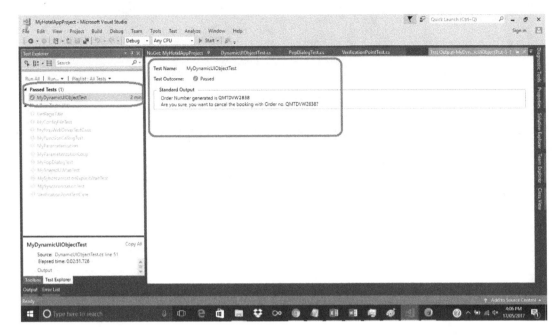

Figure 17.9 – Test Results

17.2. Handling Dynamic Objects using Partial Match

Another way of handling dynamic objects is using Partial Match. A partial match describes or matches a set of strings. It is often called a pattern match.

We can use the statement below for a partial match in XPath.

Syntax	Example	Description
startswith()	.//[starts-with(@id,'btn_id_')]	For example, if the ID of an element is btn_id_786, this will locate and return elements with btn_id_at the beginning of the ID.
endswith()	.// [ends-with(@id,'_btn_id')]	For example, if the ID of an element is 786_btn_id, this will locate and return elements with _btn_id at the end of the ID.
contains()	.//[contains(@id, 'btn_id_)]	For example, if the ID for an element is Test_btn_id_786, this will use the btn_id_part in the middle to match and locate the element.

Figure 17.10 – Partial Match Patterns

In our Scenario to match the XPath statement

Xpath for Cancel <Order No> = .//*[@id='btn_id_194183'] or .//*[@value= 'Cancel QMTDVW2838]

We could use any of the following partial matches to match the dynamic object

.//*[@id='btn_id_194183']	.//*[contains(@id,'btn_id_')]
	.//[starts-with(@id,'btn_id_')]
.//*[@value= 'Cancel QMTDVW2838']	.//*[contains(@value,'Cancel')]
	.//*[starts-with(@value,'Cancel')]

Figure 17.11 – Examples of Partial Match

Let us modify our existing script to use Regular Expression:

1. Double click on the newly created **"DynamicUIObjectTest.cs"** script so that you can see the script.

2. Comment out the existing statement when we click on Cancel <Order No> button and copy/paste it as a separate statement.

3. Modify the statement as shown below based on the options highlighted above.

```
driver.FindElement(By.XPath(".//*[contains(@id,'btn_id_')]")).
Click();
```

```
77    driver.FindElement(By.Id(ConfigurationManager.AppSettings["Txt_BookingHotel_CCCVVNumber"])).SendKeys( 111 );
78    driver.FindElement(By.Id(ConfigurationManager.AppSettings["Btn_BookingHotel_BookNow"])).Click();
79
80        Thread.Sleep(10);
81        //Get order no
82        String strOrderNo = driver.FindElement(By.Id(ConfigurationManager.AppSettings["Txt_BookingHotel_OrderNo"])).GetAttribute("value");
83        Console.WriteLine("Order Number generated is " + strOrderNo);
84
85        //My Itenary button click
86        driver.FindElement(By.Id(ConfigurationManager.AppSettings["Btn_BookingHotel_MyItinerary"])).Click();
87        //Search for booked itenary for the given order id
88        driver.FindElement(By.Id(ConfigurationManager.AppSettings["Txt_BookedItinerary_SearchOrderid"])).SendKeys(strOrderNo);
89        driver.FindElement(By.Id(ConfigurationManager.AppSettings["Btn_BookedItinerary_Go"])).Click();
90
91        //Cancel the itenary
92        //driver.FindElement(By.XPath(".//*[@value='Cancel " + strOrderNo + "']")).Click();
93        driver.FindElement(By.XPath(".//*[contains(@id,'btn_id_')]")).Click();
94
95        //Confirmation Prompt
96        string javascriptAlert = driver.SwitchTo().Alert().Text;
97        Console.WriteLine(javascriptAlert); // Get text on alert box
98        driver.SwitchTo().Alert().Accept();
99
100       driver.FindElement(By.LinkText(ConfigurationManager.AppSettings["Lnk_BookingHotel_Logout"])).Click();
101       driver.FindElement(By.LinkText(ConfigurationManager.AppSettings["Lnk_Logout_ClickHeretoLoginAgain"])).Click();
102
103   }
```

Figure 17.12 – Partial Match Used in Script

4. Save the changes and Click on **Build > Build Solution**.

5. Select the test and Run the test using **Run → Run the Selected Test**. Check if the test passes and shows the test results as before.

Note: Partial match should be used after generic recognition of an object. This should be used if WebDriver finds only one instance of the object. If WebDriver finds more than one object matching the string specified by WebDriver partial match, then we cannot use partial match. In that case we would have to use programming. For example, in our above exercise to delete an order, if we use partial match to identify the cancel Order No. button (e.g., Cancel.*), it will recognize all the Cancel <Order No> buttons, not just the one which we have booked (assuming that our Itinerary screen will show multiple orders). So we cannot use regular expression in the above exercise as WebDriver will not be able to identify the unique object. The best option in the above scenario would be to use programming to perform an exact match.

18. Multiple Choice Questions Set-2

1. Select the method used to Assert and compare two strings in a NUnit WebDriver script
a. Assert.True
b. Assert.NotNull
c. Assert.Equals
d. Assert.AreSame

2. Select the method used to read data from the config file script
a. ConfigurationManager.AppSettings[keyname]
b. ConfigurationManager.ReadData[keyname]
c. ConfigurationManager.ConnectionStrings[keyname]
d. ConfigurationManager.GetData[keyname]

3. Which is the preferred method for using objects in WebDriver?
a. Local Web elements
b. Shared Web elements

4. Which statement is used to return data from a function?
a. functionName
b. return
c. returnval
d. functionReturn

5. Which of the statements is used for static wait?
a. Thread.Sleep
b. wait
c. sleep
d. All of the above

6. Which class is used for Explicit Wait in WebDriver?
a. Wait
b. WebDriverSleep
c. Thread.sleep
d. WebDriverWait

7. What class of object is used to handle a confirmation pop-up?

a. Pop-up

b. IAlert

c. Alertwindow

d. Childwindow

8. Which method in WebDriver is used to move the focus to a Child window of the browser?

a. MoveTo

b. SwitchTo

c. FocusTo

d. SetFocus

9. Which is a valid Regular Expression statement to handle a dynamic id with format "txt. Book.4345"?

a. .//*[contains(@id,'Book.4345')]

b. .//[starts-with(@id,'Book.')]

c. .//*[contains(@id,'txt.Book.')]

d. .//[starts-with(@id,'txt.4345')]

10. Which method is used by Selenium WebDriver to get the Handle of a Parent window?

a. driver.GetHandle

b. driver.ParentWindowHandle

c. driver.CurrentWindowHandle

d. driver.Browserhandle

Answers

Q1. Answer: C

Explanation – Assert.Equals compares that two string values are the same.

Q2. Answer: A

Explanation – ConfigurationManager.AppSettings[keyname] is used to get the value from the Configuration file. The data is stored in key value format and we can read it by using the keyname as index to appsettings. We specifically use this method when we use SharedUIMap. config or Application configuration files.

Q3. Answer: B

Explanation – Shared Web elements is a better way to store object information instead of Local map. Shared Web elements present one central location for saving object properties making automation scripts more maintainable.

Q4. Answer: B

Explanation – Return statement is used to return values from the function.

Q5. Answer: A

Explanation – Thread.Sleep(waittime) is used for static wait in WebDriver.

Q6. Answer: D

Explanation – WebDriverWait class is used for Explicit Wait in WebDriver. Alternatively, you could also use custom wait methods to wait for objects' property values.

Q7. Answer: B

Explanation – IAlert interface is used to handle windows driven confirmation pop-ups.

Q8. Answer: B

Explanation – SwitchTo method is used to move focus to Child windows in WebDriver.

Q9. Answer: C

Explanation – Since value 4345 will keep varying and only part "txt.Book." is constant statement .//*[contains(@id,'txt.Book.')] is the correct answer.

Q10. Answer: C

Explanation – CurrentWindowHandle is used to get handle of the Parent or any other window. Before switching focus to the Child window, we use CurrentWindowHandle to store the handle id for the Parent window so that once an action on the Child window is finished the focus can be shifted back to the Parent window.

19. Debugging Scripts

I believe one cannot be an expert in any tool if he or she does not know how to debug issues, or does not know how to troubleshoot problems encountered while using the tool.

Debugging is an integrated feature of any automation tool. Automation scripts do fail, and we should be able to pinpoint exactly where the issue is, so that it can be fixed.

WebDriver within Visual Studio IDE comes with some nifty debugging features, which should be used while isolating reasons for failure of scripts. We would want to have the ability to execute one step at a time, or pause at a particular step or be able to peek at values of variables at runtime. All these features can be found within Visual Studio.

At one of our telecom clients, they had around 150 automation scripts, and they were not executable after a new build was released to the test team. The core automation team had left after the release and nobody knew how to fix the scripts. The only way we could figure out what went wrong with the script - and understand the application workflow - was by using the debugging features. This proved invaluable to us in getting the scripts up and running again!

In this chapter, we will learn how to debug WebDriver scripts.

Key objectives:

1. Debugging features.
2. Execute tests in debug mode.
3. Step commands, Variables, and Watches.

19.1. Debugging Features

Debugging allows you to run a program interactively while watching the source code and the variables during the execution. Basically, debugging is a way to pause the execution of a program so that we can examine its internals at that point in time to deduce what is going wrong. To that end, we have a few basic notions:

Breakpoints: These are locations in the code that we can specify where code execution will pause and we can examine the execution environment and gain manual control over the execution process. Setting a breakpoint in Visual Studio is as simple as going to the desired line of code and clicking F9. We will see how to insert a Breakpoint in the next section. In support of breakpoints are two main control buttons:

- **Run:** Execute the code as normal until the next breakpoint is encountered.
- **Stop:** Terminate the program execution completely.

Execution Stepping: This manual control over the execution process allows us to advance the execution one line of code at a time. Visual Studio provides convenient buttons for stepping control. There are generally 3 ways of stepping that one uses most often:

- **Step Into**: Advance to the next line of code, following the execution path into every method that is executed.

- **Step Over**: Advance to the next line of code, but do not go into any methods that are encountered.

- **Step Out**: Advance to the next line of code following the end of the current method in the calling method, i.e., finish the current method.

Variables Inspection: Once execution has stopped by a breakpoint, we can examine all the variables, fields and objects that are in scope (visible) at that moment. Visual Studio has "**Add Watch**" facility which enables you to select a particular variable and examine it. "Add Watch" adds the variable to the Watch window so that you can see its value changing as you step through the code.

Expressions Inspection: Apart from variables you might also want to see results of expressions, e.g., the Variables tab will show you the value of variables "a" and "b", but if you want to evaluate and view the value of expression "a+b", we can see this using **"Quick Watch"** feature in Visual Studio. Here you can use the **Reevaluate** button in the Quick Watch to evaluate the expression. Expressions are also referenced using the term "Watch" in programming tools.

Basic Debugging Procedure

There is really no "one right way" to debug. Debugging is as much an art as it is a skill. One has to think like a detective, looking for clues and applying deductive reasoning to explain what you've found. Always remember that the location, at which bugs manifest themselves as some sort of visible effect, is often not where the problem actually occurs. You must always keep an understanding of how all the pieces in your system relate to each other.

Most debugging scenarios can be broken down into these steps:

1. Set breakpoints at key locations in your code. Typical places to put breakpoints include:

   - Wherever the problem clearly manifests itself. If possible, put the breakpoint a few lines before the problematic line so you can step up to it in a controlled manner.

   - Wherever the key objects are constructed or key relationships are being established. For instance, null pointer errors are always due to calling a method on an object reference that is null, i.e., it was never assigned or instantiated properly.

2. Examine all variables that are visible at the breakpoint location and make sure that their values are what you expect them to be.

3. Step slowly through your code, checking all your variables as you go. Watch for the unexpected! Remember, if your code did what you expected, it would have run without any errors.

4. Use Step Over and Step Out (Step Out Of) only when you are positive, i.e., you already did a Step Into at least once already, that everything that is being skipped works properly. It is very common to get over-confident and miss where an error occurs because one has skipped right over the critical code.

5. Add more breakpoints when you see something amiss and you deduce that an error might be due to potential problems in another section of the code. You can use the "Continue" button to quickly advance to the next breakpoint.

Using breakpoints in the source code, you specify where the execution of the program should pause. Breakpoints and watch points can be summarized as pause points. Once the program is paused you can investigate variables, change their content, etc.

19.2. Run Tests in Debug mode with Breakpoints

In this section, we will execute one of our scripts in Debug mode with Breakpoints.

1. **Right-click** on your existing **MyFirstWebDriverTest.cs** script, select **Copy**.

2. Select the **project, right-click** and select **Paste.**

3. Rename the new script as **DebugModeTest.cs** and click **OK.**

4. Double click on the newly created **"DebugModeTest.cs"** script so that you can see the script.

5. Rename the class name from **MyFirstWebDriverTest** to **DebugModeTest** under TestFixture to remove conflicts and save the file.

Breakpoints

6. At the step where the user selects location ("Sydney") insert a breakpoint. To insert a breakpoint

   a. Click on the leftmost vertical bar next to the line of code at which you want to insert the Breakpoint.

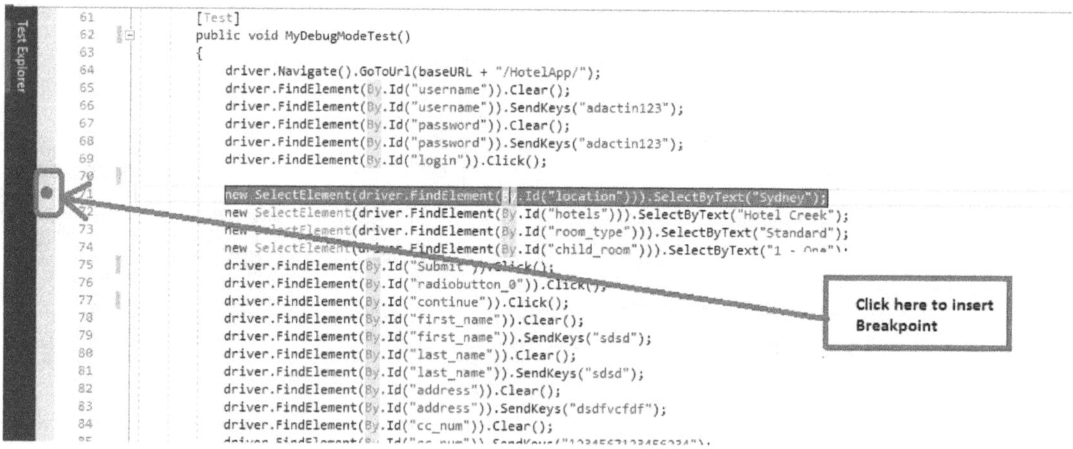

Figure 19.1 – Breakpoint Insertion

   b. Alternatively, select the step at which you would want to insert the Breakpoint and select **Debug → Toggle Breakpoint** from the menu.

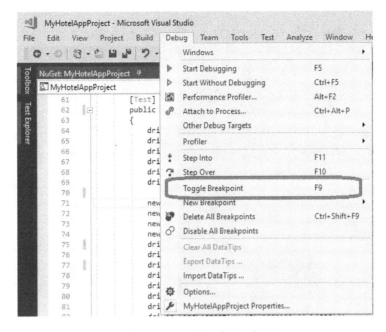

Figure 19.2 – Toggle Breakpoint

Debug Mode Run

7. Save the changes and Click on **Build > Build Solution**.

8. Once the build succeeds, all the tests appear in the Test Explorer window. Select the test **DebugModeTest** and Debug the test. Right-click on the test and select **Debug Selected Tests**.

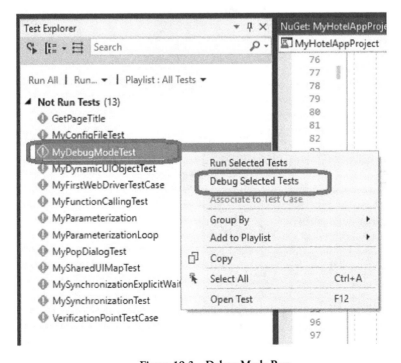

Figure 19.3 – Debug Mode Run

Note: If we run the script in normal Run mode (**Run → Run Selected Test**) our script will not pause at the breakpoint. It is only in Debug mode run that the script will pause at the breakpoint.

9. Once the test starts running you will notice that the script will pause before executing the Breakpoint step.

10. You will notice Visual Studio will open Add Watch window and call stack window. To inspect a variable, you can select it and right-click on it, then say Add Watch.

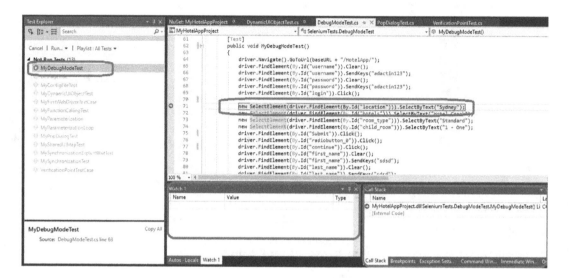

Figure 19.4 – Debug Mode Windows

11. You can also evaluate an expression using Quick Watch. Select a variable right-click and add it to Quick Watch. Make the required changes in the Expression textbox and say Reevaluate. Check to see the results.

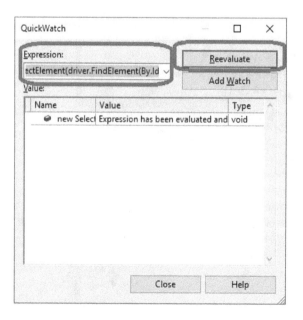

Figure 19.5 – Quick Watch

12. Go to your sample application and you will notice that execution is halted and the application is on the Search Hotel Page after login.

13. Click on the **Continue** icon at the top of the window. You can also click the **Stop** button if you want to stop debugging.

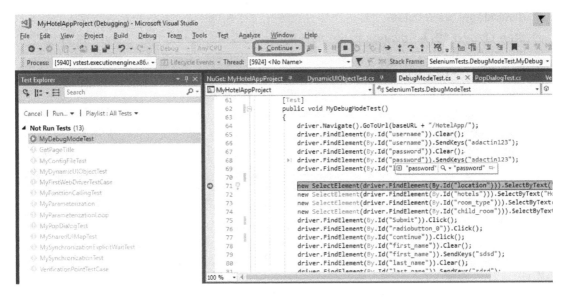

Figure 19.6 – Run Icon

14. You will notice that the test runs until completion.

Note: Breakpoint insertion is useful when you are not sure of the state of your application at a particular step of your test run. After the script pauses at the breakpoint, the user can either choose to run the script until completion or run one step at a time.

15. Visual Studio will automatically close the Add Watch and the call stack windows and go back to the original view.

19.3. Step Commands, Variables and Watch

Another benefit of running a script in debug mode is that the user can run a single step at a time which helps him to debug a specific part of the code which is causing the issue. We can achieve this using Step Into, Step Over and Step Out commands.

Also, as we are running our scripts at each step we would like to see values stored for variables used within the script or alternatively values evaluated for Expressions. We can use the Add Watch and Quick Watch windows for that.

In the following steps we will see how to use Step commands and also how to see variable values.

1. Double click on **DebugModeTest.cs** to see the script.

2. Verify that there is a breakpoint at the step where the user selects location ("Sydney"). If not, insert a breakpoint as mentioned in the previous section.

3. Once Breakpoint is inserted, build the solution, all the tests appear in the Test Explorer window. Select the test **DebugModeTest**, right-click on it and select **Debug Selected Tests**.

4. Once the test starts running, you will notice that the script will pause before executing the Breakpoint step.

5. You will notice Visual Studio will open Add Watch window and call stack window. Now let's run one step at a time using Step Into, Step Over and Step Out option.

   Step Into (F11) – Advance to the next line of code, following the execution path into every method that is executed.

   Step Over (F10) – Advance to the next line of code, but do not go into any methods that are encountered.

   Step Out (Shift + F11) – Advance to the next line of code following the end of the current method in the calling method, i.e., finish the current method.

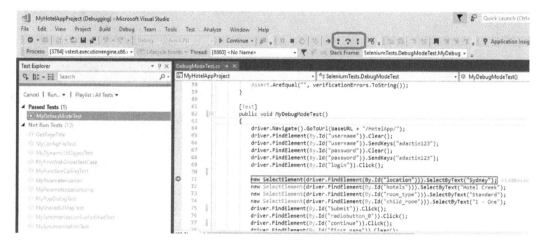

Figure 19.7 – Step Options

6. Let us use **Step Over (F10)** command to run over each step without getting into underlying methods. Click **Step Over icon** or press **F10.**

7. You would notice that the script has moved on to the next step and has again paused waiting for user action.

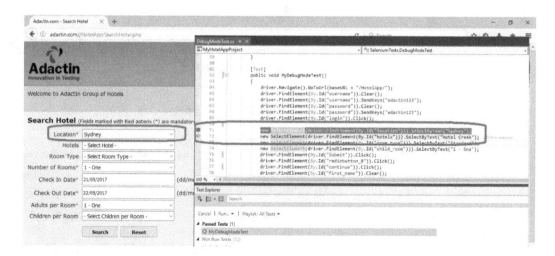

Figure 19.8 – Step Over

8. You can continue to press F10 (Step Over) and move the script one step at a time.

Variables

Let us see how to look for variable values:

9. As you are executing one step at a time and the script has paused, put your mouse cursor at variable "baseURL" which is defined in your script. You will see the variable value.

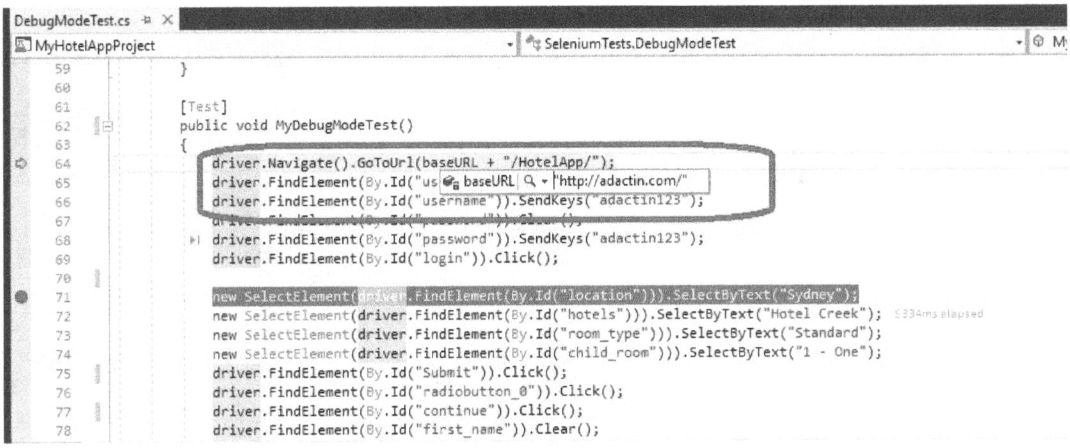

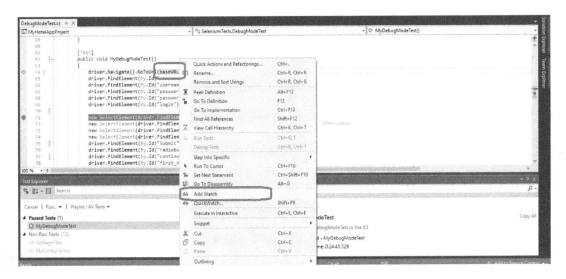

Figure 19.9 – Variable Value

10. Alternatively, right-click on the variable and select Add Watch from the context menu.

Figure 19.10 – Add Watch

11. Add Watch window appears showing the value of the variable selected.

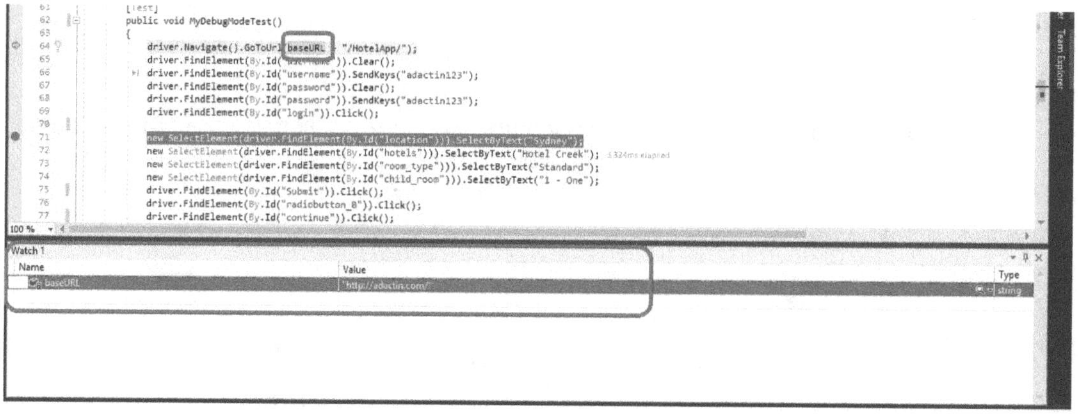

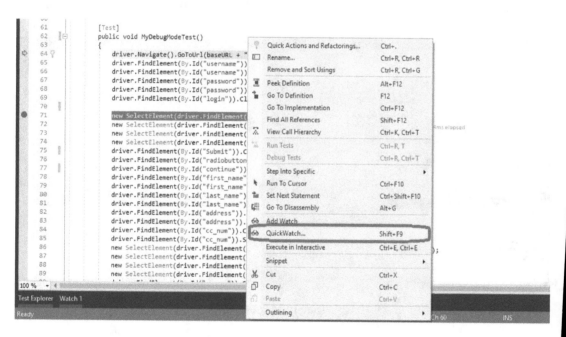

Figure 19.11 - Variable Value in Add Watch Window

Expressions

Let us see below how to look for Expression values.

12. As you are executing one step at a time and the script has paused, select the expression **baseUrl + "/HotelApp/"** which is defined in your script.

13. Right-click and select **Quick Watch**.

Figure 19.12 — Select Quick Watch

14. A Quick Watch window opens showing the selected Expression and its value.

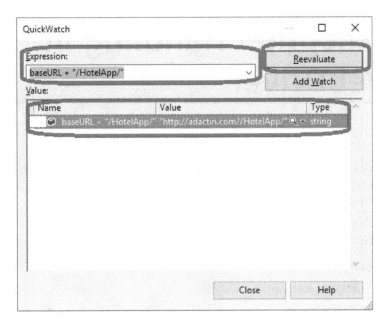

Figure 19.13 – Evaluated Expression Value

We can change the expression and say **Reevaluate**, the changed value is shown in the value column. We can use this to effectively check various conditions and values without changing the code.

15. Finish the script by clicking on the **Continue** icon. Save the script.

EXERCISE

1. Try running the ConfigFileTest.cs script in step by step mode. Insert breakpoints and verify the value of variables returned and stored in the variable sAppURL.

2. Also look for values returned for expressions "ConfigurationManager.AppSettings["Lst_ SearchHotel_Location"]"

20. Exception Handling in WebDriver

We have already learned about exceptions and their handling techniques in the earlier chapters. An *exception* is an event which occurs during the execution of a program that disrupts the normal flow of the program's instructions.

Exception handling in Selenium is also a crucial exercise. Most of the time when a selenium script fails, it is because it has landed into an exception. The cause could be anything like:

- Element not found.
- Couldn't click the element.
- Element not visible.

The moment the driver comes across an exception it will halt the test. So it's important for a tester to foresee these exception conditions and handle them according to the script or test requirements. This way the script failures are contributed to failures of test conditions and not to unhandled code exceptions. So, we have a bug corresponding to every test failure – which is our ultimate goal.

To catch an exception we first put the code which we suspect will throw an error into a **try** block like

```
IWebElement txtbox_username = driver.FindElement(By.Id("username"));
try
    {
      if (txtbox_username.Enabled)
      {
         txtbox_username.SendKeys("adactin123");
      }
    }
    catch (NoSuchElementException e)
    {
       Console.WriteLine(e.Message);
    }
```

Figure 20.1 – Code Snippet for Try-Catch block

This is followed by a **catch block** of code where we tell the system what should be done when the exception occurs. Generally, this is where we display the message of the exception object so that we know which exception has occurred and why.

20.1. Handling WebDriver Exceptions

In WebDriver, we can use **try-catch, finally** blocks or the **throw** statement with the purpose of handling the exceptions. The key point is that the exceptions we are catching here are Selenium exceptions rather than Visual Studio exceptions.

Test Scenario – If we provide an invalid username and password to the Login function, then the script should exit gracefully with a message.

Let us follow the steps to implement the above scenario.

1.   Now what visual cue tells us that a user is logged in to the application? There can be multiple visual cues but let us pick one of them as a welcome message.

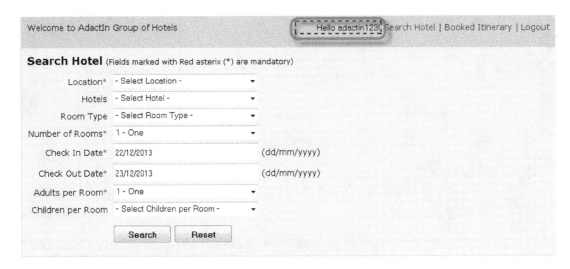

Figure 20.1 – User Welcome Message

2.   Let's use Inspect Element to get its locator value.

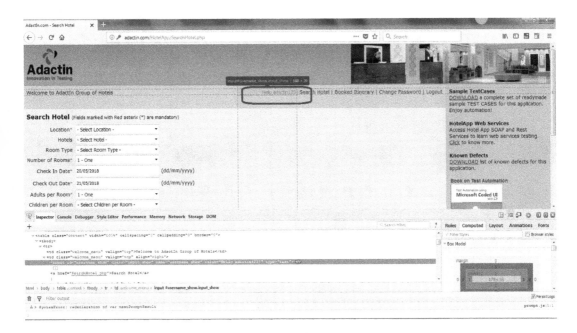

Figure 20.2 – Locator Value for Welcome Message

You see in the above snapshot the value for locator id is **username_show**.

3. Add this to our SharedUIMap.config file for further use.

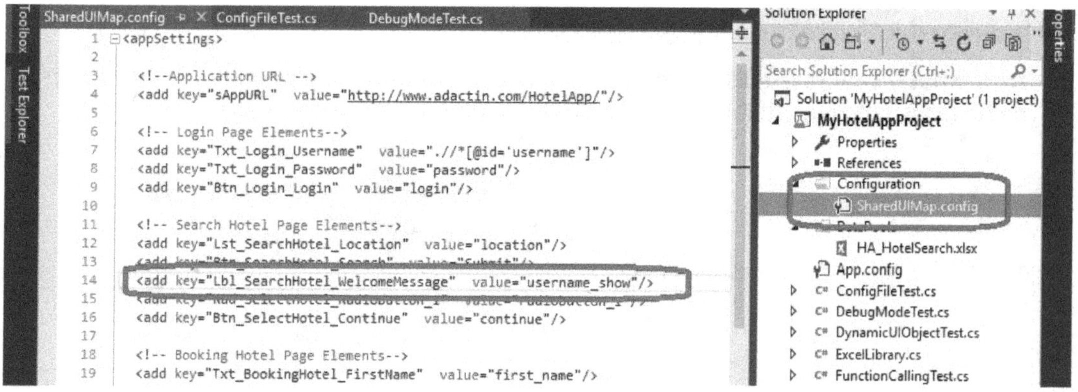

Figure 20.3 – Welcome Message Added to Shared UI Map

4. Double click and open our HotelApp_BusinessFunctions.cs script to view our existing login function.

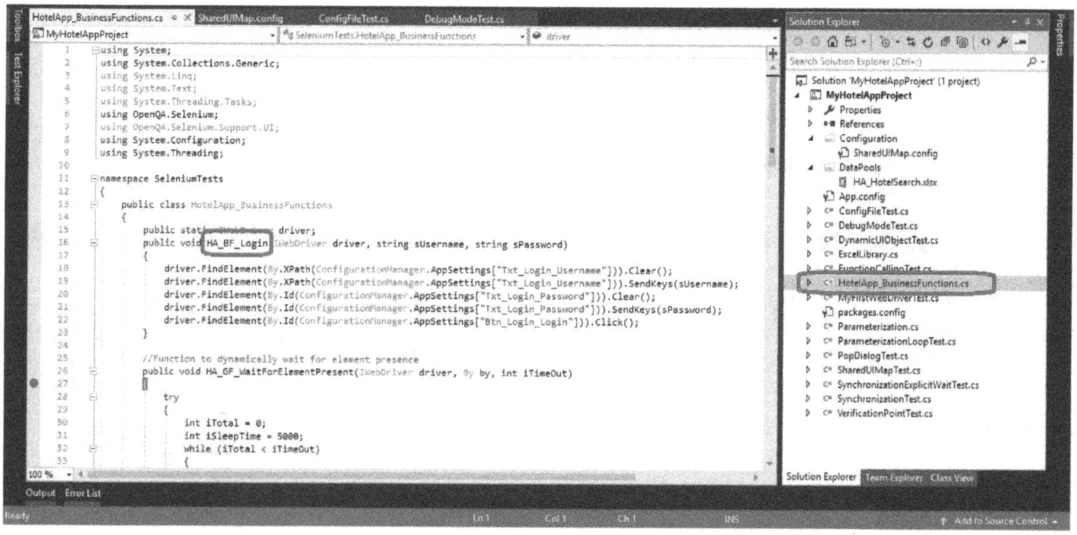

Figure 20.4 – Existing Login Function

5. Modify the function as given below to handle a successful or unsuccessful login.

```
public void HA_BF_Login(IWebDriver driver, string sUsername, string sPassword)
{
        //Provide Username
driver.FindElement(By.XPath(ConfigurationManager.AppSettings["Txt_Login_
Username"])).Clear();
driver.FindElement(By.XPath(ConfigurationManager.AppSettings["Txt_Login_
Username"])).SendKeys(sUsername);

        //Provide Password
driver.FindElement(By.Id(ConfigurationManager.AppSettings["Txt_Login_
Password"])).Clear();
driver.FindElement(By.Id(ConfigurationManager.AppSettings["Txt_Login_
Password"])).SendKeys(sPassword);

        //Click on Login button
driver.FindElement(By.Id(ConfigurationManager.AppSettings["Btn_Login_Login"])).
Click();

        // Verify for welcome message
IWebElement welcomeTxt =
driver.FindElement(By.Id(ConfigurationManager.AppSettings["Lbl_SearchHotel_
WelcomeMessage"]));
  String text = welcomeTxt.GetAttribute("value");
  if (text.Contains("Hello " + sUsername))
     Console.WriteLine("Login Test Pass for: " + sUsername);
  else
     Console.WriteLine("Login Test Fail for: " + sUsername);

}
```

Figure 20.5 – Updated Login Function

6. Right-click on your existing **FunctionCallingTest.cs** script, select **Copy**.

7. Select the **project**, **right-click** and select **Paste**.

8. Rename the new script as **ExceptionHandingTest.cs** and click **OK**.

9. Double click on the newly created **"ExceptionHandingTest.cs"** script so that you can see the script.

10. Rename the class name from **FunctionCallingTest** to **ExceptionHandingTest** under TestFixture to remove conflicts and save the file.

11. Modify the Function call in the test to call the function with an invalid username and invalid password.

```
//Comment - Call to Login Function
HA_BF_Login(driver, "InvaldUser", "InvalidPassword");
```

Figure 20.6 – Call to Login Function

12. Save the changes and Click on **Build > Build Solution**.

13. Select the test and Run the test using **Run → Run the Selected Test**. Check if the test passes and shows the test results as before.

   Our expectation would be that the system should print " **Login test Fail for: InvalidUser**".

14. But if you notice the results script fails with "NoSuchElementException" instead of throwing a valid message

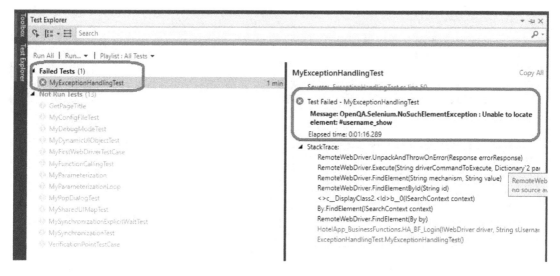

Figure 20.7 – Unable to Locate Element Exception

It is because the control never goes to the else part of the condition. Whenever you try to log in using invalid user details the browser will still display the login page only.

Figure 20.8 - Invalid Login Error

While the next line of our code is looking for a page element which is displayed on the home page of the application. This leads to a *NoSuchElementException* Exception and any line written after the findElement statement is not executed.

How do we resolve this gracefully?

15. We'll catch and report this exception and end the script gracefully.

Let's see the code for that:

```
public void HA_BF_Login(IWebDriver driver, string sUsername, string sPassword)
        {
                //Provide Username
driver.FindElement(By.XPath(ConfigurationManager.AppSettings["Txt_Login_
Username"])).Clear();
driver.FindElement(By.XPath(ConfigurationManager.AppSettings["Txt_Login_
Username"])).SendKeys(sUsername);

                //Provide Password
driver.FindElement(By.Id(ConfigurationManager.AppSettings["Txt_Login_
Password"])).Clear();
driver.FindElement(By.Id(ConfigurationManager.AppSettings["Txt_Login_
Password"])).SendKeys(sPassword);

                //Click on Login button
driver.FindElement(By.Id(ConfigurationManager.AppSettings["Btn_Login_
Login"])).Click();
                try
                {
                // Verify for welcome message.
IWebElement welcomeTxt =
driver.FindElement(By.Id(ConfigurationManager.AppSettings["Lbl_SearchHotel_
WelcomeMessage"]));
                String text = welcomeTxt.GetAttribute("value");
                if (text.Contains("Hello " + sUsername))
                {
                    Console.WriteLine("Login Test Pass for: " + sUsername);
                    return;
                }

                }
                catch (Exception e)
                {
                    //To show the results as Fail
                    Console.WriteLine ("Login Test Fail for: " + sUsername);
                }
        }
```

Figure 20.9 – Login function with Try-Catch statements

In the above code, we have inserted the exception prone code in a **try** block followed by a catch block to report proper results and not end poorly.

We do not need to explicitly print out the stack trace. Visual Studio will automatically print out the program's execution stack so that the developer or user can figure out which class, method, and line caused the exception.

16. Now if we see the NUnit test report, it comes out with a genuine message that Login Failed.

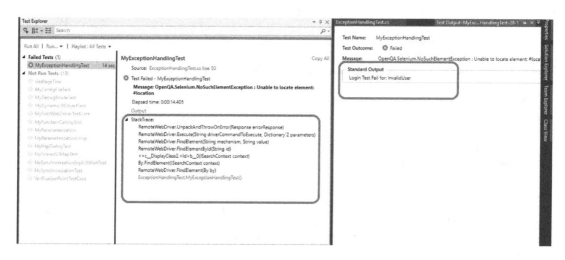

Figure 20.10 – Exception Trace

Note: You can create custom exception or wrap the exception in a new exception and throw it if you want to suppress the original exception message. In such a case, you can print the stack trace of the originally thrown exception using **StackTrace** property.

As in the above example, we should add Try-Catch blocks for all of our scripts and functions.

20.2. Handle Specific Exceptions

Note that apart from the generic way of handling exceptions we can also catch specific exceptions using multiple catch blocks.

```
    catch (ArgumentNullException Ane)
    {
        Console.WriteLine("The argument cannot be null. Please pass a
valid argument.");
    }
    catch (Exception e)
    {
        Console.WriteLine(e.Message);
    }
```

Figure 20.11 – Multiple Exception Blocks

The above example shows that we could use a specific catch block to handle *ArgumentNullException* and other generic exceptions can be handled in other common Catch blocks.

20.3. Common WebDriver Exceptions

Let us see some of the common WebDriver exceptions.

Common WebDriver Exceptions

Exception Type	Description
ElementNotInteractableException	Thrown when an element is present in the DOM but interactions with that element will hit another element do to paint order.
ElementNotSelectableException	Thrown when trying to select an unselectable element.
ElementNotVisibleException	Thrown when an element is present on the DOM, but it is not visible, and so cannot be interacted with. Most commonly encountered when trying to click or read the text of an element that is hidden from view.
ErrorInResponseException	Thrown when an error has occurred on the server side. This may happen when communicating with the Firefox extension or the remote driver server.
ImeActivationFailedException	Thrown when activating an IME engine has failed.
ImeNotAvailableException	Thrown when IME support is not available. This exception is thrown for every IME-related method call if IME support is not available on the machine.
InvalidArgumentException	The arguments passed to a command are either invalid or malformed.
InvalidCookieDomainException	Thrown when attempting to add a cookie under a different domain than the current URL
InvalidElementStateException	
InvalidSelectorException	Thrown when the selector which is used to find an element does not return a WebElement. Currently, this only happens when the selector is an XPath expression and it is either syntactically invalid (i.e. it is not an XPath expression) or the expression does not select WebElements (e.g. "count(//input)").
InvalidSwitchToTargetException	Thrown when the frame or window target to be switched doesn't exist.
MoveTargetOutOfBoundsException	Thrown when the target provided to the ActionsChains move() method is invalid, i.e. out of document.
NoAlertPresentException	Thrown when switching to no presented alert. This can be caused by calling an operation on the Alert() class when an alert is not yet on the screen.
NoSuchAttributeException	Thrown when the attribute of the element could not be found. You may want to check if the attribute exists in the particular browser you are testing against. Some browsers may have different property names for the same property.
NoSuchElementException	Thrown when element could not be found. If you encounter this exception, you may want to check the following: • Check your selector used in your find_by... • Element may not yet be on the screen at the time of the find operation.
NoSuchFrameException	Thrown when frame target to be switched doesn't exist.
NoSuchWindowException	Thrown when window target to be switched doesn't exist.

`RemoteDriverServerException`	
`StaleElementReferenceException`	Thrown when a reference to an element is now "stale". Stale means the element no longer appears on the DOM of the page. Possible causes of StaleElementReferenceException include, but not limited to: • You are no longer on the same page, or the page may have refreshed since the element was located. • The element may have been removed and re-added to the screen, since it was located. Such as an element being relocated. This can happen typically with a javascript framework when values are updated and the node is rebuilt. • Element may have been inside an iframe or another context which was refreshed.
`TimeoutException`	Thrown when a command does not complete in enough time.
`UnableToSetCookieException`	Thrown when a driver fails to set a cookie.
`UnexpectedAlertPresentException`	Thrown when an unexpected alert appears. Usually raised when an expected modal is blocking the WebDriver from executing any more commands.
`UnexpectedTagNameException`	Thrown when a support class did not get an expected web element.
`WebDriverException`	Base WebDriver exception.

Table 20.1 – WebDriver Exceptions

Note: You can find more on common WebDriver Exceptions at https://seleniumhq.github.io/selenium/docs/api/py/common/selenium.common.exceptions.html.

EXERCISE

1. Add a breakpoint at the beginning of the exception. Step and verify that code gets into Catch Block by running script in Debug mode.

21. Reporting in Selenium

One of the very important features of a test automation solution is its reporting structure. After test execution, we inspect the test report for results and defect detection. Selenium does not have its own mechanism for reporting results. Rather, it allows the automation tester to build their own reporting structure, customized to their needs, using features of the programming language of your choice.

As part of this section, we are going to try to understand Test Framework Reporting tools.

Key objectives:

- Test Framework Reporting Tools.
- Generation of HTML Report using ReportUnit.
- Generation of report using Extent Reports.
- Custom Excel or Database reports.

21.1. Test Framework Reporting Tools

Building your own reporting structure! It's great! But what if you simply want something quick that's already done for you? Often an existing library or test framework can meet your needs faster than developing your own test reporting code.

Test frameworks are available with all programming languages. Along with their primary function of providing a flexible test engine for executing your tests, they also include library code for reporting results. For example, .NET also has its own NUnit.

What's The Best Approach?

Most people new to testing frameworks will begin with the framework's built-in reporting features since that's less time-consuming than developing your own.

As you begin to use Selenium no doubt you will start putting in your own "print statements" for reporting progress. That may gradually lead to you developing your own reporting, possibly in parallel to using a library or test framework. Regardless, after the initial but short learning curve, you will naturally develop what works best for your own situation, existing testing frameworks or your custom framework.

Test Reporting Examples in .Net

We'll direct you to some specific tools supported by Selenium. The ones listed here are the latest tools which are available:

- If Selenium Test cases are developed using NUnit then we can use ReportUnit to generate HTML reports.
- We can also use Extent Reports if we want a richer UI, screenshots, and logging.

21.2. Creating XML file using NUnit Console

Before we use ReportUnit to generate an HTML report we need to generate an XML file for the Test Results. ReportUnit uses this XML file to generate the HTML file. There is no GUI which generates an XML file for the NUnit test results. The Visual Studio IDE just shows the Test summary in the Output window. In order to generate an XML file, we need to use NUnit Console. Follow the steps below:

1. Go to Solution Explorer, right-click on the project. Click on **Manage NuGet Packages.**

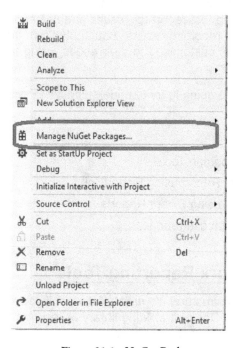

Figure 21.1 - NuGet Package

2. Go to Manage NuGet Packages and click on the **Browse** tab. Search for the Console and you will be able to see a lot of options. Select **NUnit.Console.** On the right-hand side, the versions will be displayed. Choose **Version: 3.6.1.** Click on **Install**.

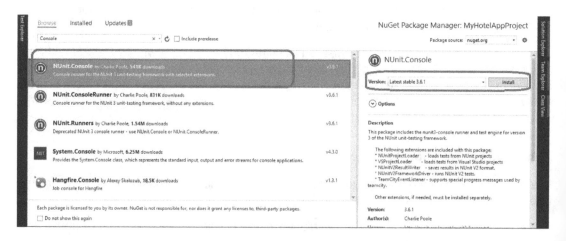

Figure 21.2 – Install NUnit Console

3. An installation pop-up window opens up showing the DLLs that will be installed. Click OK.

Figure 21.3 – Installation Pop-up

4. Once the installation is complete, we need to run the NUnit console to generate the xml file. For that open the **Windows command prompt** by going to **Start > Run > cmd**. Navigate to the directory where the NUnit3-console executable is present.

5. Give the command below to create the XML file.

```
nunit3-console.exe
"C:\Selenium_CS\MyHotelAppProject\MyHotelAppProject\bin\Debug\MyHotelAppProject.
dll" --
work="C:\Selenium_CS\MyHotelAppProject\TestReports "
```

The first argument is the project dll which contains all the tests.

The second argument is **work** which specifies the directory where the output files should go.

💡 **Note: TestReports** folder will be created in the local path to hold all the report files.

To include in IDE copy TestReports folder, right-click on MyHotelAppProject project in solution explorer and paste.

Figure 21.4 – NUnit Console Executable

6. The command gets executed and the tests are run and the TestResult XML file is created in the file path where the NUnit Console is present.

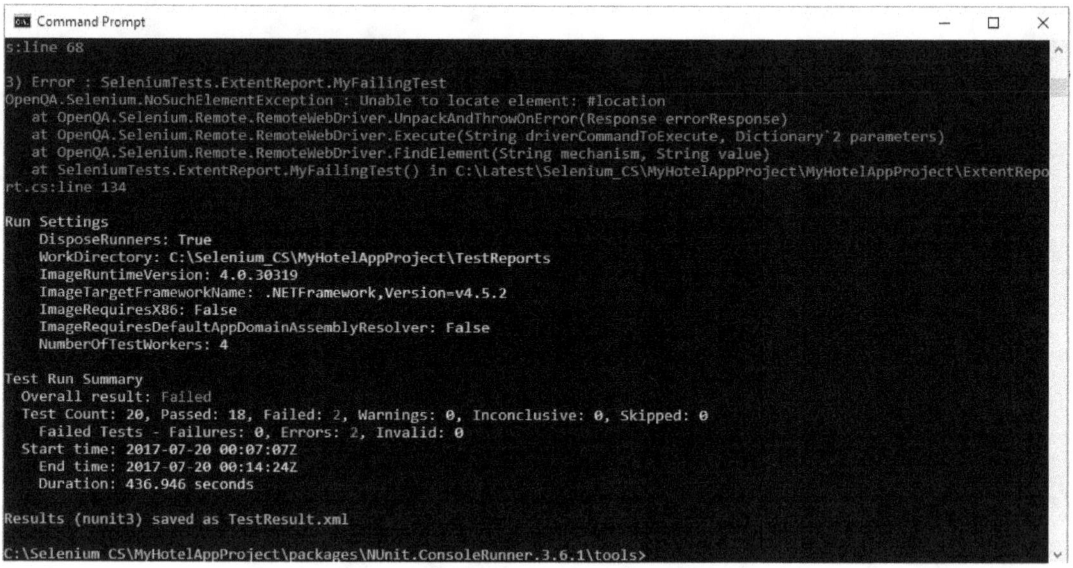

Figure 21.5 – Test Output

The above screenshot shows the Test Summary, Detailed error messages, and Run Settings.

21.3. Configuring ReportUnit for HTML Reports

ReportUnit is a report generator for the test-runner family. It uses stock reports from NUnit, MsTest, xUnit, TestNG and Gallio and converts them to HTML reports with dashboards.

Features:

- Single tool to create reports for NUnit, MsTest, xUnit, TestNG and Gallio.
- Adds dashboard to both folder-level and file-level summaries.
- Creates responsive pages.
- Provides easy navigation for report files from the sidebar.
- Filters for tests and suites.

Usage:

You can either generate a report for all files in a folder or simply convert a given file. Both methods are shown below:

1. Folders

If there are multiple files to process, simply move them to a folder and run one of the commands below:

ReportUnit "input-folder-path"

ReportUnit "input-folder-path" "output-folder-path"

2. Files

Use below steps to process single files:

ReportUnit "input-file"

ReportUnit "input-file" "output-file"

Follow the steps below to create HTML reports using ReportUnit:

1. In order to install ReportUnit into your Visual Studio project, go to Solution Explorer, right-click on the project. Click on Manage NuGet Packages.

2. Go to Manage NuGet Packages and click on the Browse tab. Search for ReportUnit and you will be able to see it. On the right-hand side, the versions will be displayed. Choose Version: 1.2.1. Click on Install.

Figure 21.6 – Browse for ReportUnit

3. A pop-up screen will appear. Click OK.

Figure 21.7 – ReportUnit Install Pop-up

4. The ReportUnit package is added to your project. Now in order to generate the HTML report we need to run the ReportUnit executable. For that, open the Windows command prompt by going to Start > Run > cmd. Navigate to the directory where ReportUnit.exe file is there.

Figure 21.8 – Windows Command Prompt

5. Now using ReportUnit.exe create an HTML file. As we can see below, we are passing two arguments for ReportUnit.exe. The first one is the path to the TestResult.xml file. The second is the path as to where the HTML file should be generated. Here we use the TestResults.xml already created using NUnit console which is present in the TestReports folder.

As you can see, the XML file is parsed and the test results are converted to a readable HTML file.

Figure 21.9 – Execute ReportUnit

6. When you go to the Specified file path and open the HTML file, you can see a rich UI clearly showing the number of tests passed, number of tests failed, and the entire tests summary.

Figure 21.10 – Test Report

7. You can click on individual test cases and examine its status.

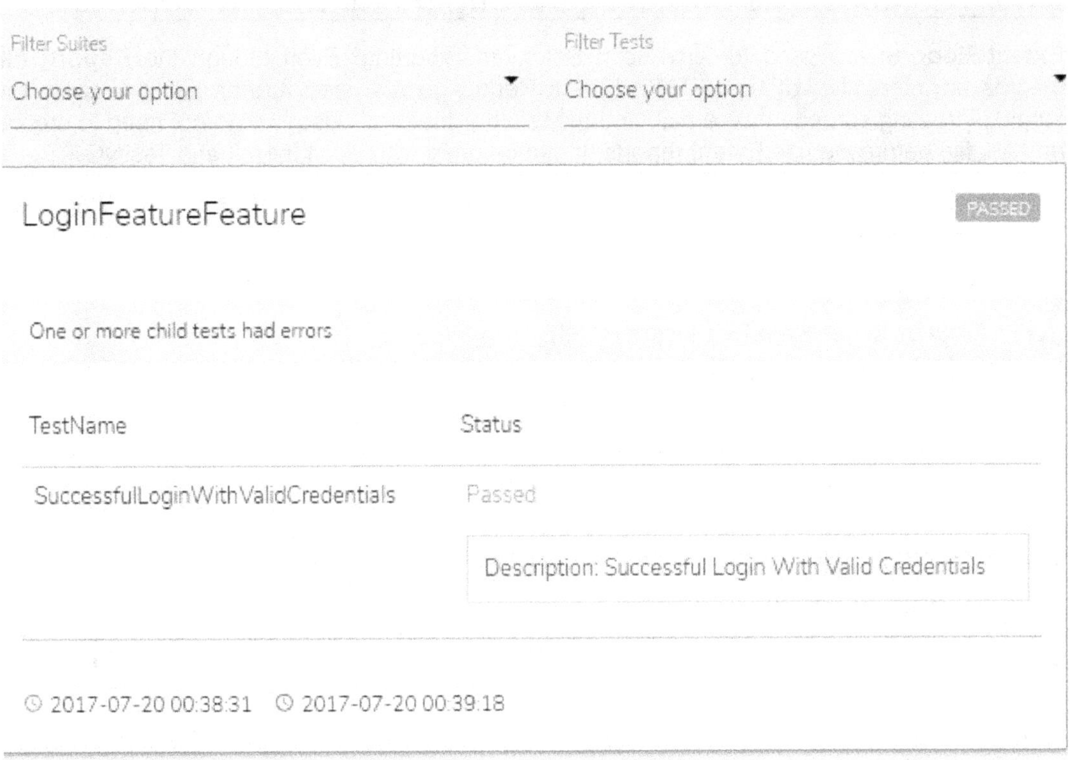

Figure 21.11 – Individual Tests

8. You can also use filters for showing the required tests, whether you want to see passed, failed or any other tests..

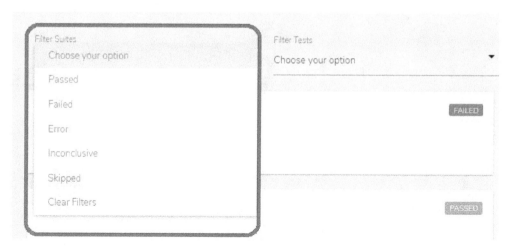

Figure 21.12 – Filters

21.4. Advanced Selenium Reporting using Extent Reports

Extent Reports are used for advanced Selenium reporting. Even though the **ReportUnit** creates an interactive UI rich HTML, Extent Report goes a step further with its facility for logging, creating screenshots, email, and many other features. Also, we do not need to create an XML file before we use Extent reports. It can be used with JUnit, NUnit and TestNG.

In order to use Extent Reports in .Net, you need to download the DLLs into your solution. This can be done using the NuGet package library.

Features of Extent Report:

- Allow us to generate logs inside HTML.
- Generate PIE Chart based on test case status.
- Generate Step summary.
- We can filter reports depending on status.
- It provides execution history.
- It fetches system details like OS, Java Version, and Memory and so on.
- Allow us the attached screenshot in the report that is the most important feature.
- It facilitates Logging.

So, let's start creating Extent Reports. We start by adding the DLLs into our project. To do that, follow the steps below:

1. In order to install Extent Reports into your Visual Studio project, go to Solution Explorer, right-click on the project. Click on **Manage NuGet Packages**.

2. Go to Manage NuGet Packages and click on the **Browse** tab. Search for **Extent** and you will be able to see it. On the right-hand side, the versions will be displayed. Choose **Version: 3.0.2.** Click on **Install**.

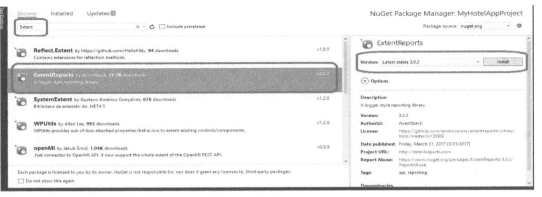

Figure 21.13 – Install Extent Reports

3. An Installation pop-up appears. Click OK. This installs the Extent Report package into your solution.

Figure 21.14 – Extent Report Installation Pop-up

4. You can see the Extent Report assembly under References.

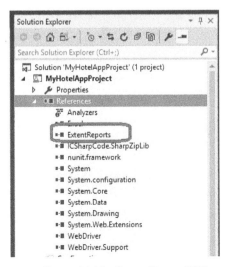

Figure 21.15 – Extent Report DLL

5. Right-click on your existing **FunctionCallingTest.cs** script, select **Copy**.

6. Select the **project**, **right-click** and select **Paste.**

7. Rename the new script as **ExtentReport.cs** and click **OK**.

8. Double click on the newly created **"ExtentReport.cs"** script so that you can see the script.

9. Rename the class name from **FunctionCallingTest** to **ExtentReport** under TestFixture to remove conflicts and save the file.

Initializing Report

It is required to start and attach reporters to **ExtentReports** class in order to successfully generate test information. Failure to start reporters or attaching them will result in **InvalidOperationException** when creating tests or flushing out run content to the report.

```
var htmlReporter = new ExtentHtmlReporter(reportPath);
extent.AttachReporter(htmlReporter);
```

Writing to Report

Simply call the **Flush()** method to write or update test information to your reporter. Below is what each reporter does to write/update results:

- ExtentHtmlReporter: builds a new report using the html template each time upon Flush with the cumulative test information.
- ExtentEmailReporter:pro-only: builds a new report using the email template each time upon Flush with the cumulative test information.
- ExtentXReporter: updates database at each listener event.

Creating Tests

To create tests, use the CreateTest or CreateNode methods:

```
test = extent.CreateTest("MyPassingTest","Test with valid user");
```

Note: it is only possible to create tests and nodes if at least one reporter is attached to ExtentReports.

Remove Tests

To remove a test simply call the RemoveTest method

```
extent.RemoveTest(test);
```

Creating Log Events

You can create logs for the events by using Log method:

```
test.Log(Status.Pass, "Test passed as it is a valid user");
```

Adding System Information

You can add the relevant system information to your report using *AddSystemInfo*

```
extent.AddSystemInfo("Host Name", "Adactin");
```

ExtentHtmlReporter Configuration

Each reporter supports several configuration items to change the look and feel, add content, manage tests, etc. You can either change the configuration in the code or you can use an external XML file to change the configuration settings.

- **Using code**

```
// make the charts visible on report open
htmlReporter.Configuration().ChartVisibilityOnOpen = true;
// create offline report (pro-only)
htmlReporter.Configuration().OfflineReport = true;
// automatic screenshot management (pro-only)
htmlReporter.Configuration().AutoCreateRelativePathMedia = true;
// report title
htmlReporter.Configuration().DocumentTitle = "HotelApp - ExtentReports";
// encoding, default = UTF-8
htmlReporter.Configuration().Encoding = "UTF-8";
// protocol (http, https)
htmlReporter.Configuration().Protocol = Protocol.HTTPS;
// report or build name
htmlReporter.Configuration().ReportName = "Hotel App Report";


// chart location - top, bottom
htmlReporter.Configuration().ChartLocation = ChartLocation.BOTTOM;
// theme - standard, dark
htmlReporter.Configuration().Theme = Theme.Dark;
// add custom css
htmlreporter.Configuration().CSS = "css-string";
// add custom javascript
htmlreporter.Configuration().JS = "js-string";
```

Figure 21.16 - Configuring HtmlReporter in Code

- **Using xml file**

1. Go to the solution explorer, right-click on Configuration folder, Add New Item. When the Add New Item dialog box opens, select XML file, rename it to extent-config.xml. Click on Add.

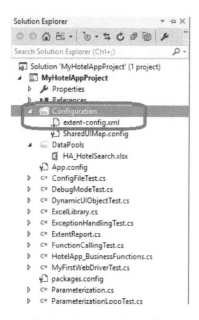

Figure 21.17 - extent-config xml

2. Go to your browser and navigate to the URL: http://extentreports.com/docs/versions/3/net/#htmlreporter-features. You will find the template for extent-config. There will be config files for community and professional. Choose the community config file. Copy the contents into your xml file.

```xml
<?xml version="1.0" encoding="UTF-8"?>
<extentreports>
  <configuration>
    <!-- report theme -->
    <!-- standard, dark -->
    <theme>standard</theme>

    <!-- document encoding -->
    <!-- defaults to UTF-8 -->
    <encoding>UTF-8</encoding>

    <!-- protocol for script and stylesheets -->
    <!-- defaults to https -->
    <protocol>https</protocol>

    <!-- title of the document -->
    <documentTitle>HotelApp - Extent Reports</documentTitle>

    <!-- report name - displayed at top-nav -->
    <reportName>Hotel App Project Test Report</reportName>

    <!-- location of charts in the test view -->
    <!-- top, bottom -->
    <testViewChartLocation>bottom</testViewChartLocation>

    <!-- custom javascript -->
    <scripts>
      <![CDATA[
        $(document).ready(function() {

        });
      ]]>
    </scripts>
```

Figure 21.18 - Configuration in extent-config

3. Now in your code, you can reference the XML file by navigating to the directory where it resides.

```csharp
htmlReporter.LoadConfig(projectPath + "Configuration\\extent-config.xml");
```

Note: You can change various properties through this XML file like Document Title, Report Name, etc.

10. Now write a script for the passing test which is basically just logging into HotelApp project with a valid user and booking it.

```
[Test]
public void MyPassingTest ()
{
    test = extent.CreateTest("MyPassingTest","Test with valid user");

    driver.Navigate().GoToUrl(ConfigurationManager.AppSettings["sAppURL"]);
    driver.Manage().Window.Maximize();
    HA_BF_Login(driver, "adactin123", "adactin123");
            new
SelectElement(driver.FindElement(By.Id(ConfigurationManager.AppSettings["Lst_
SearchHotel_Location"]))).SelectByText("Sydney");
driver.FindElement(By.Id(ConfigurationManager.AppSettings["Btn_SearchHotel_
Search"])).Click();
driver.FindElement(By.Id(ConfigurationManager.AppSettings["Rad_SelectHotel_
RadioButton_1"])).Click();
driver.FindElement(By.Id(ConfigurationManager.AppSettings["Btn_SelectHotel_
Continue"])).Click();
driver.FindElement(By.Id(ConfigurationManager.AppSettings["Txt_BookingHotel_
FirstName"])).Clear();
driver.FindElement(By.Id(ConfigurationManager.AppSettings["Txt_BookingHotel_
FirstName"])).SendKeys("test");
driver.FindElement(By.Id(ConfigurationManager.AppSettings["Txt_BookingHotel_
LastName"])).Clear();
driver.FindElement(By.Id(ConfigurationManager.AppSettings["Txt_BookingHotel_
LastName"])).SendKeys("test");
driver.FindElement(By.Id(ConfigurationManager.AppSettings["Txt_BookingHotel_
Address"])).Clear();
driver.FindElement(By.Id(ConfigurationManager.AppSettings["Txt_BookingHotel_
Address"])).SendKeys("test");
driver.FindElement(By.Id(ConfigurationManager.AppSettings["Txt_BookingHotel_
CCNumber"])).Clear();
driver.FindElement(By.Id(ConfigurationManager.AppSettings["Txt_BookingHotel_
CCNumber"])).SendKeys("12121212121212121212");
new SelectElement(driver.FindElement(By.Id(ConfigurationManager.AppSettings["Lst_
BookingHotel_CCType"]))).SelectByText("American Express");
new SelectElement(driver.FindElement(By.Id(ConfigurationManager.AppSettings["Lst_
BookingHotel_CCExpMonth"]))).SelectByText("March");
new SelectElement(driver.FindElement(By.Id(ConfigurationManager.AppSettings["Lst_
BookingHotel_CCExpYear"]))).SelectByText("2015");
driver.FindElement(By.Id(ConfigurationManager.AppSettings["Txt_BookingHotel_
CCCvvNumber"])).Clear();
driver.FindElement(By.Id(ConfigurationManager.AppSettings["Txt_BookingHotel_
CCCvvNumber"])).SendKeys("111");
driver.FindElement(By.Id(ConfigurationManager.AppSettings["Btn_BookingHotel_
BookNow"])).Click();
driver.FindElement(By.LinkText(ConfigurationManager.AppSettings["Lnk_BookingHotel_
Logout"])).Click();
driver.FindElement(By.LinkText(ConfigurationManager.AppSettings["Lnk_Logout_
ClickHeretoLoginAgain"])).Click();

    test.Log(Status.Pass, "Test passed as it is a valid user");
}
```

Figure 21.19 – Test Pass

As you can see, we are calling CreateTest method at the beginning of the test and passing test name and description as its arguments.

At the end of the test we are logging the Status.

11. Now write a script for the Failing test. This test uses invalid use and fails.

```
[Test]
public void MyFailingTest()
{
    test = extent.CreateTest("MyFailingTest", "Test with invalid user");
    driver.Navigate().GoToUrl(ConfigurationManager.AppSettings["sAppURL"]);
    driver.Manage().Window.Maximize();
    HA_BF_Login(driver, "InvalidUser", "InvalidPassword");
            new
SelectElement(driver.FindElement(By.Id(ConfigurationManager.AppSettings["Lst_
SearchHotel_Location"]))).SelectByText("Sydney");
    driver.FindElement(By.Id(ConfigurationManager.AppSettings["Btn_SearchHotel_
Search"])).Click();
    driver.FindElement(By.Id(ConfigurationManager.AppSettings["Rad_SelectHotel_
RadioButton_1"])).Click();
    driver.FindElement(By.Id(ConfigurationManager.AppSettings["Btn_SelectHotel_
Continue"])).Click();
    driver.FindElement(By.Id(ConfigurationManager.AppSettings["Txt_BookingHotel_
FirstName"])).Clear();
    driver.FindElement(By.Id(ConfigurationManager.AppSettings["Txt_BookingHotel_
FirstName"])).SendKeys("test");
    driver.FindElement(By.Id(ConfigurationManager.AppSettings["Txt_BookingHotel_
LastName"])).Clear();
    driver.FindElement(By.Id(ConfigurationManager.AppSettings["Txt_BookingHotel_
LastName"])).SendKeys("test");
    driver.FindElement(By.Id(ConfigurationManager.AppSettings["Txt_BookingHotel_
Address"])).Clear();
    driver.FindElement(By.Id(ConfigurationManager.AppSettings["Txt_BookingHotel_
Address"])).SendKeys("test");
    driver.FindElement(By.Id(ConfigurationManager.AppSettings["Txt_BookingHotel_
CCNumber"])).Clear();
    driver.FindElement(By.Id(ConfigurationManager.AppSettings["Txt_BookingHotel_
CCNumber"])).SendKeys("1212121212121212");
            new
SelectElement(driver.FindElement(By.Id(ConfigurationManager.AppSettings["Lst_
BookingHotel_CCType"]))).SelectByText("American Express");
            new
SelectElement(driver.FindElement(By.Id(ConfigurationManager.AppSettings["Lst_
BookingHotel_CCExpMonth"]))).SelectByText("March");
            new
SelectElement(driver.FindElement(By.Id(ConfigurationManager.AppSettings["Lst_
BookingHotel_CCExpYear"]))).SelectByText("2015");
    driver.FindElement(By.Id(ConfigurationManager.AppSettings["Txt_BookingHotel_
CCCvvNumber"])).Clear();
    driver.FindElement(By.Id(ConfigurationManager.AppSettings["Txt_BookingHotel_
CCCvvNumber"])).SendKeys("111");
    driver.FindElement(By.Id(ConfigurationManager.AppSettings["Btn_BookingHotel_
BookNow"])).Click();
    driver.FindElement(By.LinkText(ConfigurationManager.AppSettings["Lnk_BookingHotel_
Logout"])).Click();
    driver.FindElement(By.LinkText(ConfigurationManager.AppSettings["Lnk_Logout_
ClickHeretoLoginAgain"])).Click();

    test.Log(Status.Pass, "Test failed as it is an invalid user");
}
```

Figure 21.20 – Test Fail

12. Now under the **OneTimeSetup** annotation write the following code. This code executes just once.

```
[OneTimeSetUp]
 public void StartReport()
 {
            string filepath =
Path.GetDirectoryName(Assembly.GetExecutingAssembly().CodeBase);
            string actualPath = filepath.Substring(0, filepath.LastIndexOf("bin"));
            string projectPath = new Uri(actualPath).LocalPath;

            string reportPath = projectPath + "TestReports\\SampleExtentReport.
html";

            var htmlReporter = new ExtentHtmlReporter(reportPath);

            // make the charts visible on report open
            htmlReporter.Configuration().ChartVisibilityOnOpen = true;
            htmlReporter.LoadConfig(projectPath + "Configuration\\extent-config.
xml");

            extent = new ExtentReports();

            extent.AddSystemInfo("Host Name", "Adactin");
            extent.AddSystemInfo("Environment", "QA");
            extent.AddSystemInfo("User Name", "adactin123");

            extent.AttachReporter(htmlReporter);

 }
```

Figure 21.21 – One Time Setup

The code above creates the HTML file in the TestReports folder by deriving the path from the Executing Assembly. It loads the extent-config xml file to change various attributes in the report generated. It also adds system info like host name, environment, username. Then it attaches the html reporter to the extent report.

13. Now under the TearDown annotation write the code to log the error message and stacktrace information for the failed tests.

```
[TearDown]
public void TeardownTest()
{
     try
     {
            var status = TestContext.CurrentContext.Result.Outcome.Status;
            var stackTrace = "<pre>" + TestContext.CurrentContext.Result.
StackTrace + "</pre>";
            var errorMessage = TestContext.CurrentContext.Result.Message;
            if(status == NUnit.Framework.Interfaces.TestStatus.Failed)
            {
                test.Log(Status.Fail, stackTrace + errorMessage);
            }
            driver.Quit();

     }
     catch (Exception)
     {
            // Ignore errors if unable to close the browser
     }
     Assert.AreEqual("", verificationErrors.ToString());
}
```

Figure 21.22 – Tear Down

14. Now add the OneTimeTearDown annotation. Here you can Flush() to write or update the htmlreporter. This will just be called once. You can use RemoveTest to remove the test.

```
[OneTimeTearDown]
public void EndReport()
{
    extent.Flush();
    extent.RemoveTest(test);
}
```

Figure 21.23 – One Time Tear Down

15. Save the changes and Click on **Build > Build Solution**.

16. Once the build succeeds all the tests appear in the Test Explorer window. Select the tests **MyPassingTest** and **MyFailingTest** and run the test. Right-click on the test and select **Run Selected Tests**.

17. The tests will execute and the HTML file is created in the TestReports folder. Go to the folder and open it.

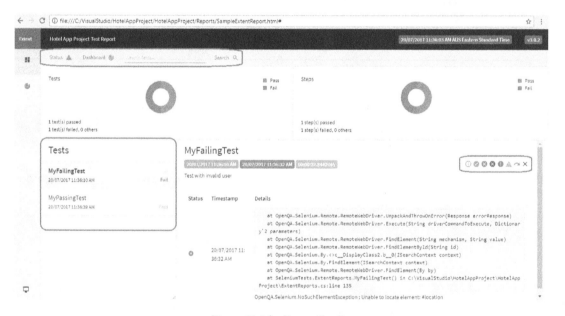

Figure 21.24 – Extent Test Report

As you can see a UI rich interactive report is created. It shows the number of tests passed and failed along with their description. It also shows tests in the form of a pie chart. You can search for a test and filter tests based on their status.

18. You can also see the environment information when you click on the button highlighted in the top left corner.

Figure 21.25 – Extent Test Report Environment

21.5. Custom Reporting in Excel Sheets or Databases

Apart from using ReportUnit and Extent reporting options, another option which is widely used is custom reporting in Excel sheets or in databases.

As seen in one of the previous chapters we can use the .Net class library to read or write into an Excel sheet. So we can create our own custom functions to write results in the Excel-based sheet which can be kept in a central location.

See the snapshot below containing a sample results format.

	A	B	C	D	E
1	BuildNo	ScriptName	StepName	Result	Date-Time
2	15	MyFirstWebDriverTest	MyFirstWebDriverTest - Test to Verify Booking Hotel		
3			Step1	Pass	
4			Step2	Pass	
5			Step3	Pass	
6			Step4	Pass	
7			Step5	Pass	
8	15	MyFirstWebDriverTest	FINAL RESULT - MyFirstWebDriverTest -Test to Verify Booking Hotel	Pass	
9	15	VerificationPointTest	VerificationPointTest - Test to Verify Search Location		
10			Step1	Pass	
11			Step2	Pass	
12	15	VerificationPointTest	FINAL RESULT - VerificationPointTest -Test to Verify Search Location	Pass	
13					
14					
15					

Figure 21.26 – Excel Results Format

We can drive the Result and Step Name based on our custom function which will write into Excel based result sheet.

Note: We are not covering how to report into Excel based sheets, as it would be done purely using C# language and using class library. You can find a lot of reference material on the internet on how to write into an Excel sheet.

Apart from Excel based reporting, we can also report into Databases. The mysql database is pretty popular along with WebDriver since they are free. You can report results into mysql database and create a small php based Web page to read and show data in that page. You can also use SQL database and using ADO.NET connect to the database and read and store the test reports. You could display this report using a simple ASP.NET web page. This is my personal favorite as we would have results in a central location and anyone can see the results using the Web-based URL.

EXERCISE

1. Create HTML reports for VerificationPointTest and SharedUIMapTest using ReportUnit and ExtentReports.

2. Create a custom function call ExcelReporter (stepname, stepstatus) which will report results to an Excel sheet. Call this custom function from one of your WebDriver scripts.

22. Batch Execution

A batch run means executing all the scripts in a suite at the same time, unattended.

There are multiple ways to achieve this:

- Use ReportUnit to run scripts in batch by using an XML file. The XML file contains all the scripts you need to run.
- Use Extent Reports for batch execution by selecting the **Run Selected Tests** in the Visual Studio Test Explorer.
- The third way is to create a Master WebDriver script which will execute calls to other WebDriver scripts as call to classes defined in those scripts.

 Note: If you want to run the tests in parallel just add **Parallelizable** attribute at the start of the test. Whichever tests you want to run in parallel, you can add the annotation and those tests will run at the same time.

You can use any of the above three ways to run your script as a batch suite.

In this chapter, we will see how to run WebDriver scripts as Batch using

- Master WebDriver script

22.1. Batch Execution with Master WebDriver Script

We can also control the execution of WebDriver scripts using a master script. This means that when we run that file it will internally make calls to other WebDriver scripts defined in that master file. We will run this suite as NUnit Tests.

Note: This option is most useful if you are reporting into an Excel sheet or Database.

Let us see how.

Step1 - Changes to Test

1. Right-click on your existing **MyFirstWebDriverTest.cs** script, select **Copy**.
2. Select the **project**, **right-click** and select **Paste.**
3. Rename the new script as **CalledbyTestSuiteTest.cs** and click **OK**.
4. Double click on the newly created **"CalledbyTestSuiteTest.cs"** script so that you can see the script.
5. Rename the class name from MyFirstWebDriverTest to **CalledbyTestSuiteTest** under TestFixture to remove conflicts and save the file.
6. You would have noticed that steps to create a new driver and set timeouts are defined in the setup function.

```
driver = new FirefoxDriver();
ExceptionHandingTest = "http://adactin.com/";
driver.Manage().Timeouts().ImplicitWait = TimeSpan.FromSeconds(10);
```

7. Cut and paste these steps at the start of MyFirstWebDriverTestCase function (which is the main test)

8. You would have noticed that step to quit the Driver is in teardown function.

```
driver.Quit();
```

9. Cut and Paste this step at the end of the function MyFirstWebDriverTestCase function.

10. So your final **"CalledbyTestSuiteTest.cs" script will appear as shown below:**

```
[Test]
  public void MyFirstWebDriverTestCase()
{
            driver = new FirefoxDriver();
            baseURL = "http://adactin.com/";
            driver.Manage().Timeouts().ImplicitWait = TimeSpan.FromSeconds(10);

            driver.Navigate().GoToUrl(baseURL + "/HotelApp/");
            driver.FindElement(By.Id("username")).Clear();
            driver.FindElement(By.Id("username")).SendKeys("adactin123");
            driver.FindElement(By.Id("password")).Clear();
            driver.FindElement(By.Id("password")).SendKeys("adactin123");
            driver.FindElement(By.Id("login")).Click();
                        new  SelectElement(driver.FindElement(By.Id("location"))).
SelectByText("Sydney");
        new SelectElement(driver.FindElement(By.Id("hotels"))).SelectByText("Hotel
Creek");
                        new  SelectElement(driver.FindElement(By.Id("room_type"))).
SelectByText("Standard");
        new SelectElement(driver.FindElement(By.Id("child_room"))).SelectByText("1
- One");
            driver.FindElement(By.Id("Submit")).Click();
            driver.FindElement(By.Id("radiobutton_0")).Click();
            driver.FindElement(By.Id("continue")).Click();
            driver.FindElement(By.Id("first_name")).Clear();
            driver.FindElement(By.Id("first_name")).SendKeys("sdsd");
            driver.FindElement(By.Id("last_name")).Clear();
            driver.FindElement(By.Id("last_name")).SendKeys("sdsd");
            driver.FindElement(By.Id("address")).Clear();
            driver.FindElement(By.Id("address")).SendKeys("dsdfvcfdf");
            driver.FindElement(By.Id("cc_num")).Clear();
            driver.FindElement(By.Id("cc_num")).SendKeys("1234567123456234");
                        new  SelectElement(driver.FindElement(By.Id("cc_type"))).
SelectByText("American Express");
                     new  SelectElement(driver.FindElement(By.Id("cc_exp_month"))).
SelectByText("March");
                        new  SelectElement(driver.FindElement(By.Id("cc_exp_year"))).
SelectByText("2018");
            driver.FindElement(By.Id("cc_cvv")).Clear();
            driver.FindElement(By.Id("cc_cvv")).SendKeys("214");
            driver.FindElement(By.Id("book_now")).Click();
driver.FindElement(By.LinkText("Logout")).Click();
    driver.FindElement(By.LinkTextt("Click here to login again")).Click();
    driver.Quit();
  }
```

Figure 22.1 – Updated Test Script

Note that the reason we are adding both invoking of the driver and quit on driver in the same method is that it will make it much easier to call just one method from any other external script.

Step2 – Create a Suite Script

1. Again, right-click on your existing **MyFirstWebDriverTest.cs** script, select **Copy**.

2. Select the **project**, **right-click** and select **Paste.**

3. Rename the new script as **HA_TestSuite.cs** and click **OK**.

4. Double click on the newly created **"HA_TestSuite.cs"** script so that you can see the script.

5. Rename the class name from MyFirstWebDriverTest to **HA_TestSuite** under TestFixture to remove conflicts and save the file.

6. Remove the code within the function [Test] so we have only the following empty declaration

   [Test]

   public void MyFirstWebDriverTestCase()

   {

   }

7. Add the code below:

```
[Test]
public void MyFirstWebDriverTestCase()
{
    //Instantiating Object for each of the tests
    SeleniumTests.CalledByTestSuiteTest bp1 = new
SeleniumTests.CalledByTestSuiteTest();

    // More tests can be added in similar fashion
    // VerificationPointTest bp2 = new VerificationPointTest();
    //SynchronizationTest bp3 = new SynchronizationTest();
    //SharedUIMapTest bp4 = new SharedUIMapTest();
    // Defining which tests to run

    Boolean bCalledbyTestSuiteTest = true;
    // More variables can be added in similar fashion for other tests
    // Boolean bVerificationPointTest = false;
    // Boolean bSynchronizationTest = false;
    // Boolean bSharedUIMapTest = false;
    //Call and run tests

    if (bCalledbyTestSuiteTest)
        bp1.MyFirstWebDriverTestCase();
}
```

Figure 22.2 – Test Suite Script

If you look at the above code, the first section instantiates all the script classes. Note that we first need to add all the scripts and instantiate them if you would want them to be executed as part of the suite.

The second section defines variables which tell us whether we want to run a particular script or not. If a value is true, it means that the script will be executed as part of the current run of the suite. We might choose not to run a few scripts if they are not relevant for that run cycle.

Note: Alternatively we can also keep this variable's value in an Excel sheet and read from it using a custom method to read from Excel.

The third section is where we call the test method within the script and run the script.

1. Save the changes and Click on **Build > Build Solution**.

8. Once the build succeeds, all the tests appear in the Test Explorer window. Select the test **TestSuite** and run the test. Right-click on the test and select Run **Selected Tests Test** and verify that the scripts run one after the other as a suite.

EXERCISE

1. Add 2 more scripts (VerificationPointTest and bSynchronizationTest) to the suite file. Modify the above script and confirm all scripts execute as a suite.

23. Continuous Integration with Visual Studio Team Services

Introduction

Why do we need Continuous Integration tools for test automation?

Continuous integration (CI) and Continuous Deployment (CD) help you reliably deliver quality apps to your customers at a faster pace. From code through build, test, and deployment you can define efficient and fully managed pipelines that automate and control the entire process.

Continuous Integration (CI) tools assist in creating frequent builds (usually on a daily basis) and running developer driven tests (unit tests) to provide timely feedback on application quality.

We can integrate our Selenium-based functional test automation scripts with CI tools to execute our scripts as soon as a new build is created which will provide instant feedback on application issues.

Popular open source tools include Hudson, Jenkins (the offspring of Hudson), CruiseControl and CruiseControl.NET.

Popular continuous integration tools include Microsoft's Team Foundation Server, Visual Studio Team Services, ThoughtWorks' Go, Jetbrains' Team City, Hudson, Jenkins and Cruise Control.

As part of this chapter, we will learn how Selenium scripts integrate with Visual Studio Team Services one of the popular CI tools provided by Microsoft.

Visual Studio Team Services and Team Foundation Server

Visual Studio Team Services is a cloud based service which provides source code management, Devops - automated builds, tests and release management, package management and code search, tracking work using various agile tools, scale-up facility.

Team Foundation Server (commonly abbreviated to TFS) is a Microsoft product which provides source code management (either via Team Foundation Version Control or Git), reporting, requirements management, project management (for both agile software development and waterfall teams), automated builds, lab management, and testing and release management capabilities. It covers the entire application lifecycle. TFS can be used as a back end to numerous integrated development environments but is tailored for Microsoft Visual Studio and Eclipse (on Windows and non-Windows platforms).

Visual Studio Team Services and Azure cloud services help remove barriers between teams, encourage collaboration, and improve the flow of value to your customers. Otherwise, use an on-premises server, Team Foundation Server (TFS), when you want to maintain your data within your network.

Both options are enterprise-ready, supporting teams of any size, from tens to thousands. Team Services provides a scalable, reliable, and globally available hosted service. It is backed by a 99.9% SLA, monitored by a 24/7 operations team, and available in local data centers around the world.

Also, you can quickly expand the power of these tools through integration with other.

Which one to choose?

Choose Team Services when you want quick setup, maintenance-free operations, easy collaboration across domains, elastic scale, and rock-solid security. You'll also have access to cloud load testing, cloud build servers, and application insights.

Choose on-premises TFS when you need your data to stay within your network or you want access to SharePoint sites and reporting services that integrate with TFS data and tools.

For the purpose of this document, we will start by using **Visual Studio Team Services**.

Key objectives:

- Visual Studio Team Services.
- Code Repository.
- Setting up Build Definition.
- Build and Test the application.

23.1. Visual Studio Team Services

Get setup with Team Services

1. Create a new account in Team Services.

2. If you're prompted, then sign in using your personal Microsoft account or your work or school account.

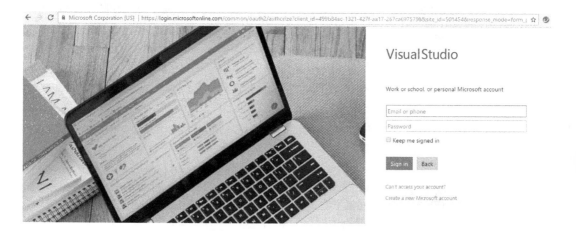

Figure 23.1 – Sign in from Microsoft account

3. Create a Visual Studio Team Service account. Keep the option to use Team Foundation Version Control selected.

Figure 23.2 - Create a Team Service Account

4. You see the home page for your first team project with a simple README.md file.

5. You also see a Setup Build button which you can use in the later stages.

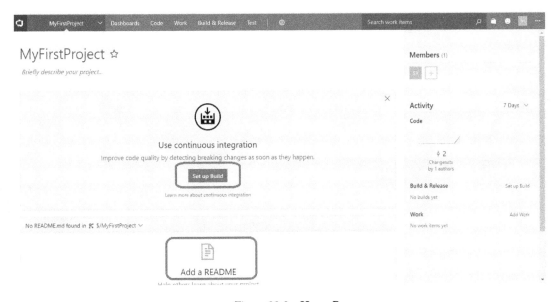

Figure 23.3 – Home Page

23.2. Code Repository

1. Once the Team Services is setup, we will start to create a project. For that click on **Browse** in the menu.

Figure 23.4 – Browse

2. It will take you to the project menu. You will find a New Project button. Click on it.

Figure 23.5 – New Project

3. Fill in the Project name, Description, Version Control and Work item process details. Click Create.

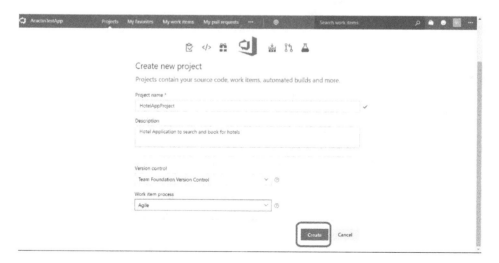

Figure 23.6 – Create New Project

4. Open Visual Studio and sign with the same account as VSTS.

5. Open the Team Explorer window. If the Team Explorer window isn't visible, click on the Team menu and then click on Manage Connections or go to View and then click on Team Explorer.

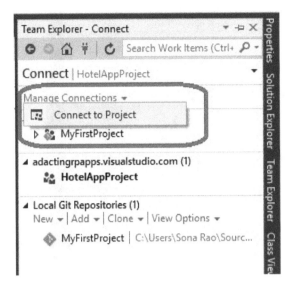

Figure 23.7 – Connect to Project

6. Click Connect to Project a new window opens showing the host repositories and the projects that are hosted. Select the account you used to create VSTS for the host repositories. Then select the recently created project. Click Connect.

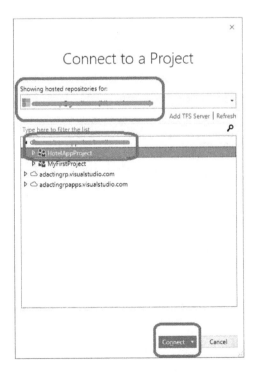

Figure 23.8 – Connect to Project Pop-up

7. Now you need to map your project to a folder in your local machine. Then Click Map & Get.

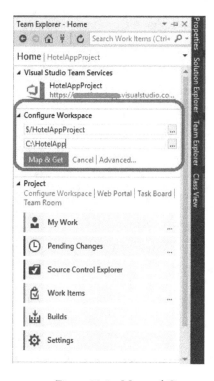

Figure 23.9 – Map and Get

8. If you selected just one team project, you'll see the Home page for that project. The pages that appear differ based on the resources enabled and the source control system selected for your team project.

Figure 23.10 – Team Explorer Home

9. Now, open HotelApp solution in Visual Studio. Once your solution and its projects are opened in Solution Explorer, right-click on the solution and select Add Solution to Source Control.

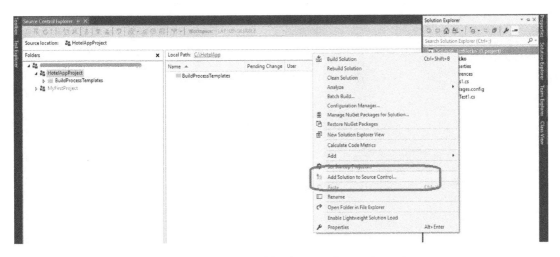

Figure 23.11 – Add Solution to Source Control

10. Now your HotelApp solution containing Selenium Tests is connected to the Visual Studio Team Services. Go to Source Control window in Visual Studio. This can be opened from View->Other Windows->Source Control Explorer as shown below.

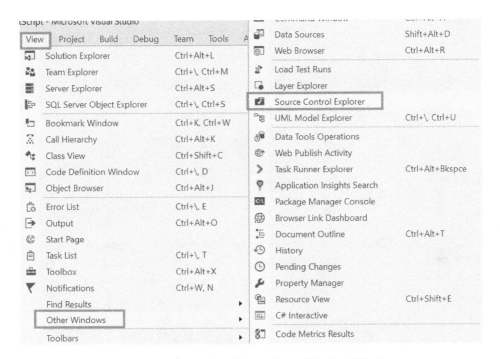

Figure 23.12 – Open Source Control Explorer Window

11. In the Source Control Explorer, you will observe that your project is shown below the Team Foundation Server as shown below:

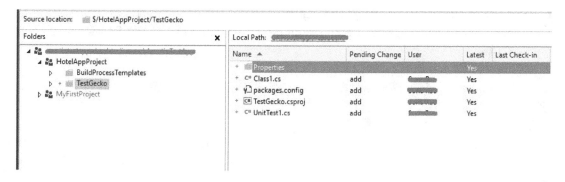

Figure 23.13 – Add Solution to VSTS

12. We now need to check-in the project into the source control. To do that we need to right-click on HotelAppProject and select Check-In Pending Changes.

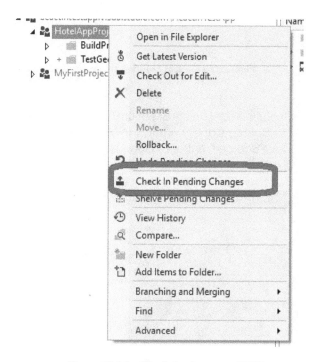

Figure 23.14 – Check-in changes to VSTS

13. On selecting this option, you will be presented with a Team Explorer – Pending Changes window on the right-hand side. By default, all files will be selected for check-in. You need to click the Check In button.

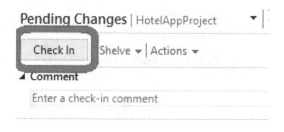

Figure 23.15 – Check-in

14. Now your HotelApp project with Selenium tests has been pushed to the Visual Studio Team Services on cloud. We will verify this by going to the browser and opening the Team Foundation Server URL: https://adactingrpapps.visualstudio.com/HotelAppProject/_versionControl?path=%24%2FHotelAppProject

If it is already opened, then refresh the web page. You will observe that all of your Selenium test project has been loaded into VSTS source control.

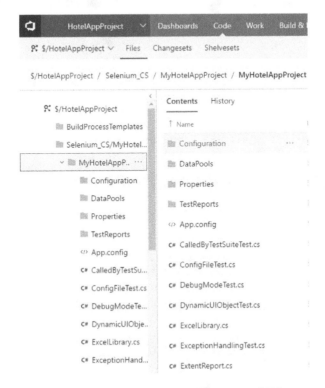

Figure 23.16 – Project in VSTS

This completes linking the Visual Studio project with the Visual Studio Team Services. In the next section, we will see how we can configure build definitions.

23.3. **Setting up Build Definition**

It is a good practice to capture bugs at an early stage and also maintain the quality of the code. If we specify Continuous Integration of cloud based build services, the quality of the product can be monitored. Every time the code is checked-in, the build will be executed (configurable). The build definition needs to be created using the Build section of Visual Studio Team Services.

The build can be automatically triggered with each check-in. The queued build can be viewed with the Build tab under Build & Release menu item. All the build definitions can be viewed in the Mine Tab. You can select individual build definitions and see the summary of builds. Double-clicking the completed build will provide the detailed summary of that particular build. The log and diagnostics can be viewed as well. With all of these features, the build can be created with quality checkpoints.

Note: The below mentioned continuous integration steps vary with projects and the type of project implementation. This activity is carried by Build Engineer or DevOps team.

To achieve this, we need to setup a build definition.

1. Go to your VSTS URL.

2. Click the Build & Release menu item. Click on Builds. You will find a New/New Definition button. Click on it.

Figure 23.17 – New Build Definition Button

3. We will select ASP.NET Core (.NET Framework) to the create build and say Apply.

Figure 23.18 – Build Template

Note: ASP.NET Core is a lean and composable framework for building web and cloud applications.

4. Build definition is a stepwise process to fetch your latest code, compile your code, deploy executable files on remote servers and execute the test scripts. The build definition should look something like this:

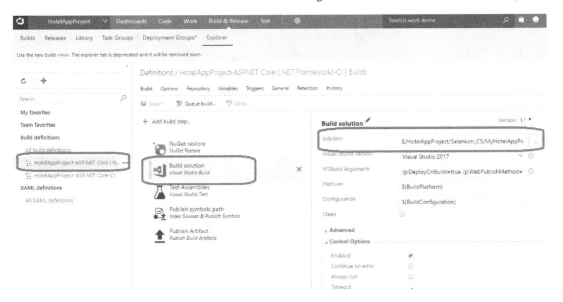

Figure 23.19 – Visual Studio Build Solution definition

Here we are providing the source control path of our solution which we checked in earlier.

5.   Next, you give the Test Assemblies which we want to use to run our test cases.

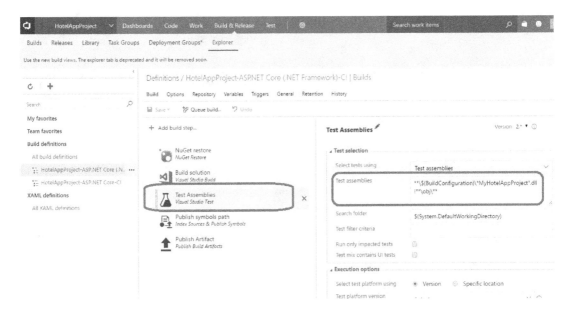

Figure 23.20 – Test Assemblies Used

💡 **Note:** In order to get an idea about the various build steps go to this URL: https://adactingrpapps.visualstudio.com/HotelAppProject/_build/explorer?definitionId=1&_a=simple-process.

You can also add build steps to suit your requirements. Apart from changing what is shown in the screenshots, default values are used for other fields.

6. Now go to the Triggers sub-tab and check the Continuous Integration check box. This makes sure that every time any new check-in happens a build is automatically scheduled. This helps in finding and resolving problems early.

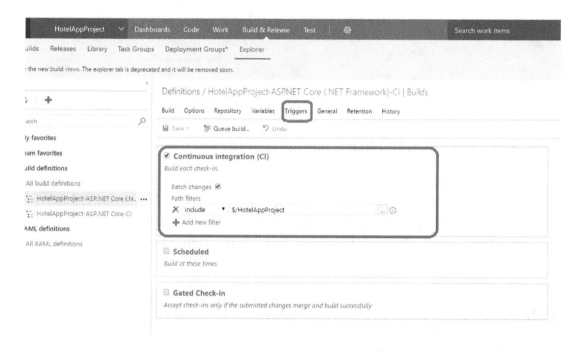

Figure 23.21 – Continuous Integration

7. Now Save the Build Definition.

8. Before starting to Queue the build, we need to add Agents to the build.

   In the section below let us learn a little bit about Agents.

Build and Release Agents

To build your code or deploy your software you need at least one agent. As you add more code and people, you'll eventually need more.

When your build or deployment runs, the system begins one or more jobs. An agent is installable software that runs one build or deployment job at a time.

Hosted Agents

If you're using Team Services, you've got the option to build and deploy using a hosted agent. When you use a hosted agent, VSTS takes care of the maintenance and upgrades. So, for many teams, this is the simplest way to build and deploy.

For Visual Studio 2017 we have to use Hosted VS2017 agent queue and lesser versions can use Hosted agent queue.

Note: Hosted agents are available only in Team Services, not in Team Foundation Server (TFS).

Private agents

An agent that you set up and manage on your own to run build and deployment jobs is a private agent. You can use private agents in Team Services or Team Foundation Server (TFS). Private agents give you more control to install dependent software needed for your builds and deployments.

You can install the agent on Windows, Linux, or OSX machines. You can also install an agent on a Linux Docker container.

After you've installed the agent on a machine, you can install any other software on that machine as required by your build or deployment jobs.

Instead of managing each agent individually, you organize agents into agent pools. An agent pool defines the sharing boundary for all agents in that pool. An agent queue provides access to an agent pool. When you create a build or release definition, you specify which queue it uses.

Hosted agents do not offer interactive mode. Selenium Tests will generally be run interactively, which would fail when we use Hosted Agents. In order to overcome this issue, we need to create our own private agent.

If you run your build with the Hosted Agent it fails. The failed build using Hosted Agent is shown below:

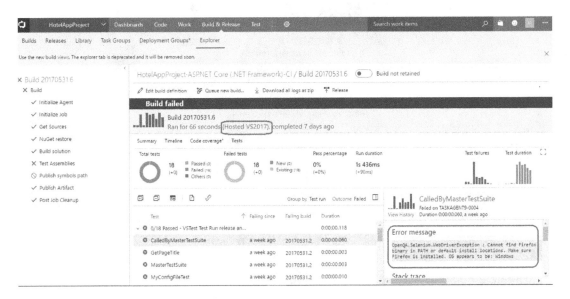

Figure 23.22 – Failed Build

Creating Private Agent

Check prerequisites.

Make sure your machine is prepared with our <u>Windows system prerequisites</u>.

Prepare permissions

Decide which user account you're going to use to register the agent.

Authenticate with a personal access token (PAT) to Team Services or TFS 2017

1. Sign in with the user account you plan to use in either your Visual Studio Team Services account (https://{your-account}.visualstudio.com) or your Team Foundation Server web portal (https://{your-server}:8080/tfs/).

2. Currently, we use the already opened VSTS account.

3. From your home page, open your profile. Go to your security details.

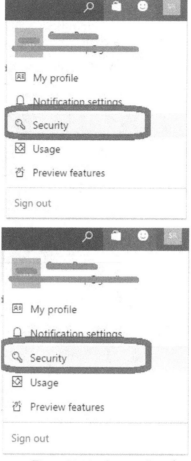

Figure 23.23 – Security Details

4. Create a Personal Access Token. Click Add.

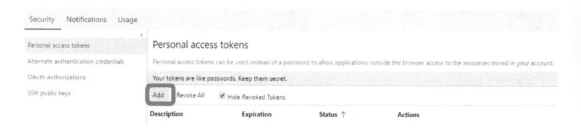

Figure 23.24 – Create Personal Access Token

Give a Description to your token. For the scope select Agent Pools (read, manage) and make sure all the other boxes are cleared. Click Create Token.

Confirm the user has permission

Make sure the user account that you're going to use has permission to register the agent.

💡 **Note**: Is the user you plan to use a Team Services account owner or a TFS server administrator? If so, then skip these steps. Otherwise, you might see a message like this: Sorry, we couldn't add the identity. Please try a different identity.

1. Open a browser and navigate to the *Agent pools* tab for your Team Services account or TFS server:

    o Team Services: https://{your_account}.visualstudio.com/_admin/_AgentPool

    o TFS 2017: https://{your_server}/tfs/DefaultCollection/_admin/_AgentPool

    o TFS 2015: http://{your_server}:8080/tfs/_admin/_AgentPool

2. Click the pool on the left side of the page and then click **Roles**.

3. If the user account you're going to use is not shown, then get an administrator to add it. The administrator can be an agent pool administrator, a Team Services account owner, or a TFS server administrator.

Download and configure the agent

1. Log on to the machine using the account for which you've prepared permissions as explained above.

2. In your web browser, sign on to Team Services or TFS, and navigate to the **Agent pools** tab:

    o Team Services: https://{your_account}.visualstudio.com/_admin/_AgentPool

    o TFS 2017: https://{your_server}/tfs/DefaultCollection/_admin/_AgentPool

    o TFS 2015: http://{your_server}:8080/tfs/_admin/_AgentPool

3. Click **Download agent**.

4. On the **Get agent** dialog box, click **Windows**.

5. Click the **Download** button.

6. Follow the instructions on the page.

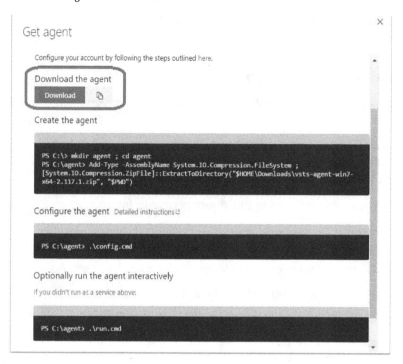

Figure 23.25 – Download Agent

7. When you run the .\config.cmd you will be asked to enter the server URL, authentication type, and other parameters.

Server URL

- Team Services: https://{your-account}.visualstudio.com

- TFS 2017: https://{your_server}/tfs

- TFS 2015: http://{your-server}:8080/tfs

Authentication type

Choose **PAT**, and then paste the PAT token you created into the command prompt window.

Note: When using PAT as the authentication method, the PAT token is used only for the initial configuration of the agent. Also when the PAT is created initially you have to copy the token and save it to your clipboard because once you navigate the page, it will not be available again. This token is required when you configure the agent.

Other Parameters like Agent pool name, work folder, etc., can be given any descriptive names.

Choose interactive or service mode

If you configured the agent to run interactively, to run it:

.\run.cmd

If you configured the agent to run as a service, it starts automatically. You can view and control the agent running status from the services snap-in. Run services.msc and look for «VSTS Agent (*name of your agent*)".

The Powershell script for creating, configuring, and running Agent is shown below.

Open Powershell using Start > Run > powershell and configure it as shown:

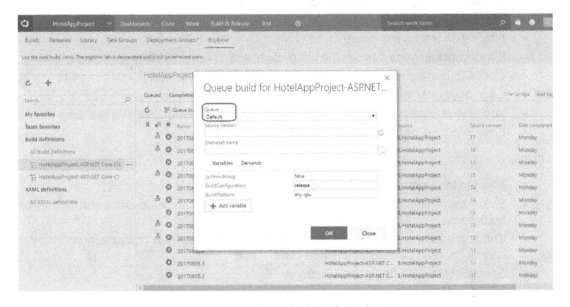

Figure 23.26 – Powershell Script for Agent Configuration

Once the private agent is configured and running. We can queue our build using Default Agent.

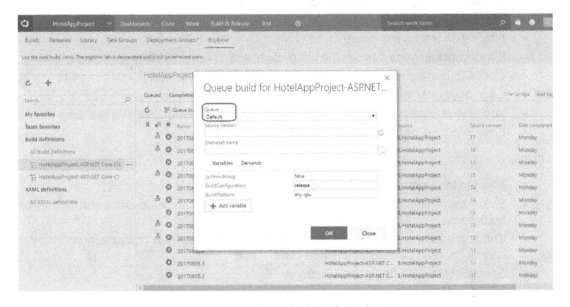

Figure 23.27 – Queue the build for Default Agent

The build succeeds showing the Build Summary, No. of Tests passed, No. of Tests failed and the logs.

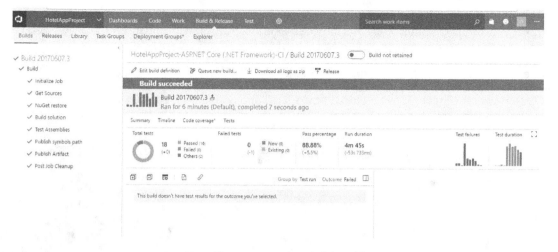

Figure 23.28 – Successful Build

Note: The latest version of geckodriver used is version 0.16.1. The build fails showing it cannot start up if you use the earlier versions.

23.4. Advantages and Disadvantages of Continuous Integration

These are some of the advantages of continuous integration:

- You catch build breaks early on.
- In a distributed development environment where developers do not always communicate with one another, continuous integration is a great way to assure the developer that the build he or she is building is the latest one.
- Continuous integration also causes less regression.
- The feedback loop is smaller.
- Integration testing moves up in the chain.
- Every check-in goes through the integration testing where problems are caught early.
- Continuous integration enforces better development processes.
- Each developer is held accountable.
- You always have a latest-and-greatest build to use in demos, showcases, etc.
- Easy integration and execution of automated scripts

On the other hand, there are some disadvantages:

- Maintenance overhead often increases.
- Some teams find that the level of discipline required for continuous integration causes bottlenecks.
- The immediate impact of a check-in often causes a backup because programmers cannot check in partially completed code.
- Specialist DevOps Engineer is required.

Note: The above points are taken from MSDN (https://msdn.microsoft.com/en-us/library/ms364045(v=vs.80).aspx) and personal experiences. These might differ based on your project.

24. Behavior Driven Development

Introduction

Behavior Driven Development or BDD is an approach to development that improves communication and bridges the gap between business stakeholders and technical teams to create software with business value. BDD uses a common language for communication which is easily understandable.

Let us understand in detail about BDD and how it works.

Test Driven Development (TDD)

BDD is an extension of TDD so we have to understand TDD before we go further.

TDD is an iterative development process. Each iteration starts with a set of tests written for a new piece of functionality. These tests are supposed to fail during the start of iteration as there will be no application code corresponding to the tests. In the next phase of the iteration Application code is written with an intention to pass all the tests written earlier in the iteration. Once the application code is ready tests are run.

Any failures in the test run are marked and more Application code is written/re-factored to make these tests pass. Once application code is added/re-factored the tests are run again. This cycle keeps on happening till all the tests pass. Once all the tests pass, we can be sure that all the features for which tests were written have been developed.

Benefits of TDD

- Unit test proves that the code actually works.
- Can drive the design of the program.
- Refactoring allows improving the design of the code.
- Low Level regression test suite.
- Test first reduces the cost of the bugs.

Drawbacks of TDD

- The developer can consider it as a waste of time.
- The test can be targeted on verification of classes and methods and not on what the code really should do.
- Test becomes part of the maintenance overhead of a project.
- Rewrite the test when requirements change.

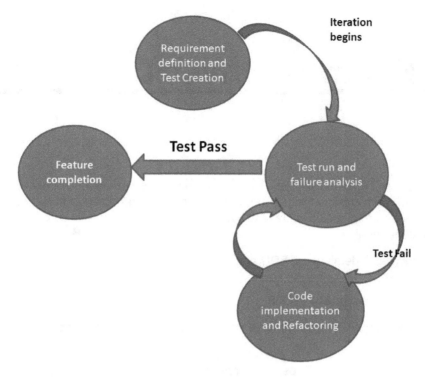

Figure 24.1 – Test Driven Development

With this understanding of TDD we will move to BDD which will form the basis of understanding **Gherkin** and eventually **SpecFlow**.

Behavior Driven Development

In the last section, we discussed what TDD is. We discussed how TDD is test-centered development process in which we start writing tests firsts. Initially, these tests fail but as we add more application code these tests pass. This helps us in many ways:

- We write application code based on the tests. This gives a test first environment for development and the generated application code turns out to be bug free.

- With each iteration, we write tests and as a result, with each iteration, we get an automated regression pack. This turns out to be very helpful because, with every iteration, we can be sure that earlier features are working.

- These tests serve as documentation of application behavior and reference for future iterations.

Behavior Driven testing is an extension of TDD. Like in TDD, in BDD also we write tests first and then add application code. The major differences that we get to see here are:

- Tests are written in plain descriptive English type grammar.

- Tests are explained as behavior of the application and are more user-focused.

- Using examples to clarify requirements.

- This difference brings in the need to have a language which can define, in an understandable format.

Features of BDD:

- Shifting from thinking in "tests" to thinking in "behavior".
- Collaboration between Business stakeholders, Business Analysts, QA Team, and developers.
- Ubiquitous language, it is easy to describe
- Driven by Business Value.
- Extends Test Driven Development (TDD) by utilizing natural language that non-technical stakeholders can understand.
- BDD frameworks such as Cucumber or JBehave are an enabler, acting as a "bridge" between Business & Technical Language.

24.1. What is Cucumber?

Cucumber is a testing framework which supports **Behavior Driven Development (BDD).** It lets us define application behavior in plain meaningful English text using a simple grammar defined by a language called **Gherkin**. Cucumber itself is written in **Ruby**, but it can be used to "test" code written in *Ruby* or other languages including but not limited to *Java, C#,*, and *Python.*

24.2. What is SpecFlow?

SpecFlow is inspired by **Cucumber** framework. **Cucumber** uses plain English in the Gherkin format to express user stories. Once the user stories and their expectations are written, the Cucumber gem is used to execute those stories. **SpecFlow brings the same concept to the .NET world** and allows the developer to express the feature in plain English language. It also allows writing specifications in human readable **Gherkin Format.**

Why BDD Framework?

Let's assume there is a requirement from a client for an E-Commerce website to increase the sales of the product with implementing some new features on the website. The only challenge for the development team is to convert the client idea into something that actually delivers the benefits to the client.

The original idea is awesome. But the only challenge here is that the person who is developing the idea is not the same person who has this idea. If the person who has the idea happens to be a talented software developer, then we might be in luck: the idea could be turned into working software without ever needing to be explained to anyone else. Now the idea needs to be communicated and has to travel from Business Owners (Client) to the development teams or many other people.

Most software projects involve teams of several people working collaboratively together, so high-quality communication is critical to their success. As you probably know, good communication isn't just about eloquently describing your ideas to others; you also need to solicit feedback to ensure you've been understood correctly. This is why agile software teams have learned to work in small increments, using the software that's built incrementally as the feedback that says to the stakeholders: "Is this what you mean?"

With the help of Gherkin language, SpecFlow helps facilitate the discovery and use of a ubiquitous language within the team. Tests written in SpecFlow directly interact with the development code, but the tests are written in a language that is quite easy to understand by the business stakeholders. The SpecFlow test removes many misunderstandings long before they create any ambiguities in the code.

The main feature of the SpecFlow is that it focuses on Acceptance testing. It makes it easy for anyone in the team to read and write test and with this feature it brings business users into the test process, helping teams to explore and understand requirements.

What is *Gherkin* – BDD *Language*?

Before diving into Gherkin, it is necessary to understand the importance and need of a common language across different domains of project. By different domains, I mean **Clients**, **Developers**, **Testers**, **Business analysts,** and the **Managerial team**.

As we might have experienced the requirements given by the business team may have been very crude and basic. So, this leads to many interpretations and doubts. For better understanding, easier implementation, and bug-free code, both the business team and the technical team should be in sync with each other. They need a common language which is easily understandable by both the teams. When the requirements are clear and specific, the overhead of defects due to ambiguous requirements is reduced.

So, to summarize we need a language which takes care of the following:

1. *Different teams in the project need a common language to express requirements. This language should be simple enough to be understood by Business team members and should be explicit enough to remove most of the ambiguities for developers and testers.*

2. *This language should open up the thinking of team members to come up with more scenarios. As you express more details you try to visualize the system more and hence you end up making more user scenarios.*

3. *This language should be good enough to be used as project documentation.*

To answer these problems **Gherkin** was created. **Gherkin** is a simple, lightweight and structured language which uses regular spoken language to describe requirements and scenarios. By regular spoken language, we mean English, French, and around 30 more languages.

Example of Gherkin

As Gherkin is a structured language it follows some syntax let us first see a simple scenario described in gherkin.

Feature: Search feature for users important because it will allow users to filter products.

Scenario: When the user searches, without spelling mistake, for a product name present in inventory, all the products with similar name should be displayed.

Given User is on the main page of www.myshoppingsite.com
When User searches for laptops
Then search page should be updated with the lists of laptops

Gherkin contains a set of keywords which define different premise of the scenario. As we can see above, the colored parts are the keywords. The key points to note are:

- *The test is written in plain English which is common to all the domains of your project team.*

- *This test is structured that makes it capable of being read in an automated way, thereby creating automation tests at the same time while describing the scenario.*

  You can get more information about Gherkin language from http://toolsqa.com/cucumber/gherkin-keywords/.

24.3. Steps to Configure or Setup SpecFlow

Now we have a complete understanding of *What is TDD, What is BDD* and Why & When these are used. In this section, we will learn *How to Configure or SetUp SpecFlow*.

SpecFlow tests are defined as "*features*" that have multiple scenarios. There is a small amount of project setup that needs to be done, but it's not too bad and you can be up and running in just a few minutes.

Let us start configuring SpecFlow for our HotelApp application:.

1. Open your HotelApp application in Visual Studio. Go to **Tools > Extensions and Updates**.

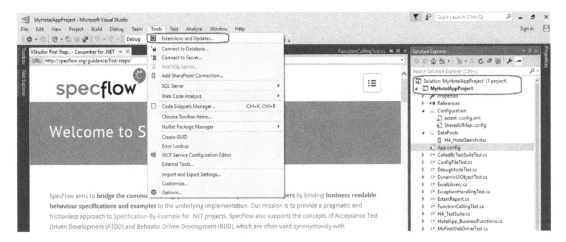

Figure 24.2 – Extensions and Updates

2. Make sure you are in the *Online* branch on the left and type *SpecFlow* into the *search area* in the upper right corner of the dialog. Search will display the *SpecFlow Tool* at the center, *select* it and *click* on *Download*.

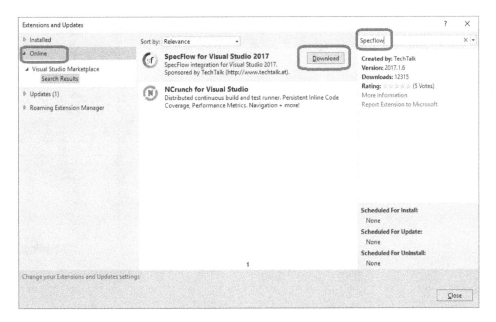

Figure 24.3 – Download SpecFlow

3. Once you click Download the installation will be scheduled. Close your Visual Studio for the installation to start. Click on **Modify**. The SpecFlow will be downloaded and installed.

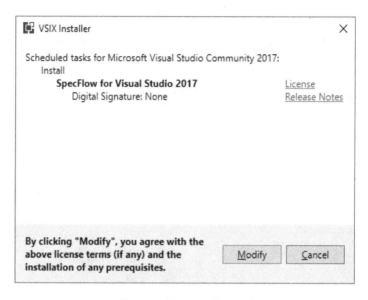

Figure 24.4 – Install SpecFlow

4. Open HotelApp application in Visual Studio. Now we need to add the project reference to SpecFlow. Navigate to *Tools -> NuGet Package Manager -> Manager NuGet Packages for Solutions...* **or right-click on the project and click on** *Manage NuGet Packages...*

5. Click on **Browse** tab and in the search field type SpecFlow. Select the project and the latest version of SpecFlow and click on **Install**.

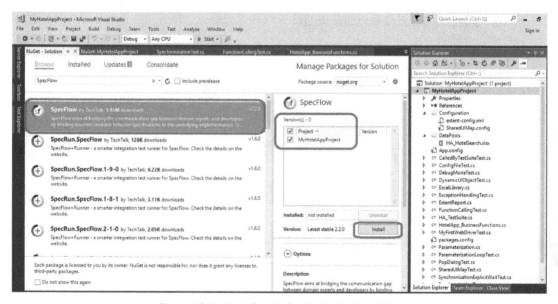

Figure 24.5 – SpecFlow in the NuGet Package Manager

6. An installation pop-up appears. Click **OK.** SpecFlow is installed successfully in the project.

Figure 24.6 – SpecFlow Installation Pop-up

24.4. Creating your First SpecFlow Test

Create a Feature File

1. Now that you have the environment setup, you can actually use *SpecFlow*. Before adding any new files, let us create two new folders called **Features** and **Steps** in the project. To do this, right-click on the **project** and select **Add → New Folder**. The purpose of this step is to add all the feature files into the Features folder and all the Step Definitions into the Steps folder. This helps in code readability. We will understand it in detail as we proceed further.

2. To create your first feature file, you can right-click on the *Feature* **folder** and select **Add –> New Item...** from the context menu. Select **SpecFlow Feature File**. Give it a logical name. When you name your *SpecFlow* feature files, try to name them similar to the feature it will be testing. Click **Add.** The Feature file will be added to your project **Features** folder.

Figure 24.7 – Add Feature File

3. The ***feature file*** will have a sample of how the feature will be setup. This is just a sample and the purpose of it is to display the pattern of the feature file. So, you will be changing this file a lot when you move forward in this tutorial. As you can see Gherkin language is used and the keywords are highlighted in blue.

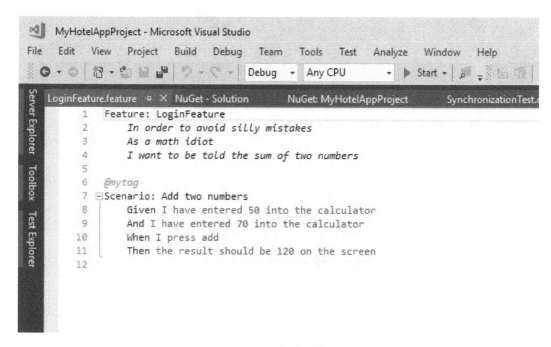

Figure 24.8 – Sample Feature File

4. Now let us change this feature file for our Login functionality.

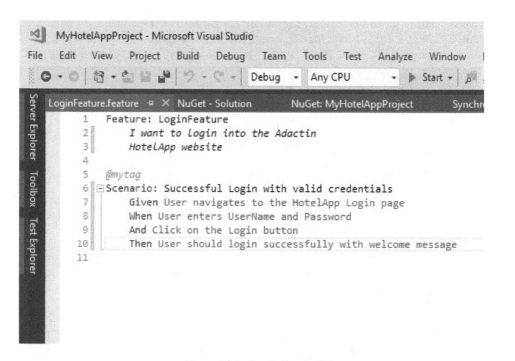

Figure 24.9 – Login Feature File

Feature keyword defines the logical test functionality you will test in this feature file.

Each Feature will contain some number of tests to test the feature. Each test is called a ***Scenario*** and is described using the ***Scenario****:* keyword.

Given defines a precondition to the test.

When keyword defines the test action that will be executed. By test action we mean the user input action.

And keyword is used to add conditions to your steps.

Then keyword defines the Outcome of previous steps.

In the above scenario when the user enters a valid username and password and then clicks on login, the user should successfully login with a welcome message.

Generate Step Definition File

In order to test our scenario, the next thing to do is to create a Step Definition file. This is a regular C# file with a Binding attribute added. The file that SpecFlow will generate will match the template they provided in the feature file. Yes, it can automatically generate a skeleton for the automation code that you can then extend as necessary:

1. Right-click on your feature file in the code editor and select Generate Step Definitions from the pop-up menu.

Figure 24.10 – Generate Step Definition

2. This displays a pop-up window, which will ask to select the statements for which Step Definition file is to be created. Select all, give a valid name and click on the **Generate** button.

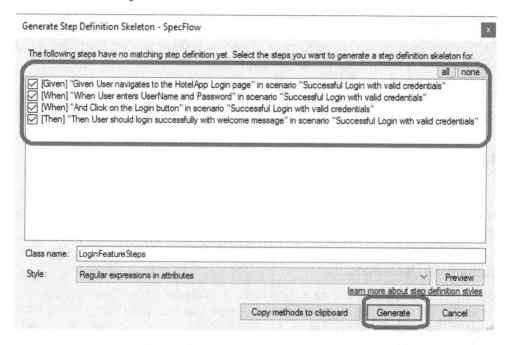

Figure 24.11 – Generate Step Definition Skeleton

3. It will ask to specify the folder path to save the *Step Definition* file, choose the **Steps** folder in the project location and hit the **Save** button.

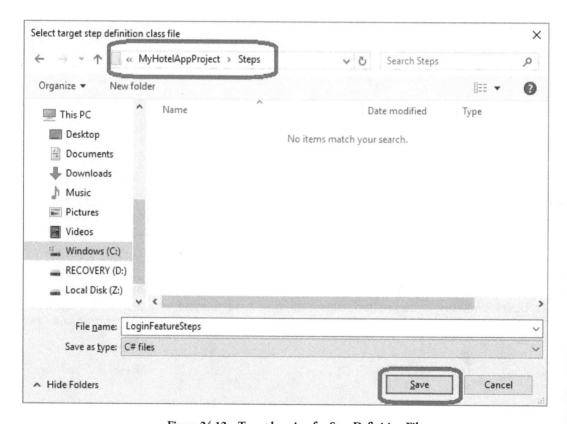

Figure 24.12 – Target location for Step Definition File

4. All the statements will change color now, it means these Feature statements are linked with Step Definitions.

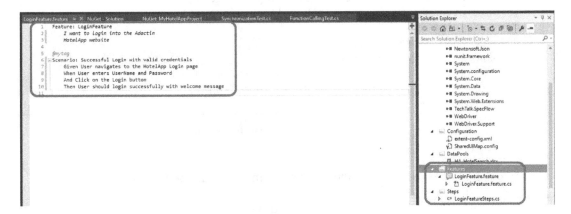

Figure 24.13 – Feature linked to Step Definition

5. To have a look at the attached definitions, click on any statement and press the **F12** button. This will open up the linked definition file and the cursor will be pointing to the linked definition.

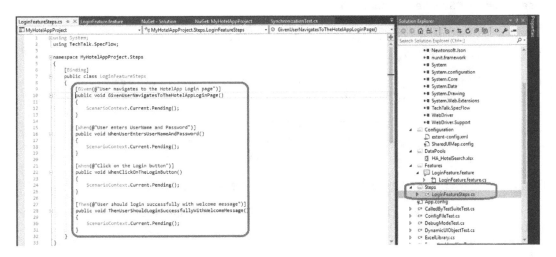

Figure 24.14 – Step Definition Code File

As you can see, there are method definitions for each of the keywords in the feature file. Currently, there is a default code inside each method. As and when we proceed, we need to add our own definition into these methods.

6. Let us add Login functionality to these methods.

In the `GivenUserNavigatesToTheHotelAppLoginPage()` method add the following code to navigate to the HotelApp web page.

```
private IWebDriver driver;
private string baseURL;
[Given(@"User navigates to the HotelApp Login page")]
public void GivenUserNavigatesToTheHotelAppLoginPage()
{
    driver = new FirefoxDriver();
    baseURL = "http://adactin.com/";
    driver.Manage().Timeouts().ImplicitWait = TimeSpan.FromSeconds(10);
    driver.Navigate().GoToUrl(baseURL + "/HotelApp/");
}
```

Figure 24.15 – Navigate to the Page

In the `WhenUserEntersUserNameAndPassword()` method add the following code

```
[When(@"User enters UserName and Password")]
public void WhenUserEntersUserNameAndPassword()
{

driver.FindElement(By.XPath(ConfigurationManager.AppSettings["Txt_Login_
Username"])).Clear();

driver.FindElement(By.XPath(ConfigurationManager.AppSettings["Txt_Login_
Username"])).SendKeys("adactin123");

driver.FindElement(By.Id(ConfigurationManager.AppSettings["Txt_Login_
Password"])).Clear();

driver.FindElement(By.Id(ConfigurationManager.AppSettings["Txt_Login_
Password"])).SendKeys("adactin123");
}
```

Figure 24.16 – Enter Valid Credentials

This piece of code is used for entering a valid username and password.

In the `WhenClickOnTheLoginButton()` method add the following code to click on the login button.

```
[When(@"Click on the Login button")]
public void WhenClickOnTheLoginButton()
{

driver.FindElement(By.Id(ConfigurationManager.AppSettings["Btn_Login_
Login"])).Click();
}
```

Figure 24.17 – Click Login Button

The user should be logged in successfully with a welcome message. The
ThenUserShouldLoginSuccessfullyWithWelcomeMessage() checks if the user logs in
successfully. Then close the window.

```
[Then(@"User should login successfully with welcome message")]
public void ThenUserShouldLoginSuccessfullyWithWelcomeMessage()
{
    Assert.AreEqual("Hello adactin123!",
driver.FindElement(By.Id(ConfigurationManager.AppSettings["Lbl_SearchHotel_
WelcomeMessage"])).GetAttribute("value"));
driver.Quit();
}
```

Figure 24.18 – Successful Login

Executing a SpecFlow Test

1. Once the code is written, we need to build the tests. Go to **Build → Build Solution**. The
    build should succeed and all the tests should appear in the **Test Explorer**. Go to **Test →
    Windows → Test Explorer** to identify the tests in the feature file.

2. If the tests do not appear in the Test Explorer_open **App.config** file from the Solution
    Explorer window and make sure that **unitTestProvider** name should contain only one
    entry, either **NUnit** or SpecFlow as shown in the screenshot below:

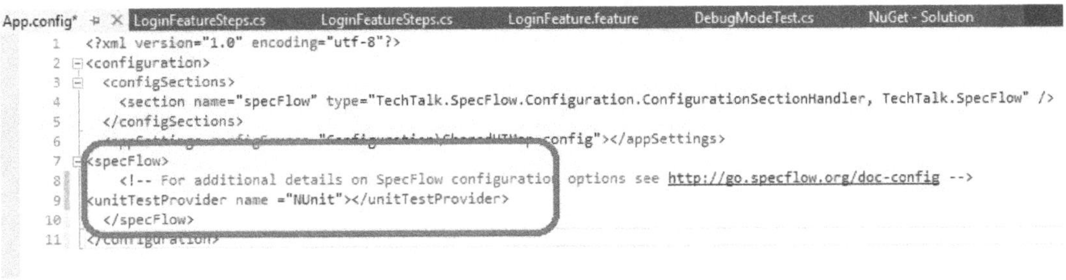

```
App.config* ⊕ ✕  LoginFeatureSteps.cs      LoginFeatureSteps.cs      LoginFeature.feature      DebugModeTest.cs      NuGet - Solution
 1    <?xml version="1.0" encoding="utf-8"?>
 2  ⊟ <configuration>
 3  ⊟   <configSections>
 4        <section name="specFlow" type="TechTalk.SpecFlow.Configuration.ConfigurationSectionHandler, TechTalk.SpecFlow" />
 5      </configSections>
 6        <appSettings configSource="Configuration\SharedHTMap.config"></appSettings>
 7  ⊟   <specFlow>
 8        <!-- For additional details on SpecFlow configuration options see http://go.specflow.org/doc-config -->
 9        <unitTestProvider name ="NUnit"></unitTestProvider>
10      </specFlow>
11    </configuration>
```

Figure 24.19 – unitTestProvider in App.config

3. Now to run a Feature Test, right-click on the test in the Test Explorer window and select
    Run Selected Tests. This will run the selected test and display the output in the console
    window.

💡 **Note**: Feature File can also be run by right-clicking in the feature and choosing **Run
SpecFlow Scenarios**. But sometimes it creates issues.

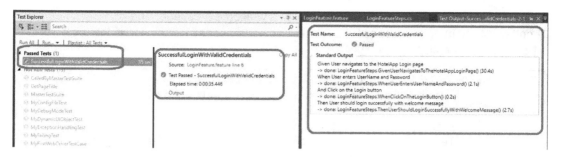

Figure 24.20 — Successful Login

As you can see the Feature test executes successfully and the result is **Pass**. The output window shows each of the steps executed. This is easily understandable and the readability increases the efficiency in tracking issues and building bug-free applications.

We have now clearly understood in depth about **Behavior Driven Development**, using **SpecFlow** and **Gherkin** to create BDD tests.

25. Automation Frameworks

Being a part of the software testing domain, we would have heard the term "Automation Frameworks" many times. Again, it is a very common question one encounters at interviews too. In this chapter we will try to understand the answers to these basic questions:

- Why do we need a framework? What are the advantages of frameworks?
- What exactly is an automation framework? What are the components of the framework?
- How do we implement frameworks? What are the different types of frameworks?

25.1. Why do we need Automation Frameworks?

1. Maintainability

One of the key reasons behind creating an automation framework is to reduce the cost of script maintenance. If there is any change in the functionality of the application, then we need to get our scripts fixed and working utilizing the least amount of time and effort.

Ideally, there should not be too much need to update the scripts, in case the application changes. Most of the fixes should be handled at the framework level.

2. Productivity

If we ask how many manual test cases we can automate in a day that might be a difficult question to answer. But the important thing to ask is whether we can increase our productivity by automating more test cases per day?

Yes, we can. If we have an effective framework, we can increase the productivity manifold. In one of our previous projects, we increased the productivity from 3-4 test cases a day to 10-12 test cases a day, mainly through effective framework implementation.

3. Learning curve

If you have a new person joining your team, you would like to reduce the effort in training the person, and have him/her up and running on the framework as soon as possible.

Creating an effective framework helps reduce the learning curve.

As a best practice, we always advise our clients to keep the framework as simple as possible.

4. Make result analysis easier

Once the test cases are automated, a lot of time is spent by the testing team on analyzing the results. Sometimes they are not detailed enough, which might make it hard to pinpoint the error. Most often, it is not script failure but environment or data issues that turn out to be the source of problems. A better reporting format in the framework will cut down on result analysis time considerably.

25.2. What Exactly is an Automation Framework?

Frameworks are a set of guidelines which define how we will structure the various components in an automation environment. These components include object repository, test data, functions, reports and batch execution scripts.

When the development team begins development, it creates a high-level design of the application. Similarly, we, as an automation team, need to create an automation framework to define how different automation components will interact with each other. We can also call it high-level design for automation components.

So what are the components of the frameworks? Let us see below:

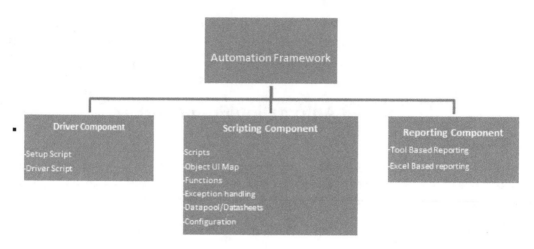

Figure 25.1 – Automation Framework

At a high level, an Automation Framework can be divided into three components:

- **Driver Component** – How will you execute the script as a batch? What setup will you need before you start execution?
- **Scripting Component** – How will you structure all of the key components of your automation framework?
- **Reporting Component** – How will you get your results?

Together, all these components make up an **Automation Framework.**

So, let us understand what exactly is stored within these components.

- **Setup Script** – This script defines what setup you need before you can start script execution.

example

In one of our projects, we had to install the new desktop thick client application, before we could kick off the automation test execution. So we created a setup script to download the latest thick client and install it on the test machines to setup the environment.

- **Driver Script** – Most of the time we need to run our scripts overnight. So we need a driver script which can run the scripts as a suite (one after another).
- **Scripts** – These are the actual automation programs, which execute just like manual test cases

- **Shared UI Map** – A common place where all object properties and information are stored.
- **Functions** – Modular programs which can be reused across scripts.
- **Configuration File** – File in which we can setup the application URL and other variable parameters in our application.
- **Exception Handling** – Exception handling scenarios in our application.
- **Data Pool** –Test data that will drive our scripts.
- **Tool Based Reporting** – Most of the automation tools will have their own reporting format. For instance, Selenium can run tests and create TestNG or JUnit reports. Similarly, in Microsoft Coded UI, results can be viewed in the MTM or TFS.

It is also important to think about where to store these results for future reference and the ease of drilling down to the results you are looking for.

With Selenium, we can store results in a database and read them using a custom Web-based interface. This does not come with Selenium but can be developed.

- **Excel Based Reports** – Not all tools have corresponding test management tools to store results. Quite often, and as part of a framework, the automation team has to develop their own excel drivers (at times database driven) to store results in Excel Sheets for easy viewing and analysis.

25.3. Types of Frameworks

This brings us to the next important question of how to implement frameworks and what the different types of frameworks are.

Automation developers have different reasons for following a particular framework and every framework has its own advantages and disadvantages.

We can divide frameworks into the following categories:

- Level 1- Record- Replay
- Level 2- Data Driven Framework
- Level 3- Test Modularity Framework
- Level 4 - Hybrid Framework
- Level 5 - Keyword Driven Framework

We will call Level 1 the lowest level framework and Level 5 the highest.

Let's understand more about each of the different levels.

Level 1 - Record-Replay

This is not really a framework but helps as a starting point to an introduction to frameworks.

- This framework provides the ability to capture/record the user actions and later to play them back.
- Also called Capture/Replay approach.
- Enhance the recorded script with verification points, where some property or data is verified against an existing baseline.
- Also note that as part of this framework, we use a shared object repository across all the scripts.

Advantages

- Fastest way to generate scripts.
- Automation expertise not required.

Disadvantages

- Little reuse of scripts.
- Test data is hard coded into the script.
- New scripts always take the same time to automate as previously automated scripts.
- Maintenance is a nightmare.

One of the key issues with this framework is that if the application workflow changes or if the test data changes, we need to go into each script and modify the script.

For instance, if you have 500 automation scripts for your application and username or password changes for your login page, you would need to go into each of the scripts and fix them, which can be a nightmare.

This leads us to our next level of framework, which resolves this issue.

Level 2 – Data Driven Framework

In this framework, while test case logic resides in test scripts, the test data is separated and kept outside the test scripts. Test data is read from the external files (Excel files, Text files, CSV files, and database) and loaded into the variables inside the test script. Variables are used both for storing input values and verification values. Test scripts themselves are prepared using the record replay approach.

Since the data is stored outside the script, if as in our previous example the username or password changes, we would need to change just one datasheet and all our 500 scripts will be fit for execution. So we avoided a huge maintenance effort using this framework.

Also, we can use the same script to run multiple sets of data defined in external datasheets helping us achieve more return on investment.

Advantages

- Test data can be changed at one central place and there is no need to modify the scripts.
- Changes to the Test data do not affect the Test scripts.
- Test cases can be executed with multiple sets of data.

Disadvantages

- If functional workflow of the application changes, it will be a maintenance nightmare.
- No reuse of code.

One of the key issues with the above framework is that if the workflow of the application changes, you would need to go back and fix all the scripts again.

For instance, assuming you have 500 scripts, and in each script you login to the application. Due to a new business requirement, apart from just username and password, your application now also requires your business unit name to be entered before login. This represents a change in application. Even though your data resides outside the script, you still need to go into each of the scripts and add extra lines of code to enter the business unit name. This approach is still a nightmare!

Let us look at the next level of frameworks which helps to handle this issue.

Level 3– Test Modularity Framework

As part of this framework we divide the application-under-test into libraries (Functions or Action based). These library files are then directly invoked from the test case script. This framework embodies the principle of abstraction.

In this framework, we can reuse a lot of the existing code, which helps to improve productivity.

Considering our earlier example where our login workflow has changed. We will be able to handle that issue using this framework more simplistically, as we would have created login as a separate function. This login function will be invoked from all our scripts. So we just need to add a step in the login function to enter a value in the business Unit field and all our scripts should be fine.

So, as we would have understood, modular and data driven frameworks work differently; one utilizes a modular approach and the other focuses around data.

Advantages

- Higher level of code reuse is achieved in Structured Scripting compared to "Record & Playback".
- Automation scripts are less costly to develop due to higher code reuse.
- Easier Script Maintenance.

Disadvantages

- Technical expertise is necessary to write Scripts using Test Library Framework.
- More time is needed to plan and prepare test scripts.
- Test Data is hard coded within the scripts.

Level 4– Hybrid Framework

In the previous section, we saw the advantages of a data driven framework and test modularity framework. Should we not get benefits of both the data driven and modular approach?

This is exactly what we do in a hybrid framework. We keep data outside our scripts and create modular functions.

Advantages

- Higher level of code reuse.
- Test Data is at a central location and can be changed on demand.
- Higher productivity and more scripts can be automated as we build the libraries.
- Easier script maintenance.

Disadvantages

- Technical expertise is necessary to write scripts and understanding of existing functions could take time.
- More time is needed to plan and prepare test scripts.
- Can be used by expert automation testers only.

Note: Hybrid frameworks constitute 80-90% of the frameworks, which are highly successful.

Level 5– Keyword Driven Framework

Hybrid frameworks have a lot of advantages, but the disadvantage is that they get too technical. Inherently testers are not programmers and so automation gets limited to automation testers only and cannot be done by functional testers or business analysts.

Keyword driven framework makes it easier for functional testers and business analysts to be involved in automation. Let us see how.

The keyword-driven or table-driven framework requires the development of data tables (usually Excel Sheets) and keywords, **independent of the test automation tool** used to execute them. Tests can be designed with or without the application.

For example, instead of recording a script to login to the application, if we had an Excel Sheet to store username and password and reuse, wouldn't that be easy enough for functional testers? See table below.

Object Object Repository	Action (KEYWORD)	TestData
uIUsernameEdit(UserName)	Set	adactin123
uIPasswordEdit(Password)	Set	Xxxxx
uILoginButton(Login)	Click	
browserWindow(Adactin.com)	Verify	Loads

But how will the script actually run?

Embedded within the back-end, there will be an intermediate component, which will translate this Excel Sheet at runtime and create an automation script on the fly.

The key point to remember about this framework is that the intermediate component which will translate high-level Excel sheet statements written by non-programmers is the complex part and can take time. Usually, we would need expert programmers to write the intermediate component.

Advantages

- Provides high code re-usability.
- Test tool independent.
- Independent of Application under Test (AUT), same function works for other applications (with some limitations).
- Tests can be designed with or without AUT.

Disadvantages

- Initial investment being pretty high, the benefits of this can only be realized if the application is considerably bigger, and the test scripts are to be maintained for a few years.

- Debugging of this kind of framework can be very hard.

- Test data is hard-coded within every Excel-based test script, which leads to data issues.

- A high level of automation expertise is required to create the keyword driven framework

Even though keyword driven framework might look like the coolest thing to work on, we have seen a lot of keyword-driven frameworks fail due to their disadvantages. Most commonly, I have seen that keyword driven frameworks end up being so complicated, that it is hard for anyone to debug and isolate the problem in case the script fails.

Personally, we prefer implementing the hybrid framework since it is simple to debug and hand over to functional teams. Some of the keyword-driven frameworks that we encountered or developed were too hard for the client teams to understand and they ended up not using the framework.

26. Sample Naming and Coding Conventions

26.1. Sample Naming Conventions

Standardized naming and coding conventions ensure that automation components including names of scripts, functions, Web elements and variables are consistent throughout our framework. This reflects good coding practice and assists in code maintenance later on. Generally, two forms of naming conventions are followed:

- **Pascal casing:** The first character of all words is upper case and the other characters are lower case.

- **Camel casing:** The first character of all words, except the first word, is upper case and other characters are lower case.

In C#, we mostly follow Pascal casing as described in the table below:

Identifier	Casing	Example
Name-space	Pascal	`namespace System.Security { ... }`
Type	Pascal	`public class StreamReader { ... }`
Interface	Pascal	`public interface IEnumerable { ... }`

Method	Pascal	`public class Object {`
		`public virtual string ToString();`
		`}`

Property	Pascal	`public class String {`
		`public int Length { get; }`
		`}`

Event	Pascal	`public class Process {`
		`public event EventHandler Exited;`
		`}`

Field	Pascal	`public class MessageQueue {`
		`public static readonly TimeSpan`
		`InfiniteTimeout;`
		`}`
		`public struct UInt32 {`
		`public const Min = 0;`
		`}`

Enum value	Pascal	`public enum FileMode {`
		`Append,`
		`...`
		`}`

Parameter	Camel	`public class Convert {`
		`public static int ToInt32(string value);`
		`}`

Table 26.1 – Pascal Notation

1. **Automation components naming convention** – You can follow these naming conventions for automation components:

Subtype	Syntax	Example
Tests	**[Product]_ [TestCaseID]_ [TestType]_[Test Name]**	*HA_TC101_BP_FindHotel*
Functions	**[Product]_[FunctionType]_[FunctionName]**	*HA_GBF_HotelBooking.cs*
Data Table	**[Product]_ [DataTableType]_[Table Name]**	*HA_DE_FindHotel.xls*
Objects	**ul[Object Description][Object Type]**	*ulSubmitButton*

Table 26.2 – Naming Convention

Syntax Description

- **Product/Project [Product]**

    - **HA** - Hotel Application (Name of the project/product)

- **TestCase ID [TestCaseID]**

    - **TC101 –** Represents Testcase id TC101

- **Test Types [TestType]**

    - **BP**: Business Process Script (End to end test)

    - **TC**: Test Case Script (test that maps to functional test case)

    - **UT**: Utility Script (test that assists as a utility script, e.g., test data creation test)

    - **UI**: User Interface Script (test that validates User Interface)

- **Test Name [TestName]**

    - **VerifyValidLogin –** Brief description of test case objective

- **Function Types [FunctionType]**

    - **GBF**: Global Business Function

    - **LBF**: Local Business Function

    - **VF**: Verification Function

    - **UF**: Utility Function

    - **RF**: Recovery Function

- **Function Name [Function Name]**

  - **Login** – Brief description of Function Objective

- **Data Table Types [DataTableType]**

  - **DE**: Data Entry Data table (Datasheet used with the objective of reading data from a particular row of sheet, e.g., Login with row id 3.)

  - **DL**: Data Loop Data Table (Datasheet used with the objective of data driving the test with multiple data values.)

- **UI Map Name [UI Map Name]**

  - **SharedUIMap** – Brief description of Shared UI Map

26.2. Coding Conventions

1. C# Coding Conventions

Variable Naming Convention

For purposes of readability and consistency, use Camel casing for variables and method parameters in your C# code.

```
public class HelloWorld
{
int totalCount = 0;
void SayHello(string name)
{
  string fullMessage = „Hello „ + name;
  ...
}
}
```

Table 26.3 – Variable Naming Convention

Descriptive Variable and Procedure Names

The body of a variable or procedure name should use mixed case and should be as complete as necessary to describe its purpose. In addition, procedure names should begin with a verb, such as **InitNameArray** or **CloseDialog**.

For frequently used or long terms, standard abbreviations are recommended to help keep name length reasonable. In general, variable names greater than 32 characters can be difficult to read.

When using abbreviations, make sure they are consistent throughout the entire script. For example, randomly switching between Cnt and Count within a script or set of scripts may lead to confusion.

2. Code Commenting Conventions

Comments are an integral part of any programming language. They help maintenance engineers understand the objective of lines of code. As a good coding practice, key logic in the code should have comments.

Guidelines for Comments for Functions

Heading	Mandatory	Comment Contents
Function	Mandatory	Name of the function and the description.
Inputs	Mandatory	List of variables passed into the function as the parameters.
Outputs	Mandatory	List of variables as the output of the function.
Returns	Mandatory	List of variables returned by the function.
Usage	Optional	Specific information about how the function is implemented, and how that might affect its usage in a script.
See Also	Optional	Linking to any related topic – similar/opposite functions, type definitions.

Example:
```
/*
* * * * * * * * * * * * * * * * * * * * * * * * * * * * * * * * * * * * * * * * * * * * * *
```

public static String Function: string HA_GF_readXL (**int** rownum, String columnname, String filepath)
A sample function for demonstrating comment format.

Inputs:

rownum – An integer representing the row of the Excel sheet to be read.
columnname – A string used to represent the name of the column to be read.
filepath – A string path of the location of the Excel file.

OutPuts:

content– A String value for data read from an Excel sheet and returned by the function.

Returns:

A valid String for success.
In case of failure will return an exception and message.

History:

QA1   Create   Version 1.0   06/06/2015
QA2   Update   Version 1.1   07/07/2015 - Updated for error handling

Usage / Implementation Notes:

Make sure file is of extension .xls and not .xlsx.
Make sure datasheet ends with extension.

See Also:

<HA_GF_WriteXl>
```
*****************************************************************
*/
```

```
public static string HA_GF_readXL (int rownum, String columnName, String filePath)
{
        // lines of code
}
```

27. Sample Test Cases for Automation

TEST CASE ID	OBJECTIVE	STEPS	TEST DATA	EXPECTED RESULTS
TC-101	To verify valid login Details	1. Launch hotel reservation application using URL as in test data. 2. Login to the application using username and password as in test data.	URL:http://adactin.com/HotelApp/index.php User:{test username} Password:{test password}	User should login to the application.
TC -102	To verify whether the check-out date field accepts a later date than check-in date.	1. Launch hotel reservation application using URL as in test data. 2. Login to the application using user-name and password as in test data. 3. Select location as in test data. 4. Select hotel as in test data. 5. Select room type as in test data. 6. Select no-of-rooms as in test data. 7. Enter check-in-date later than the check-out-date field as in test data. 8. Verify that system gives an error saying "check-in-date should not be later than check-out-date".	URL: http://adactin.com/HotelApp/index.php User:{test username} Password:{test password} Location: Sydney Hotel: Hotel Creek Room type: standard No-of-rooms:1 Check-in-date: today + 7 date Checkout date:today+5 date	System should report an error message.
TC -103	To check if error is reported if check-out date field is in the past	1. Launch hotel reservation application using URL as in test data. 2. Login to the application using user-name and password as in test data. 3. Select location as in test data. 4. Select hotel as in test data. 5. Select room type as in test data. 6. Select no-of-rooms as in test data. 7. Enter check-out-date as in test data. 8. Verify that application throws error message.	URL: http://adactin.com/HotelApp/index.php User:{test username} Password:{test password} Location: Sydney Hotel: Hotel Creek Room type: standard No-of-rooms:1 Check-in-date: today's - 5 date Check-out date: today's -3 date	System should report an error message "Enter Valid dates".
TC-104	To verify whether loca-tions in Select Hotel page are displayed according to the location selected in Search Hotel.	1. Launch hotel reservation application using URL as in test data. 2. Login to the application using username and password as in test data. 3. Select location as in test data. 4. Select hotel as in test data. 5. Select room type as in test data. 6. Select no-of-rooms as in test data. 7. Enter check-out-date as in test data. 8. Select No-of-adults as in test data. 9. Select No-of-children as in test data. 10. Click on Search button. 11. Verify that hotel displayed is the same as selected in search Hotel form.	URL: http://adactin.com/HotelApp/index.php User:{test username} Password:{test password} Location: Sydney Hotel: Hotel Creek Room type: standard No-of-rooms:1 Check-in-date: today's date Check-out-date:today+1 date No-of-adults:1 No-of-children: 0	Location displayed in Select Hotel should be the same as location selected in search hotel form.

TEST CASE ID	OBJECTIVE	STEPS	TEST DATA	EXPECTED RESULTS
TC-105	To verify whether Check-in date and Check-out date are being displayed in Select Hotel page according to the dates selected in search Hotel.	1. Launch hotel reservation application using URL as in test data. 2. Login to the application using username and password as in test data. 3. Select location as in test data. 4. Select hotel as in test data. 5. Select room type as in test data. 6. Select no-of-rooms as in test data. 7. Enter check-out-date as in test data. 8. Select No-of-adults as in test data. 9. Select No-of-children as in test data. 10. Click on Search button. 11. Verify that check-in-date and check-out-dates are the same as selected in search hotel form.	URL: http://adactin.com/HotelApp/index.php User:{test username} Password:{test password} Location: Sydney Hotel: Hotel Creek Room type: standard No-of-rooms:1 Check-in-date: today's date Checkoutdate:today+1 date No-of-adults:1 No-of-children:0	Check-in-date and check-out-date should be displayed according to the data entered in search hotel form.
TC-106	To verify whether no. of rooms in Select Hotel page is same as the Number of rooms selected in search hotel page	1. Launch hotel reservation application using URL as in test data. 2. Login to the application using username and password as in test data. 3. Select location as in test data. 4. Select hotel as in test data. 5. Select room type as in test data. 6. Select no-of-rooms as in test data. 7. Enter check-out-date as in test data. 8. Select No-of-adults as in test data. 9. Select No-of-children as in test data. 10. Click on Search button. 11. Verify that no-of-rooms is reflected according to the number of rooms selected in search hotel page.	URL: http://adactin.com/HotelApp/index.php User:{test username} Password:{test password} Location: Sydney Hotel: Hotel Creek Room type: standard No-of-rooms:3 Check-in-date: today's date Checkoutdate:today+1 date No-of-adults:1 No-of-children: 0	No-of-rooms should be displayed and match with number of rooms in search hotel page
TC-107	To verify whether Room Type in Select Hotel page is same as Room type selected in search hotel page.	1. Launch hotel reservation application using URL as in test data. 2. Login to the application using username and password as in test data. 3. Select location as in test data. 4. Select hotel as in test data. 5. Select room type as in test data. 6. Select no-of-rooms as in test data. 7. Enter check-out-date as in test data. 8. Select No-of-adults as in test data. 9. Select No-of-children as in test data. 10. Click on Search button. 11. Verify that room type reflected is the same as selected in search hotel page.	URL: http://adactin.com/HotelApp/index.php User:{test username} Password:{test password} Location: Sydney Hotel: Hotel Creek Room type: Deluxe No-of-rooms:1 Check-in-date: today's date Checkoutdate:today+1 date No-of-adults:1 No-of-children:0	Room type displayed should be the same as selected in search hotel page.

TEST CASE ID	OBJECTIVE	STEPS	TEST DATA	EXPECTED RESULTS
TC-108	To verify whether the total price (excl.GST) is calculated as "price per night * no. of nights* no of rooms".	1. Launch hotel reservation application using URL as in test data. 2. Login to the application using username and password as in test data. 3. Select location as in test data. 4. Select hotel as in test data. 5. Select room type as in test data. 6. Select no-of-rooms as in test data. 7. Enter check-out-date as in test data. 8. Select No-of-adults as in test data. 9. Select No-of-children as in test data. 10. Click on Search button. 11. Select the hotel and click on continue button 12. Verify that total-price(excl.GST) is being calculated as (price-per-night*no-of-nights*no-of-rooms)	URL: http://adactin.com/HotelApp/index.php User:{test username} Password:{test password} Location: Sydney Hotel: Hotel Creek Room type: standard No-of-rooms:2 Check-in-date: today's date Check-out-date:today+1 date No-of-adults:1 No-of-children: 0	Total price =125*1*2 =250$
TC-109	To verify when pressed, logout button logs out from the application.	1. Launch hotel reservation application using URL as in test data. 2. Login to the application using username and password as in test data. 3. Select location as in test data. 4. Select hotel as in test data. 5. Select room type as in test data. 6. Select no-of-rooms as in test data. 7. Enter check-out-date as in test data. 8. Select No-of-adults as in test data. 9. Select No-of-children as in test data. 10. Click on Search button. 11. Select the hotel and click on continue button. 12. Enter the details and click on book now. 13. Click on logout and verify we have been logged out of the application.	URL: http://adactin.com/HotelApp/index.php User:{test username} Password:{test password} Location: Sydney Hotel: Hotel Creek Room type: standard No-of-rooms:2 Check-in-date: today's date Check-out-date:today+1 date No-of-adults:1 No-of-children:0	User should logout from the application.
TC-110	To check correct total price is being calculated as "price per night*no of days*no of rooms in Book a hotel page.	1. Launch hotel reservation application using URL as in test data. 2. Login to the application using username and password as in test data. 3. Select location as in test data. 4. Select hotel as in test data. 5. Select room type as in test data. 6. Select no-of-rooms as in test data. 7. Enter check-out-date as in test data. 8. Select No-of-adults as in test data. 9. Select No-of-children as in test data. 10. Click on Search button. 11. Select the hotel and click on continue button 12. Verify that total-price is being calculated as (price-per-night*no-of-rooms*no-of-days + 10% GST").	URL: http://adactin.com/HotelApp/index.php User:{test username} Password:{test password} Location: Melbourne Hotel: Hotel Creek Room type: standard No-of-rooms:2 Check-in-date: today's date Check-out-date:today+1 date No-of-adults:1 No-of-children: 0	Total price should be calculated as (price-per-night*no-of-rooms*no-of-days Total Price= 125*2*1 = 250$ In book a hotel page

TEST CASE ID	OBJECTIVE	STEPS	TEST DATA	EXPECTED RESULTS
TC-111	To check Hotel name, Location, room type, Total Day, price per night are same in Booking confirmation page as they were selected in the previous screen.	1. Launch hotel reservation application using URL as in test data. 2. Login to the application using username and password as in test data. 3. Select location as in test data. 4. Select Hotel as in test data. 5. Select room type as in test data. 6. Select no-of-rooms as in test data. 7. Enter check-out-date as in test data. 8. Select No-of-adults as in test data. 9. Select No-of-children as in test data. 10. Click on Search button. 11. Select the hotel and click on continue button 12. Verify Hotel name, Location, room type, Total Day, price per night are same in Booking confirmation page as they were selected in previous screen	URL: http://adactin.com/HotelApp/index.php User:{test username} Password:{test password} Location: Sydney Hotel: hotel Creek Room type: standard No-of-rooms:2 Check-in-date: today's date Check-out-date:today+1 date No-of-adults:1 No-of-children: 0	Data should be the same as selected in the previous screen.
TC-112	To check correct Final billed price is Total Price + 10% Total price in Book a Hotel page.	1. Launch hotel reservation application using URL as in test data. 2. Login to the application using username and password as in test data. 3. Select location as in test data. Select Hotel as in test data. 4. Select room type as in test data. 5. Select no-of-rooms as in test data. 6. Enter check-out-date as in test data. 7. Select No-of-adults as in test data. 8. Select No-of-children as in test data. 9. Click on Search button. 10. Select the hotel and click on continue button 11. Verify that Final Billed Price is being calculated as (price-per-night*no-of-rooms*no-of-days	URL: http://adactin.com/HotelApp/index.php User:{test username} Password:{test password} Location: Sydney Hotel: Hotel Creek Room type: standard No-of-rooms:2 Check-in-date: today's date Check-out-date:today+1 date No-of-adults:1 No-of-children: 0	Final billed Price= 125+12.5 =137.5 in Book a Hotel page
TC-113	To verify whether the data displayed is same as the selected data in Book hotel page.	1. Launch hotel reservation application using URL as in test data. 2. Login to the application using user-name and password as in test data. 3. Select location as in test data. 4. Select Hotel as in test data. 5. Select room type as in test data. 6. Select no-of-rooms as in test data. 7. Enter Check-out-date as in test data. 8. Select No-of-adults as in test data. 9. Select No-of-children as in test data. 10. Click on Search button. 11. Select the hotel and click on contin-ue button 12. Verify displayed data is same as the selected data in Book hotel page	URL: http://adactin.com/HotelApp/index.php User:{test username} Password:{test password} Location: Sydney Hotel: Hotel Creek Room type: standard No-of-rooms:2 Check-in-date: today's date Check-out-date:today+1 date No-of-adults:1 No-of-children: 0	Hotel: hotel Creek Room type: Standard No-of-rooms:2 Check-in-date: 27/07/2012 Check-out-date: 28/07/2012 No-of-adults:1 No-of-children: 0

TEST CASE ID	OBJECTIVE	STEPS	TEST DATA	EXPECTED RESULTS
TC-114	Verify Order number is generated in booking confirmation page.	1. Launch hotel reservation application using URL as in test data. 2. Login to the application using username and password as in test data. 3. Select location as in test data. 4. Select hotel as in test data. 5. Select room type as in test data. 6. Select no-of-rooms as in test data. 7. Enter check-out-date as in test data. 8. Select No-of-adults as in test data. 9. Select No-of-children as in test data. 10. Click on Search button. 11. Select the hotel and click on continue button 12. Verify Order number is generated	URL: http://adactin.com/HotelApp/index.php User:{test username} Password:{test password} Location: Sydney Hotel: hotel Creek Room type: standard No-of-rooms:2 Check-in-date: today's date Check-out-date:today+1 date No-of-adults:1 No-of-children: 0	Order No. should be generated.
TC-115	To verify whether the booked itinerary details are not editable.	1. Launch hotel reservation application using URL as in test data. 2. Login to the application using username and password as in test data. 3. Select location as in test data. 4. Select Hotel as in test data. 5. Select room type as in test data. 6. Select no-of-rooms as in test data. 7. Enter check-out-date as in test data. 8. Select No-of-adults as in test data. 9. Select No-of-children as in test data. 10. Click on Search button. 11. Select the hotel and click on continue button 12. Fill the form and click on Book now button. 13. Click on My itinerary button 14. Verify that the details are not editable	http://adactin.com/HotelApp/index.php User:{test username} Password:{test password} Location: Adelaide Hotel: Hotel Cornice Room type: standard No-of-rooms:2 Check-in-date: today's date Check-out-date:today+1 date No-of-adults:1 No-of-children: 0	Details once accepted should not be editable.
TC-116	To check whether the booked itinerary reflects the correct information in line with the booking.	1. Launch hotel reservation application using URL as in test data. 2. Login to the application using username and password as in test data. 3. Select location as in test data. 4. Select hotel as in test data. 5. Select room type as in test data. 6. Select no-of-rooms as in test data. 7. Enter check-out-date as in test data. 8. Select No-of-adults as in test data. 9. Select No-of-children as in test data. 10. Click on Search button. 11. Select the hotel and click on continue button 12. Fill the form and click on Book now button. 13. Click on My itinerary button 14. Verify that the details are reflected correctly as per the booking	http://adactin.com/HotelApp/index.php User:{test username} Password:{test password} Location: Sydney Hotel: Hotel Creek Room type: standard No-of-rooms:2 Check-in-date: today's date Check-out-date:today+1 date No-of-adults:1 No-of-children: 0	Itinerary should reflect the correct information in line with the booking.

TEST CASE ID	OBJECTIVE	STEPS	TEST DATA	EXPECTED RESULTS
TC-117	To check whether "search order id" query is working and displaying the relevant details.	1. Launch hotel reservation application using URL as in test data. 2. Login to the application using username and password as in test data. 3. Click on booked itinerary link. 4. Enter the order id. 5. Verify that the relevant details are displayed	http://adactin.com/HotelApp/index.php User:{test username} Password:{test password} Order id:pick existing order id	Search Order ID query should display the relevant details for Order ID.
TC-118	Verify that all the details of newly generated order number in booked itinerary page are correct and match with data during booking.	1. Launch hotel reservation application using URL as in test data. 2. Login to the application using username and password as in test data. 3. Book an order as in previous test cases. 4. Click on My itinerary button. 5. Search for Order number. 6. Verify that all the details of order number are correct as entered while saving order.	http://adactin.com/HotelApp/index.php User:{test username} Password:{test password} Location: Sydney Hotel: Hotel Creek Room type: standard No-of-rooms:2 Check-in-date: today's date Check-out-date:today+1 date No-of-adults:1 No-of-children: 0	All the details in booked itinerary page should be same as those entered during booking.
TC-119	To verify that the order gets canceled after click on Cancel order number link.	1. Launch hotel reservation application using URL as in test data. 2. Login to the application using username and password as in test data. 3. Book the Hotel as in previous test cases. Keep a note of order number generated. 4. Click on Booked Itinerary link. 5. Search for order number booked. 6. Click on Cancel <Order Number> 7. Click Yes on pop-up which asks to cancel order or not 8. Verify that order number is canceled and no longer exists in the Booked Itinerary page.	http://adactin.com/HotelApp/index.php User:{test username} Password:{test password}	Order number should no longer be present in booked itinerary page after cancellation.
TC-120	To Verify Title of every Page reflects what the page objective is. For example, Title of Search Hotel page should have "Search Hotel"	9. Launch hotel reservation application using URL as in test data. 10. Login to the application using username and password as in test data. 11. Verify that the title of each page is the same as the page objective. 12. Click on the Search hotel link and verify whether the application directs to search the hotel form. 13. Click on booked itinerary link and verify that the application directs to the booked itinerary form.	http://adactin.com/HotelApp/index.php User:{test username} Password:{test password}	The title of each page should reflect its objective and the buttons should redirect as specified, to the relevant page.

CPSIA information can be obtained
at www.ICGtesting.com
Printed in the USA
FSHW022116141020
74856FS

9 780992 293567